lo

NEW ENGLAN

Bob Curley, Lisa Halvorsen, Stasha Mills Healy,
Peggy Newland, Alexandra Pecci, Mara Vorhees

Meet our writers

THOMAS H. MITCHELL/500PX ©

Bob Curley
@rhodytravel

Bob's hometown of North Kingstown is centrally positioned between Newport and Providence, making it easy to split time between his favorite activities, like strolling the Cliff Walk in the summer and warming up cool evenings beside the braziers of WaterFire.

Lisa Halvorsen

Lisa's favorite experience is sampling a new flavor at an artisan ice-cream shop after spending the day in the Northeast Kingdom, observing birds, and secretly hoping to spot a moose.

Stasha Mills Healy
@stashastravels

Stasha has been everywhere from Abu Dhabi to Albuquerque but one of her happiest places is in her idyllic hometown of Greenwich, Connecticut.

Peggy Newland

Peggy is on the perpetual search for the nooks and crannies of this world. She writes travel features for the *Nashua Telegraph* and has been awarded fellowships and grants for her fiction. She is currently writing a book with her dog, Lucy, called *Dear Lucy: Life Lessons from a Lab*. See peggynewland.com.

Boston 42

Around Boston 76

Rhode Island 106

Connecticut 128

New Hampshire 186

Experience New England online

Gulf of Maine
Atlantic Ocean
NEW YORK
MASSACHUSETTS
Ticonderoga
Middlebury
Rutland
Woodstock
Lebanon
Plymouth
Conway
Bridgton
Brunswick
Damariscotta
Boothbay Harbor
Monhegan Island
Portland
Boston 2½hrs
Kennebunkport
Saco River
Claremont
Rochester
Hudson Falls
Concord
Portsmouth
Manchester
Bennington
Connecticut River
Brattleboro
Newburyport
Lawrence
Albany
Greenfield
Fitchburg
Lowell
Pittsfield
Hudson River
Concord
Salem
Lenox
Hudson
Worcester
Massachusetts Bay
Hartford 1½hrs
Providence 1hr
Springfield
Provincetown
Plymouth
Putnam
Cape Cod Bay
Cape Cod
Poughkeepsie
Hartford
Providence
Fall River
Chatham
Waterbury
Norwich
Newport
Falmouth
Danbury
Mystic
Nantucket Sound
New Haven
New London
Bridgeport
Long Island Sound
Rhode Island Sound
Martha's Vineyard
Nantucket
Block Island
Stamford
Boston 4 hrs
Riverhead
Long Island
New York

0 100 km
0 50 miles

D

Discover centuries of history, from indigenous sites to industrial innovations and intellectual movements. Enjoy the sunshine in a canoe or on a schooner. While away winter days on the slopes. Indulge in fresh seafood and creative local brews. Taste the culture and cuisine of the region's dynamic cities. Marvel at timeless art and architecture. Explore offshore islands and sandy beaches. Spot birds on the wing and moose in the wild. Hike the magnificent Appalachian Mountains. Cycle the endless country roads.

This is New England.

TURN THE PAGE AND START PLANNING YOUR NEXT BEST TRIP →

Rivière-du-Loup
Baie St Paul
Edmundston
QUÉBEC
(CANADA)
Fort Kent
NEW
BRUNSWICK
(CANADA)
Caribou
St Lawrence River
Québec
City
Presque
Isle
Trois-Rivières
Houlton
Woodstock
St-Georges
St John River
Millinocket
Jackman
Montréal
Sherbrooke
Maine 212
Kennebec
River
Lincoln
St Stephen
Calais
Bingham
Penobscot
River
Newport
Lake
Champlain
Skowhegan
Pittsfield
Lubec
Plattsburgh
Errol
Farmington
Bangor
Machias
Vermont 156
Burlington
Rumford
Ellsworth
St Johnsbury
Berlin
Waterville
Belfast
Bar Harbor
Boston
3½hrs
Montpelier
Mt Washington
Augusta
Penobscot
Bay
Acadia
National
Park
Barre
Lewiston
Rockland

Woodstock, Vermont (p172)

Alexandra Pecci

@ThePreppyWitch

Alex is a Massachusetts native with family ties to the Salem witch trials. She loves low tide at Ipswich's Crane Beach, haunting Colonial cemeteries, witchcraft shopping in Salem, and polishing off a fried scallop and onion ring boat with ease.

Mara Vorhees

@mara_vorhees

A longtime resident of Somerville, Massachusetts, Mara spends her free time cycling along the River Charles and slurping oysters in Union Square. She loves exploring New England with her kids – hitting the sand in summer and the slopes in winter.

Contents

S. GREG PANOSIAN/GETTY IMAGES ©

Historical architecture, Boston (p42)

ESSAYS

VISUAL GUIDES

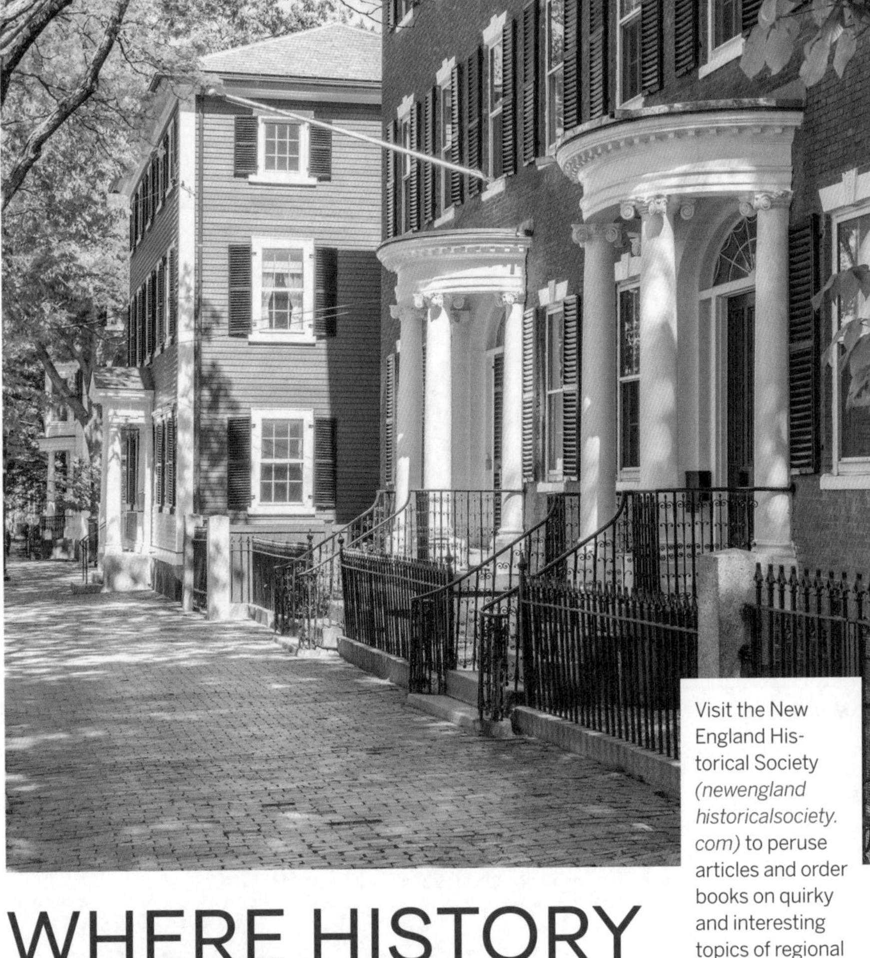

Visit the New England Historical Society *(newengland historicalsociety.com)* to peruse articles and order books on quirky and interesting topics of regional history.

WHERE HISTORY **HAPPENED**

New England is sprinkled with historical markers – museums and memorials, buildings and battlefields – of 400 years of recorded events and centuries of indigenous history before that. From the Pilgrims' landing at Plymouth to the War of Independence to the intellectual and industrial revolutions in later centuries, see where this rich history unfolded and how it is remembered in this region.

JOSEPH SOHM/SHUTTERSTOCK ©

→ OLDEST IN THE US

Public school Boston Latin (1635)

Newspaper *Hartford Courant* (1764)

Pub White Horse Tavern, Newport (1763)

Chairlift Mad River Glen, Vermont (1948)

Food truck Ocean Roll, Kennebunk (1961)

Left Historic architecture, Salem, MA. **Right** Brick flooring, Boston Latin School. **Below** Wampanoag hut, Plimoth Patuxet.

WALKS THROUGH HISTORY

- African American Heritage Trail of Martha's Vineyard (p97)
- Freedom Trail, Boston (p56)
- Independence Trail, Providence
- Portland Freedom Trail

RIGHT: JACLYN VERNACE/SHUTTERSTOCK ©, LEFT: PAUL BRADY PHOTOGRAPHY/SHUTTERSTOCK ©

↑ INDIGENOUS MUSEUMS

Learn about indigenous history and contemporary culture:

- Mashpee Wampanoag Museum, Mashpee
- Plimoth Patuxet Museums, Plymouth (p103)
- Tomaquag Museum, Exeter

Best History Experiences

▶ **Pay respects to revolutionary heroes in Boston's oldest burial grounds.** (p70)

▶ **Discover the sordid history of the Salem witch trials.** (p82 and p94)

▶ **See firsthand the sites where the true story of the slave ship *Amistad* unfolded.** (p144)

▶ **Follow in the footsteps of the country's most beloved writers.** (p98 and p150)

▶ **Marvel at the 19th-century architecture, farms and charm of Woodstock.** (p172)

Check out the Appalachian Mountain Club *(outdoors.org)* for guided hikes, educational programs and trail maps. Founded in 1876, it is the country's oldest outdoor organization.

HAVESEEN/SHUTTERSTOCK ©

ON TWO **FEET**

Don your knapsack, lace up your boots and hit the trails in New England. Appalachian hikes offer forest-shrouded paths and expansive panoramas, from the rounded mounts of the Berkshires to the glorious greens of Vermont to the rugged peaks of the White Mountains. Miles of coastal trails traverse sand dunes, salt marshes or rocky cliffs, with endless ocean breezes and sea views to urge you on.

Best Hiking Experiences

- **Discover Block Island's stunning seascapes on a network of walking trails.** (p114)
- **Hike hut to hut along New England's highest peaks in the White Mountains.** (p206)
- **Journey up to the Northeast Kingdom for lakeside strolls and mountain summits.** (p168)
- **Finish mountain treks or cliffside scrambles with a cool-down swim in Acadia.** (p232)

ON TWO WHEELS

If you're not sure about bringing your bike to New England, let's put this matter to rest. Quiet country roads and thousands of miles of off-road bike trails make this a fantastic cycling destination, not to mention the tremendous variety of landscapes (and cityscapes) and the many enticing stops along the way.

LEFT: PEGGY NEWLAND/LONELY PLANET ©; BOTTOM: ALBERT PEGO/SHUTTERSTOCK ©

→ BIKE-SHARE PROGRAMS

Boston bluebikes.com

Burlington greenridebikeshare.com

Pioneer Valley valleybike.org

Providence spin.app

Best Cycling Experiences

- **Pedal through college campuses in Boston and Cambridge.** (p48)
- **Choose between two New Hampshire rail trails – the mountains or the lakes.** (p192)
- **Cross Lake Champlain's islands by ferry and bicycle.** (p166)
- **Tackle the rock bridges and carriage roads of Acadia National Park.** (p232)
- **Cycle through coastal Maine's verdant farmland and pine forests.** (p220)

← RAILS TO TRAILS

New England has more than 1800 miles of rail trails. Get the TrailLink app *(traillink.com)* for information and maps for individual trails.

Far left Hiking, White Mountains, NH. **Above left** Carriage road, Acadia, ME. **Near left** Blue Bikes, Boston.

ARTISTIC ENDEAVORS

New England's artistic endeavors are as diverse and dynamic as the region itself, from centuries-old museums and prestigious academies, to cutting-edge contemporary galleries and smaller specialty collections. In addition to the many excellent venues, there are informal exhibitions and open-studio events in the major cities and artsy towns, as well as noteworthy architecture around the region.

Burlington

Art in unexpected places

Artists thrive in this lakeside city, where communal art space has bloomed out of abandoned warehouses, a former bottling plant and even a firehouse. Public art dots the waterfront and university campus, while murals adorn the streets.

3½hrs from Boston

▶ p162

The Berkshires

An artist's retreat

City folk have long summered in the Berkshires, for cool mountain air and artistic inspiration. See the homes and studios of some of America's most beloved artists and enjoy the region's most sophisticated outdoor cultural events.

3hrs from Boston

▶ p88

Fairfield County

An architecture scavenger hunt

There's more to Fairfield County than *The Stepford Wives:* there's also their fancy houses. But that's just the beginning of the architectural gems that grace the streets in the splendid towns of Lower Fairfield County.

/ 1hr from New Haven

▶ p134

Cornwall
St Lawrence River
Lake Champlain
Plattsburgh
Burlington
Middlebury
Watertown
Ticonderoga
Rutland
Toronto
Lake Ontario
Hamilton
Niagara Falls
Rochester
ONTARIO (CANADA)
Lake Erie
Syracuse
Hudson Falls
Bennington
NEW YORK
Erie
Albany
Pittsfield
Binghamton
Hudson
Kingston
Hudson River
PENNSYLVANIA
Poughkeepsie
CONN
Scranton
Newburgh
New Haven
Bridgeport
Long Island Sound
Stamford
NEW JERSEY
Newark
Long Island
Allentown
New York
Atlantic Ocean
Trenton
Philadelphia
Wilmington
WEST VIRGINIA
MARYLAND

Barre

From granite to grand

This quarry town shows its stuff in the buildings and monuments that have been crafted from its local granite. See the artistic creations all over town (including the cemetery) and take a tour of the quarry to learn about the granite industry.

1hr from Burlington

▶ p170

Rockland

Art Capital of Maine

Dozens of downtown galleries plus two local art museums have earned Rockland its artsy reputation. Spend a day gallery-hopping, then ferry out to Monhegan Island to see artists at work.

½hr from Portland

▶ p223 and p236

Boston

The Athens of America

World-class museums, showpiece public buildings and acclaimed private and university collections thrill art lovers. The local grassroots, street-smart art scene also has creatives churning out works in SoWa studios, hawking wares at markets and painting murals on the streets.

/ 4hrs from New York

▶ p58 and p64

Providence

The Creative Capital

It isn't called the 'Creative Capital' for nothing. Providence is home to a top art school and esteemed art club, not to mention the murals, performance art, thriving music scene and the ever-popular WaterFire.

/ 1hr from Boston

▶ p112

The three more southerly New England states – Massachusetts, Connecticut and Rhode Island – are home to nine of the 10 largest cities in the region and three-quarters of its population.

WANGKUN JIA/SHUTTERSTOCK ©

IN THE CITY

Even if you came for the serenity and scenery of the New England countryside, don't miss the chance to also experience some of the most diverse and dynamic urban areas in the US. Discover adventurous art scenes, innovative and international dining, and soul-moving music. Plus, you'll see how former manufacturing cities have transformed into postindustrial creative centers.

Best Urban Experiences

▶ **Visit local designers on Boston's snazziest shopping strip.** (p60)

▶ **Experience the industrial roots and artistic heart of revitalized Lowell.** (p92)

▶ **Discover the contemporary art scene in Boston, Burlington and Providence.** (p58, p162 and p112)

▶ **Listen to classical concerts in the park or blues jams in Portsmouth clubs.** (p204)

IN THE WILD

The wilds of New England abound with animal life. Cruise off the Massachusetts coast to see whales and dolphins, and explore the remote north in search of moose. Birders might spot common loons on northern lakes, bald eagles soaring overhead, and dozens of shorebird species on the coast. From November to March, look for the snowy owl.

LEFT: PAUL TESSIER/SHUTTERSTOCK © BOTTOM: MIERCAT PHOTOGRAPHY/SHUTTERSTOCK ©

→ MASSAUDUBON

MassAudubon *(massaudubon.org)* manages some 60 wildlife sanctuaries across Massachusetts, offering nature walks, educational programs and guides to common wildlife species.

▶ Read more about bird-watching in Massachusetts on p101

Best Wildlife Experiences

▶ **Bring your binocs for bird-watching in the salt marshes on Plum Island.** (p100)

▶ **Investigate the footprints of dinosaurs that once roamed New England.** (p152)

▶ **Go on a moose hunt in the North Woods.** (p202)

▶ **Kayak with seals off the coast of New Hampshire.** (p201)

▶ **Spot birds on the wing and on display along the Molly Stark Scenic Byway.** (p178)

← TIP FOR MOOSE-SPOTTERS

Look for moose at dawn and dusk between mid-May and July, especially in bogs and wetlands.

Far left Downtown Lowell, MA. **Above left** Moose, Baxter State Park, ME. **Near left** Cormorants, Nahant Thicket Wildlife Sanctuary, MA.

Not too long ago, lobster was a food reserved for poor folks and prisoners. Only in the late 19th century did city dwellers and non–New Englanders discover the delights of the clawed crustacean, sending demand (and prices) soaring.

LOBSTER TAILS & **CRAFT ALES**

Seafood from local waters, fresh seasonal produce, artisanal cheeses and seductively sweet maple syrup... this is the local bounty that makes its way into New England kitchens and onto menus at the region's excellent chef-driven restaurants. In urban areas, international influences are strong and spicy, thanks to the many immigrant populations in the region.

KEN WEINRICH/SHUTTERSTOCK ©

Left Lobster fishing. **Right** Steamed clams. **Below** Asian cuisine, Quincy Market, Boston.

→ MUST-TRY SEAFOOD

- Clam chowder
- Fried clams
- Oysters on the half-shell
- Steamers (steamed clams)
- Lobster roll

CRAFTY BASTARDS

Lauren Clark does a deep dive into her favorite beverage in her book *Crafty Bastards: Beer in New England from the Mayflower to Modern Day.*

RIGHT: 2P2PLAY/SHUTTERSTOCK ©, LEFT: WOODYSPHOTOS/SHUTTERSTOCK ©

↑ INTERNATIONAL INFLUENCES

Taste the culinary influence of immigrants in southern New England:

Boston Chinese, Italian, Korean, Vietnamese

Hartford Jamaican

Lowell Cambodian

Providence Italian, Latin American, Portuguese

Best Appetizing Experiences

▸ **Sample pizza and pasta, cannoli and cappuccino in Boston's North End.** (p68)

▸ **Be the judge in the ongoing contest for best fried clam in Essex.** (p91)

▸ **Taste the piquant influences of *la cocina latina* in Providence restaurants.** (p116)

▸ **Go straight to the source for Connecticut's best craft beers.** (p142)

▸ **Witness the tapping of the maples and taste the resulting treats at Vermont farms.** (p176)

There are 4600 islands in Maine (according to the Maine State Planning Office), but only 15 of them are inhabited year-round.

SANDY SHORES & **ROCKY ISLES**

The New England coastline is enticingly long and delightfully varied, from Rhode Island's sandy beaches to the cliff-lined coast of Maine. Offshore, thousands of islands dot the seascape. Spectacular sunrises greet the earliest risers. But you don't have to get up at the crack of dawn to enjoy swimming in brisk waters, beachcombing endless stretches of sand, exploring unknown islands and – of course – eating seafood galore.

→ THRILL FACTOR

Yes, surfing is a thing in New England. Catch the biggest waves in Rhode Island, especially at Narragansett and Newport.

THORNTON COHEN/ALAMY STOCK PHOTO ©

Left Bear Island, ME. **Right** Surfing, Newport, RI. **Below** Brant Point Lighthouse, MA.

CHILL FACTOR

North Atlantic waters are undeniably chilly, but temperatures vary depending where you dip. Average water temps in July:

Newport 68°F (20°C)

Martha's Vineyard 70°F (21°C)

Bar Harbor 58°F (14°C)

RIGHT: ALLAN WOOD PHOTOGRAPHY/SHUTTERSTOCK ©, LEFT: MIHAI_ANDRITOIU/SHUTTERSTOCK ©

↑ LET THE LIGHT SHINE

See New England Lighthouses: A Virtual Guide *(newenglandlighthouses.net)* for information and photographs of some 200 New England lighthouses.

▶ Find out how to spend a night in a historic lighthouse on p250

Best Coastal Experiences

- **Have an island adventure just a short ferry ride away from Boston.** (p66)
- **Savor the region's prettiest beaches and warmest waters on Martha's Vineyard.** (p96)
- **Bring your board or a book and have a blast at South County beaches.** (p120)
- **Uncover hidden beaches, take a dip and sleep under the stars on a Maine island.** (p230)
- **Catch the sunrise *and* sunset over the water from the cliffs of the Isles of Shoals.** (p196)

LET IT SNOW

Although whingeing about the weather is a New England winter tradition, we recommend giving it a pass. Instead, sample one of the other favorite pastimes, such as skiing, ice skating, snowshoeing or even dogsledding. Move your body, breathe the cold, fresh air and take in the snow-covered wonderland: it's bound to be a good day.

★ SNOWIEST STATES

US-wide rankings (average annual snowfall):

1 Vermont (89.25in)
2 New Hampshire (77.28in)
3 Maine (71.44in)
8 Massachusetts (51.05in)
13 Rhode Island (38.85in)
14 Connecticut (37.85in)

Best Winter Experiences

▶ **Bring your best friend – yes, your dog – to play and ski in the snow.** (p194)

▶ **Go off-trail in snow-shoes or skis in the mountains around Jackson.** (p194)

▶ **Embrace the winter in Vermont with dogsledding, snowshoeing or ice skating.** (p180)

▶ **Ski the rolling Nordic trails or steep mountain slopes in Bethel.** (p218)

WINTER WARM-UP ESSENTIALS

- Long underwear
- Hand/toe warmers
- Outdoor exercise
- Hot yoga
- Hot tubs
- Hot chocolate
- Hot toddies

Top left Dogsledding, VT. **Bottom left** Skiing, ME. **Top right** Canoeing, ME.

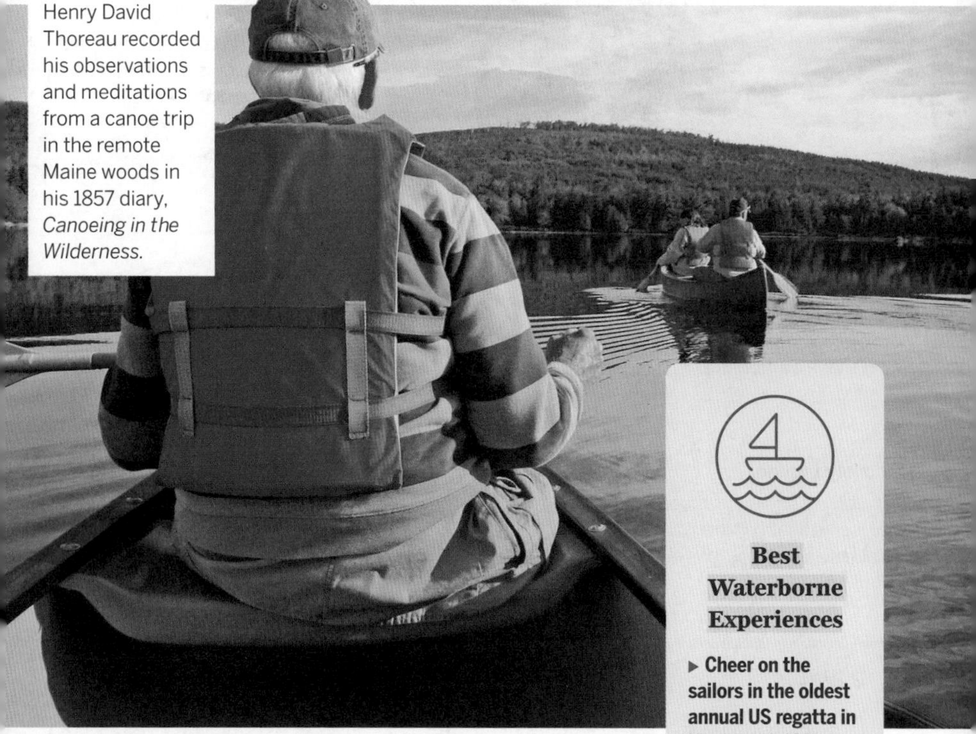

Henry David Thoreau recorded his observations and meditations from a canoe trip in the remote Maine woods in his 1857 diary, *Canoeing in the Wilderness.*

PADDLES & **SAILS**

With thousands of lakes and rivers inland and one vast blue ocean out the front door, New England offers countless opportunities to get out on the water, whether by power of the wind or by power of your own strong self. You'll find kayaks and canoes (rentals or tours) almost everywhere, from urban Boston to remotest Maine. Schooner tours set sail from harbors up and down the coast.

Best Waterborne Experiences

- **Cheer on the sailors in the oldest annual US regatta in Newport.** (p122)
- **Dive into Mystic's seafaring and shipbuilding past.** (p136)
- **Explore Connecticut's coast by kayak.** (p140)
- **Paddle north New Hampshire's rivers and lakes.** (p200)
- **Sail around the coves of Casco Bay and Penobscot Bay.** (p228)

↗ Beach Season

The water is still frigid in June, but the beaches are less crowded and accommodations more affordable.

Lovely Lupine

In early to mid-June, blooms of lupine light up New Hampshire fields with purple, pink and white.

PVD Fest

Three days in June dedicated to music, dance, food and art outdoor venues.

📍Providence, RI

▶ pvdfest.com

← Windjammer Days

The last weekend in June features boat parades, boat tours and sailing regattas.

📍Boothbay Harbor, ME

▶ boothbayharbor windjammerdays.org

▶ p227

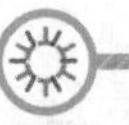

JUNE

Average daytime max: 76°F (24°C)
Days of rainfall: 12

JULY

New England in SUMMER

Polo Matches

Catch a polo match on Sunday afternoons in June, July or September.

Greenwich, CT

▶ greenwichpoloclub.com

▶ p148

→ Fourth of July Festivities

Independence Day parades and fireworks take place around the region, including the big event in Boston.

▶ july4th.org

Demand for accommodations at the beach peaks in July and August. Book tours and overnight adventures in advance.

▶ lonelyplanet.com/usa/new-england

Average daytime max: 81°F (27°C)
Days of rainfall: 11

AUGUST

Average daytime max: 80°F (26°C)
Days of rainfall: 10

Summer Cultural Festivals

Music, film, dance and theater festivals take place around the region, including Lenox, Lowell, Martha's Vineyard, Newport and Portsmouth.

Packing Notes

Moisture-wicking clothing for humid days; sunblock, sunglasses and sun hat; insect repellent.

↘ School's Back in Session

Students return to college towns, and streets are filled with U-Hauls during the first week of September.

The first few weeks in September are a great time to hit the beaches, as the water is still warm but the crowds are gone.

Labor Day

The first Monday in September is Labor Day, the official end of the summer season. Accommodation prices in beach destinations decrease after Labor Day.

Foliage Season

Nature at its most ostentatious. The colors 'peak' in late September or early October in the northern states, and in mid- to late October further south.

SEPTEMBER

Average daytime max: 72°F (22°C)
Days of rainfall: 10

OCTOBER

New England in AUTUMN

Demand for accommodations peaks during foliage season. Book tours and overnight adventures in advance.

▶ lonelyplanet.com/usa/new-england

↗ Haunted Happenings

Salem, aka 'Witch City,' celebrates Halloween throughout October. Additional Halloween fun in Keene, NH, and Providence, RI.

Salem, MA

▶ hauntedhappenings.org

The tourist season ends abruptly in November, when accommodation prices drop dramatically.

Average daytime max: 61°F (16°C)
Days of rainfall: 10

NOVEMBER

Average daytime max: 51°F (10°C)
Days of rainfall: 11

↘ Thanksgiving Day

The third Thursday in November is Thanksgiving Day. Most museums, stores and offices (as well as many restaurants) are closed.

Packing Notes

Cool and crisp temperatures mean 'sweater weather' in New England.

Jingle Bell Chocolate Tour

Take a sleigh ride through the village and collect handmade chocolates along the way. Weekends in November and December.

Jackson, NH

↗ **Boston Tea Party Reenactment**

On December 16, history buffs dress up like Mohawk warriors and dump tea into the Boston Harbor, just as their forebears did in 1773.

Boston

▸ december16.org

↓ **New Year's Day**

Many towns ring in the new year with art exhibits, parades and fireworks displays on December 31. New Year's Day is a public holiday.

▸ firstnightboston.org

DECEMBER

Average daytime max: 41°F (5°C)
Days of rainfall: 11

JANUARY

New England in WINTER

↘ Ski Season

Slopes open as early as Thanksgiving weekend in northern Vermont and New Hampshire; the season starts in earnest in December.

Presidents' Day Weekend

The third weekend in February represents the peak of ski season, and schools are closed all week for winter break.

Accommodation prices are at their lowest all around the region, with the exception of ski resorts.

Average daytime max: 36°F (2°C)
Days of rainfall: 13

FEBRUARY

Average daytime max: 39°F (3°C)
Days of rainfall: 11

Demand for accommodations at ski resorts peaks during Presidents' Day weekend. Book tours and overnight adventures in advance.

▶ lonelyplanet.com/usa/new-england

Packing Notes

Bundle up! Warm winter coats, hats, gloves and boots are required.

St Patrick's Day

Festivities around the region, including Boston *(southbostonparade.org)* and Newport, RI *(newportirish.com)*.

↙ Patriots' Day

On the third Monday in April, the first battles of the American Revolution are commemorated around New England, especially in Boston, Concord and Lexington.

Maple Open-House Weekend

Maple-sugar producers in Vermont and Maine open their doors for tastings for two days in late March.

Vermont & Maine

▶ vermontmaple.org

▶ p177

Boston Marathon

Also on the third Monday in April, tens of thousands of runners participate in the world's oldest marathon.

Boston

▶ baa.org

MARCH **APRIL**

Average daytime max: 45°F (7°C)

Days of rainfall: 13

New England in SPRING

↘ Vermont Maple Festival

In Vermont, the last weekend in April is dedicated to a celebration of the state's first agricultural 'harvest.'

St Albans, VT

▸ vtmaplefestival.org

▸ p177

↓ Memorial Day

The last Monday in May is a public holiday. Memorial Day weekend officially kicks off the summer tourist season.

Demand for accommodations peaks during big events like the Boston Marathon and college graduations. Book tours and overnight adventures in advance.

▸ lonelyplanet.com/usa/new-england

Average daytime max: 56°F (13°C)
Days of rainfall: 12

MAY

Average daytime max: 66°F (18°C)
Days of rainfall: 13

In May, the sun comes out on a semi-permanent basis, while lilac and magnolia trees bloom all around the region.

Packing Notes

Sunglasses *and* umbrella, plus plenty of layers. Anything can happen and it usually does!

MASSACHUSETTS
Trip Builder

TAKE YOUR PICK OF MUST-SEES AND HIDDEN GEMS

Everything that New England promises can be found right here – from invigorating contemporary culture and learning to complex and consequential history, and from the beaches and ports on the big blue to the gorgeous greens of the Berkshires.

Trip Notes

Hub town Boston

How long Allow 2 weeks

Getting around With the exception of the Berkshires, these destinations can be reached by train (plus a ferry for Martha's Vineyard), though traveling by car is more efficient and allows more flexibility for out-of-town destinations.

Tips Avoid some of the summer crowds and enjoy mild weather by visiting Massachusetts in late spring, early fall or (gasp!) winter.

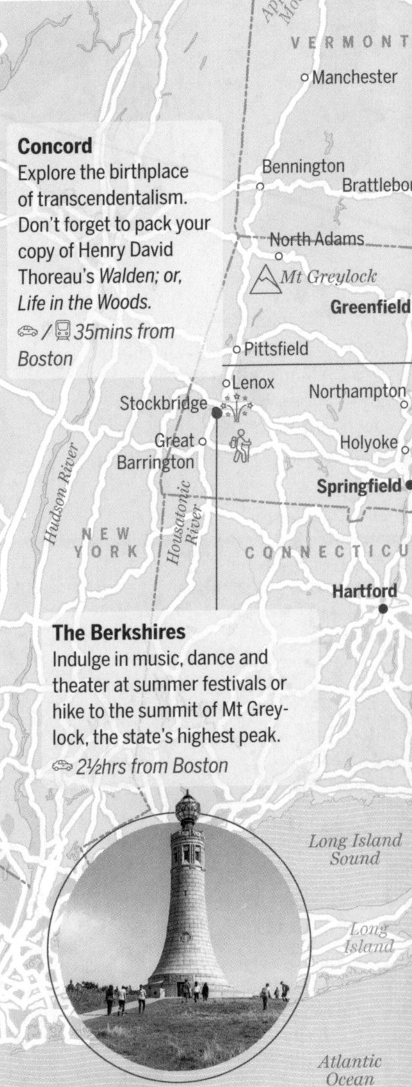

Concord
Explore the birthplace of transcendentalism. Don't forget to pack your copy of Henry David Thoreau's *Walden; or, Life in the Woods.*
35mins from Boston

The Berkshires
Indulge in music, dance and theater at summer festivals or hike to the summit of Mt Greylock, the state's highest peak.
2½hrs from Boston

Lowell

See how one town has transformed from an industrial workhorse – once home of America's textile industry – to a contemporary, cosmopolitan hub for art, music and innovation.

/ 50mins from Boston

Salem

Delve into the tragic history of the Salem witch trials at museums and memorials around town, and witness the curious Wiccan community that thrives today.

/ 45mins from Boston

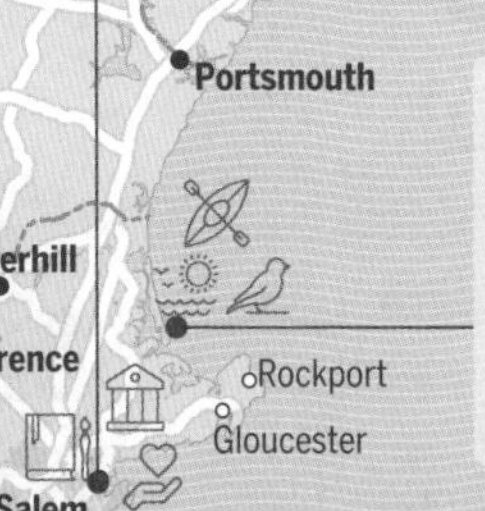

Plum Island

Lounge on pristine beaches, paddle through winding waterways and wander among the salt marshes in search of birdlife.

1hr from Boston

Plymouth

Step back in time at the Plimoth Patuxet Museums and experience the lives and times of English settlers and Native Americans in the 17th century.

/ 1hr from Boston

Boston

Marvel at the cityscape, follow the Freedom Trail, explore centers of learning, admire fabulous artwork, slurp oysters and shop till you drop in the capital of the Commonwealth.

/ 4hrs from New York

Martha's Vineyard

Discover Oak Bluffs' unique African American culture and heritage, against a spectacular backdrop of saltwater ponds, red-clay cliffs and sun-drenched beaches.

+ 2½hrs from Boston

CONNECTICUT & RHODE ISLAND
Trip Builder

TAKE YOUR PICK OF MUST-SEES AND HIDDEN GEMS

The southerly New England states are relatively compact but undeniably rewarding, rich with art and architecture, institutes of learning and historic sites. The many miles of shoreline abound in charming coastal towns, glorious sandy beaches and decadent seafood.

Trip Notes

Hub towns Hartford, New Haven, Providence

How long At least 1 week

Getting around Most of the coastal towns are connected by train, but you'll want to rent a car to get out of the cities and all around both states.

Tips Sample some hyper-local culinary specialties, like white-clam pizza in Connecticut and coffee milk in Rhode Island.

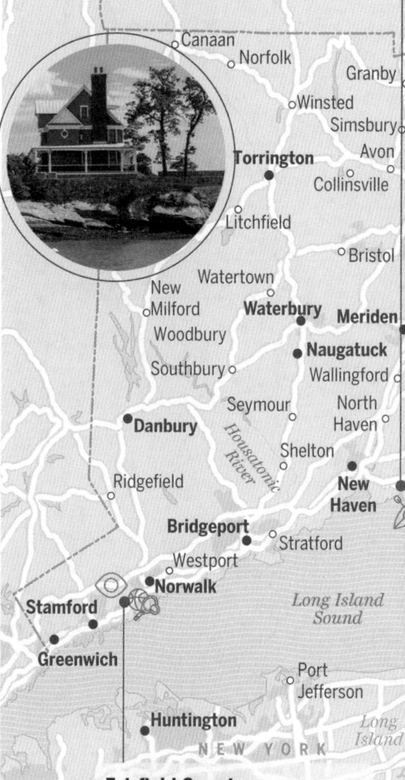

Thimble Islands
Paddle through this scenic archipelago, observing the private homes up close, for an unexpected adventure on the mid-Connecticut coast.
20mins from New Haven

Fairfield County
Don your preppiest duds to watch players and ponies face off on the polo field, or take an architecture tour around these swanky NYC suburbs.
1hr from New Haven

South County
Soak up some rays at Narragansett Beach, paddle the Pettaquamscutt River, and savor the freshest of seafood along this scenic coastline.
45mins from Providence
Providence
Stroll through the revitalized streets, peruse the many art spaces, admire the elegant architecture on College Hill and marvel at WaterFire along the Riverwalk.
/ 1hr from Boston
Newport
Feel the wind in your face, while strolling past majestic mansions on the Cliff Walk or while skimming across sparkling waters on a schooner.
45mins from Providence
Mystic
Hoist the jib and set sail out of this historic shipbuilding center, now home to the fabulous interactive Mystic Seaport Museum.
/ 1hr from New Haven
Block Island
Hike, bike or kayak around this ecofriendly island, stopping for swim breaks and bird sightings. Refuel with local treats from the weekly farmers market.
+ 2hrs from Providence
MASSACHUSETTS
Northampton
Springfield
Webster
Mansfield
Plymouth
MASSACHUSETTS
Stafford
Enfield
Windsor Locks
Putnam
Taunton
Middleborough
Rockville
Greenville
Pawtucket
Providence
CONNECTICUT
Storrs
Scituate Reservoir
Fall River
Manchester
Hartford
Warwick
Warren
Willimantic
Bristol
RHODE ISLAND
Plainfield
Narragansett Bay
Rocky Hill
Marlborough
Prudence Island
Portsmouth
Wickford
Colchester
Middletown
East Hampton
Norwich
Conanicut Island
Aquidneck Island
Connecticut River
Jamestown
Newport
Westerly
Salem
Wakefield
Uncasville
Mystic
Narragansett Pier
Charlestown
Chester
New London
Point Judith
Essex
Guilford
Niantic
Clinton
Old Saybrook
Fishers Island (NY)
Misquamicut
Stonington
Rhode Island Sound
Block Island Sound
Gardiners Island
Block Island
Greenport
Gardiners Bay
Sag Harbor
Montauk
Great Peconic Bay
East Hampton
Riverhead
Atlantic Ocean
0 50 km
0 25 miles

COASTAL NEW ENGLAND
Trip Builder

TAKE YOUR PICK OF MUST-SEES AND HIDDEN GEMS

The New England coastline is long and varied. Some of the most scenic stretches are in the northern reaches, where the rocky cliffs are punctuated by photogenic lighthouses and alluring islands, with plenty of seafood shacks.

Trip Notes

Hub towns Boston, Portland

How long Allow 10 to 12 days

Getting around Trains run between Boston and Portland, but you'll want a car to really explore all of the other destinations. Bring your bike for the East Coast Greenway and Mount Desert Island.

Tips In the busy summer season, try to avoid driving on Rte 1. Travel during shoulder seasons to experience 'real' coastal New England.

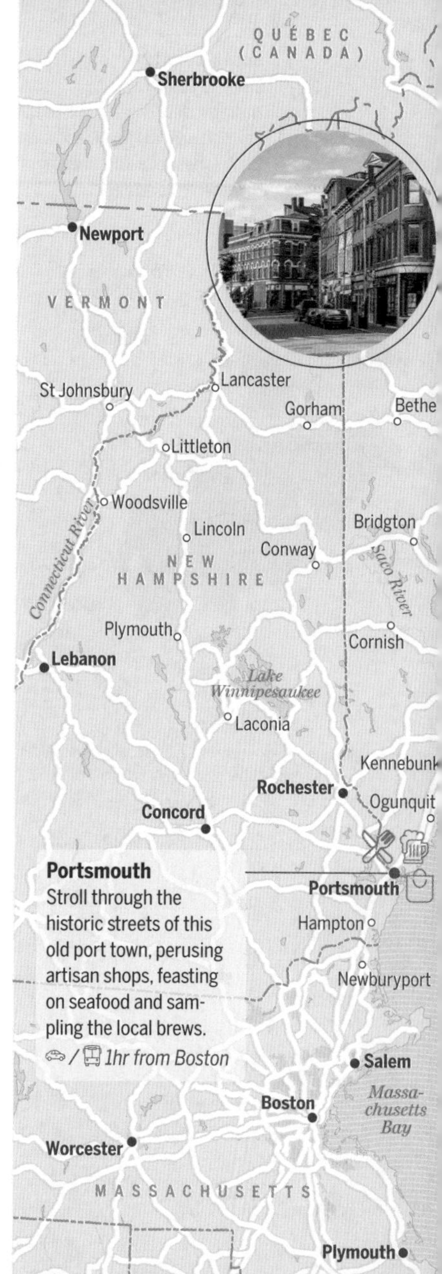

Portsmouth
Stroll through the historic streets of this old port town, perusing artisan shops, feasting on seafood and sampling the local brews.
🚗 / 🚌 *1hr from Boston*

Mid-Coast Maine

Drive slow for ocean and island views, lighthouse stops, artistic inspiration at the Farnsworth Art Museum and blooming joy at the Coastal Maine Botanical Gardens.

1½hrs from Portland

Portland

By day, island-hop around Casco Bay or visit iconic Portland Head Light; by night, ramble along the cobblestone streets of Old Port for fresh lobster and craft beer.

2½hrs from Boston

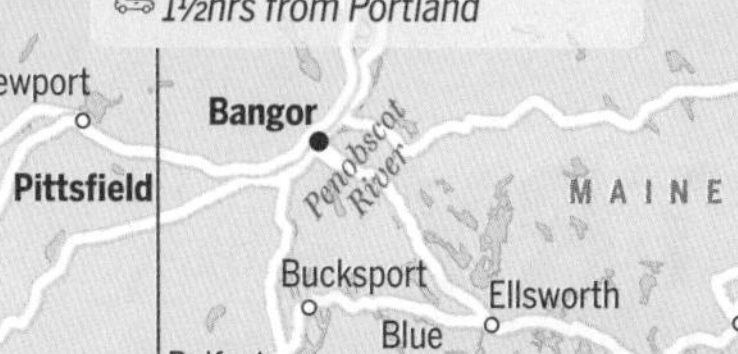

Mount Desert Island

Bike scenic carriage trails, summit Cadillac Mountain and cool off in Echo Lake, then stroll around Bar Harbor and treat yourself to a lobster ice-cream reward.

2hrs from Augusta

Monhegan Island

Gape at the stunning scenery around the 'Artist's Island' and marvel at the masterpieces it has inspired in the Monhegan Museum of Art and History.

1½hrs from Boothbay Harbor

Southern Coast

Cycle along the East Coast Greenway, stopping for breaks in delightful coastal towns with gallery-dotted main streets and lighthouses perched on seaside cliffs.

30 – 45mins from Portland

Atlantic Ocean

0 — 50 km
0 — 25 miles

NEW ENGLAND HIGH COUNTRY
Trip Builder

TAKE YOUR PICK OF MUST-SEES AND HIDDEN GEMS

How much outdoor adventure can you squeeze into one region? If the region is New England, the answer is a lot. There are lakes and rivers to paddle, mountains to climb, and miles and miles of trails to hike, bike or ski.

Trip Notes

Hub towns Bethel, Jackson

How long Allow 10 days

Getting around Travel by car, but bring your bicycle if you want to challenge yourself on the Cross New Hampshire Adventure Trail.

Tips If you're coming during foliage season, book your accommodations early, as the small inns and B&Bs fill up fast.

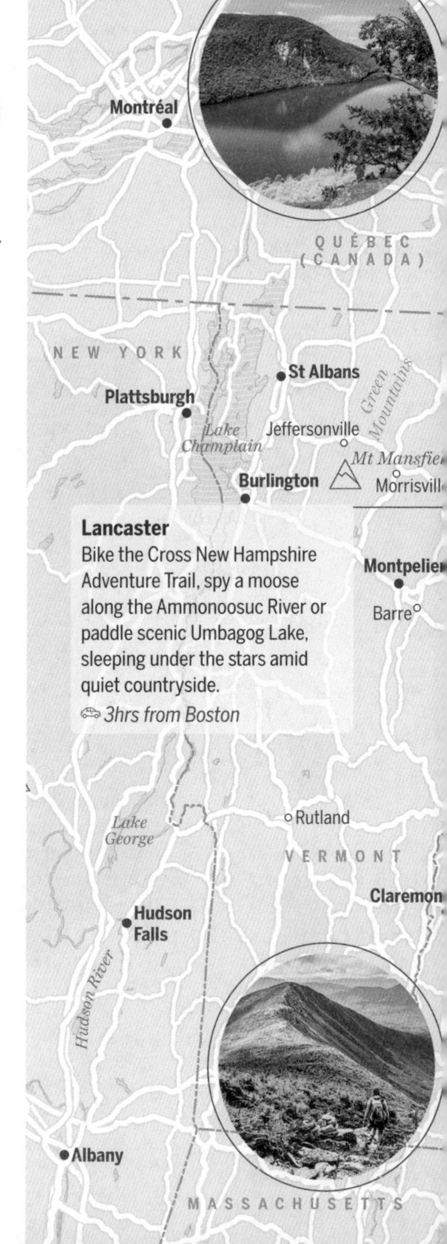

CLOCKWISE FROM TOP LEFT: EDITH ROSS/SHUTTERSTOCK ©, ADAM NIXON PHOTOGRAPHY/SHUTTERSTOCK ©, REBECCA SMITH/GETTY IMAGES ©

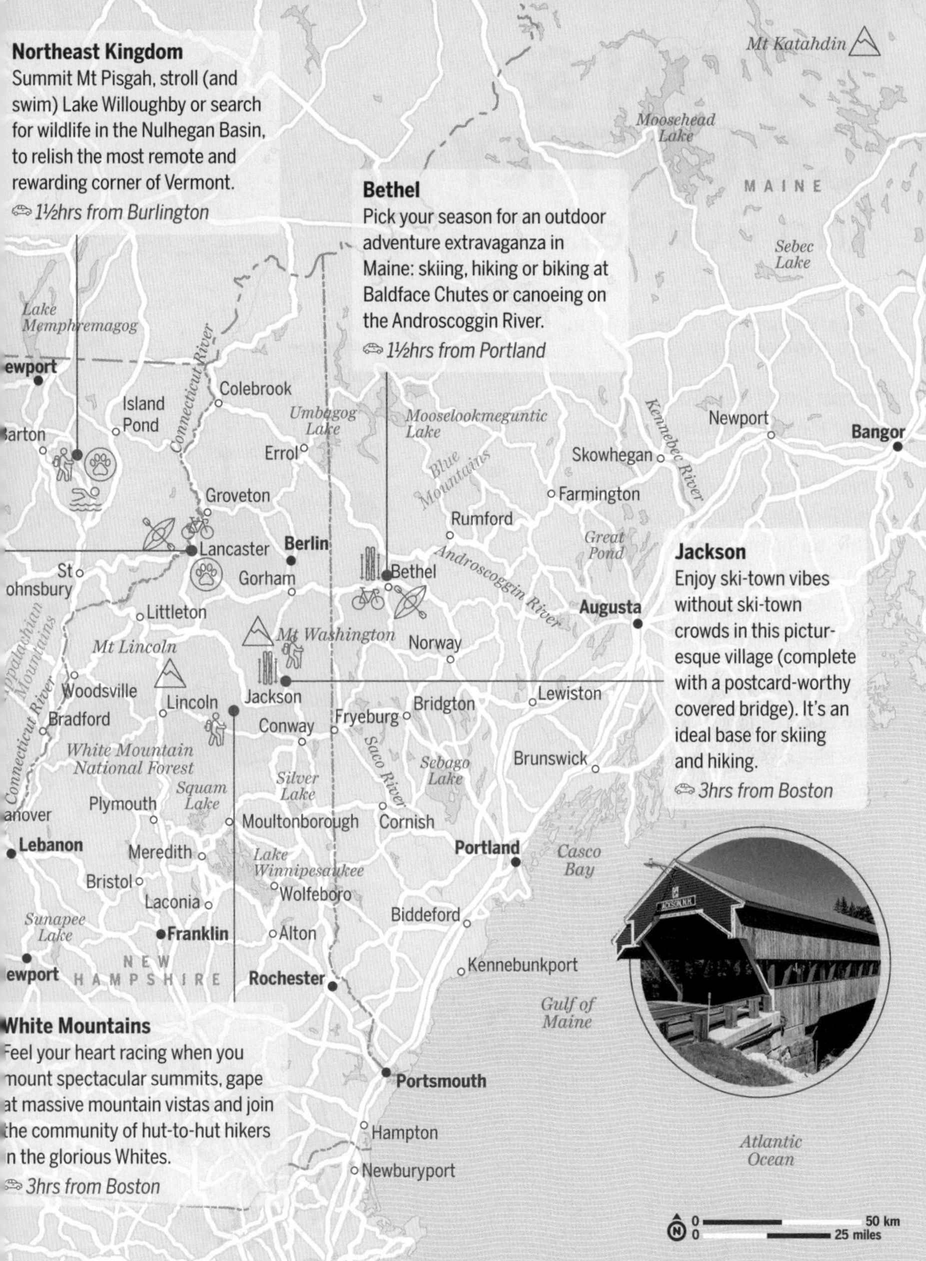
Northeast Kingdom
Summit Mt Pisgah, stroll (and swim) Lake Willoughby or search for wildlife in the Nulhegan Basin, to relish the most remote and rewarding corner of Vermont.
1½hrs from Burlington
Bethel
Pick your season for an outdoor adventure extravaganza in Maine: skiing, hiking or biking at Baldface Chutes or canoeing on the Androscoggin River.
1½hrs from Portland
Jackson
Enjoy ski-town vibes without ski-town crowds in this picturesque village (complete with a postcard-worthy covered bridge). It's an ideal base for skiing and hiking.
3hrs from Boston
White Mountains
Feel your heart racing when you mount spectacular summits, gape at massive mountain vistas and join the community of hut-to-hut hikers in the glorious Whites.
3hrs from Boston
Mt Katahdin
Moosehead Lake
MAINE
Sebec Lake
Lake Memphremagog
Newport
Colebrook
Island Pond
Connecticut River
Umbagog Lake
Mooselookmeguntic Lake
Kennebec River
Newport
Bangor
Barton
Errol
Skowhegan
Blue Mountains
Groveton
Farmington
Rumford
Great Pond
Lancaster
Berlin
St Johnsbury
Gorham
Bethel
Androscoggin River
Augusta
Littleton
Appalachian Mountains
Mt Washington
Norway
Mt Lincoln
Woodsville
Lincoln
Jackson
Lewiston
Bradford
Connecticut River
Conway
Fryeburg
Bridgton
White Mountain National Forest
Saco River
Sebago Lake
Brunswick
Silver Lake
Squam Lake
Hanover
Plymouth
Moultonborough
Cornish
Lebanon
Meredith
Portland
Casco Bay
Lake Winnipesaukee
Bristol
Wolfeboro
Laconia
Biddeford
Sunapee Lake
Franklin
Alton
NEW HAMPSHIRE
Newport
Rochester
Kennebunkport
Gulf of Maine
Portsmouth
Hampton
Atlantic Ocean
Newburyport
JACKSON, N.H.
0 50 km
0 25 miles

TOWN & COUNTRY
Trip Builder

TAKE YOUR PICK OF MUST-SEES AND HIDDEN GEMS

Rural New England is not only for backcountry explorers. The region's greatest charms include its delightful small towns and lush landscapes. Sleep in cozy inns, dine on farm-to-table delicacies, enjoy artsy enclaves and historic architecture – all amid the rich New England countryside.

Trip Notes

Hub towns Burlington, Keene

How long Allow 10 days

Getting around Travel by car, supplemented by bike on the rail trails and cycling routes.

Tips If you have a cheesy streak (as most of us do!), consult the Vermont Cheese Trail *(vtcheese.com)* to sample delicious artisanal cheeses and to see where and how they are made.

hamplain Islands
ck a route and explore the
lands by bicycle, stopping to
sit historic villages, sample
cal wine and cool off at lake-
de beaches.
25mins from Burlington
0
50 km
0
25 miles
MAINE
Flagstaff Lake
Kennebec River
Bingham
Mooselookmeguntic Lake
Newport
Colebrook
Newport
Island Pond
Connecticut River
St Albans
Green Mountains
Errol
Barton
Jeffersonville
Barre
Discover a history written in stone, among the statues, gravestones and public buildings of this granite-quarrying town.
1hr from Burlington
Morrisville
Lancaster
Berlin
Androscoggin River
urlington
Mt Mansfield
St Johnsbury
Gorham
Bethel
Waterbury
Littleton
Mt Washington
Montpelier
Barre
Vergennes
Jackson
Woodsville
Saco River
Bridgton
Lincoln
Middlebury
Bradford
Randolph
White Mountain National Forest
Woodstock
Ogle the rural landscape, admire the historic architecture, and soak up the small-town atmosphere of quintessential Vermont.
½hr from Burlington
Brunswick
VERMONT
Brandon
Plymouth
Hanover
Meredith
Lake Winnipesaukee
Fair Haven
Lebanon
Rutland
Woodstock
Laconia
Franklin
Claremont
Newport
Ludlow
Merrimack River
Connecticut River
Equinox
NEW HAMPSHIRE
Manchester
Concord
Bellows Falls
Hillsborough
Portsmouth
Keene
Manchester
Keene
Pedal the rail trails and paddle the canoe trails in the foothills and lakes surrounding this quaint college town in New Hampshire.
2hrs from Boston
Brattleboro
Bennington
North Adams
Greenfield
Fitchburg
Salem
Boston
Brattleboro
Contemplate contemporary art, choose your favorite craft-beer brewer and get a taste of this dynamic town's cutting-edge culinary scene.
2½hrs from Burlington
Housatonic River
Worcester
MASSACHUSETTS
Cape Cod
Atlantic Ocean
Plymouth
Cape Cod Bay

Things to Know About NEW ENGLAND

INSIDER TIPS TO HIT THE GROUND RUNNING

1 Beat the Crowds

Weather is unpredictable (but often lovely) and crowds are sparse from April through June.

Consider traveling off-season for cheaper lodgings and fewer crowds (think beach in September).

Come between November and March for museums, snow sports and the best travel bargains.

Avoid school vacation weeks at museums and on the slopes.

Go off the beaten track on weekends and public holidays like Independence Day. It's a big region!

▶ Read more about travel seasons on p20

2 Driving Dos & Don'ts

Do rent a car so you can explore the rural areas.

Don't hit a moose.

Do wear your seatbelt.

Don't use your cell phone unless it's in hands-free mode.

Do beware the 'Boston left,' when the first left-turning car jumps out in front of oncoming traffic as soon as the light turns green.

Don't drive in Boston if you can avoid it.

▶ See driving essentials on p244

3 Ad-Free Driving

Billboards are prohibited on roads throughout the states of Maine and Vermont. Enjoy!

4 New England Reserve

It's not customary to greet strangers or strike up a conversation, especially in urban areas. Don't be offended. That said, most New Englanders are happy to give directions, answer questions or otherwise help out.

5 Local Lingo

A guide to deciphering local expressions:

How ah yah? Standard friendly greeting.

Wicked Awesome, really cool. It can also be a modifier meaning 'extremely' – so something might be 'wicked expensive' or it could be 'wicked cold' outside. The best compliment a New Englander can give is to say something is 'wicked pisser' (usually pronounced 'wicked pissah').

U-ey A U-turn, as in 'You missed the entrance, you better pull a u-ey.'

Drinks If you order a 'regular' coffee, you'll get cream and sugar. A soda is a 'tonic.' A milkshake is a 'frappe' (or a 'cabinet' in Rhode Island). A water fountain is a 'bubbler.' Buy your beer at a 'packie' (package store).

Sweets A glazed doughnut is 'honey-dipped.' If you want sprinkles on your ice cream, ask for 'jimmies.'

Boston Common It's singular. Please don't refer to America's oldest public park as 'the Commons.'

6 New England Accents

New Englanders are notorious for dropping their r's in the middle or at the end of words, and adding r's when words end in a vowel. Alas, it's not a smaht idear to mock, imitate or comment on someone's accent. Don't say 'You can't get theyah from heah' or 'Pahk the cah in Hahvahd Yahd.' We already know.

7 Weather Woes

As Mark Twain supposedly said, 'If you don't like the weather in New England now, wait a few minutes.' The quote is unverified, but the sentiment is true. The weather is bound to change while you're out, so bring your rain hat and your sunglasses.

▶ Find out how to prepare for weather extremes on p18 and p246

Read, Listen, Watch & Follow

READ

Olive Kitteridge (Elizabeth Strout; 2008) Pulitzer Prize–winning short stories set in small-town Maine.

The Stars are Fire (Anita Shreve; 2017) Suspense and survival during the 1947 Maine wildfire.

Interpreter of Maladies (Jhumpa Lahiri; 1999) Pulitzer Prize winner about immmigration and multiculturalism in New England.

The Emperor of Ocean Park (Stephen L Carter; 2002) A legal thriller by a Yale law professor.

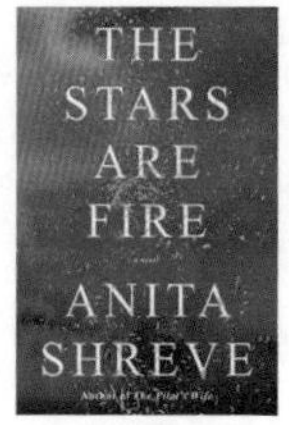

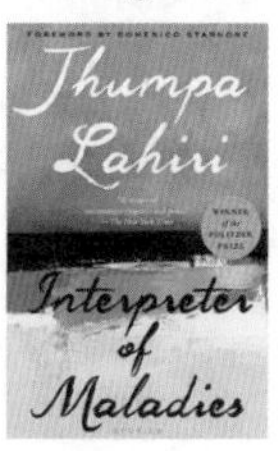

LISTEN

Chronicle the Podcast *(chronicle5.podbean.com)* The podcast version of the popular regional 'magazine show.'

New England Legends *(ournewengland legends.com/category/podcasts)* Two storytellers share strange stories and mysterious lore from around the region.

Farmhouse (Phish; 2000) Upbeat rootsy rock by beloved Vermont indie band; inspired by seeing the aurora borealis over Stowe.

Food for Thought with Billy & Jenny Foodie hosts chat with chefs, brewers and other culinary professionals on this podcast.

THE PHOTO ACCESS/ALAMY STOCK PHOTO ©

Let's Face It (The Mighty Mighty Bosstones; 1997) Rousing album by Boston ska-punk legends, including the single 'The Impression That I Get.'

WATCH

Jaws (1975) Cult classic filmed on Martha's Vineyard.

On Golden Pond (1981; pictured top right) Oscar-winning performances in a drama set on Lake Winnipesaukee.

Amistad (1997; pictured bottom right) Chronicles a Supreme Court case involving African slaves who mutinied and won freedom.

Good Will Hunting (1997) A blue-collar boy from South Boston becomes a math savant at MIT.

The Lighthouse (2019) A psychological thriller set on a remote Maine island.

TCD/PROD.DB/ALAMY STOCK PHOTO ©

UNITED ARCHIVES GMBH/ALAMY STOCK PHOTO ©

FOLLOW

@edibleboston Recipes, restaurateur profiles and culinary events.

Art New England (artnewengland.com) Contemporary art exhibits and reviews.

New England Cable Network (necn.com) Breaking regional news stories.

Nothing But New England (nothingbutnewengland.com) Outdoor activities and family fun.

YANKEE

@yankeemagazine Cultural insights and travel resources.

BOSTON
HISTORY | ART & ARCHITECTURE | OUTDOORS
Experience
Boston
online

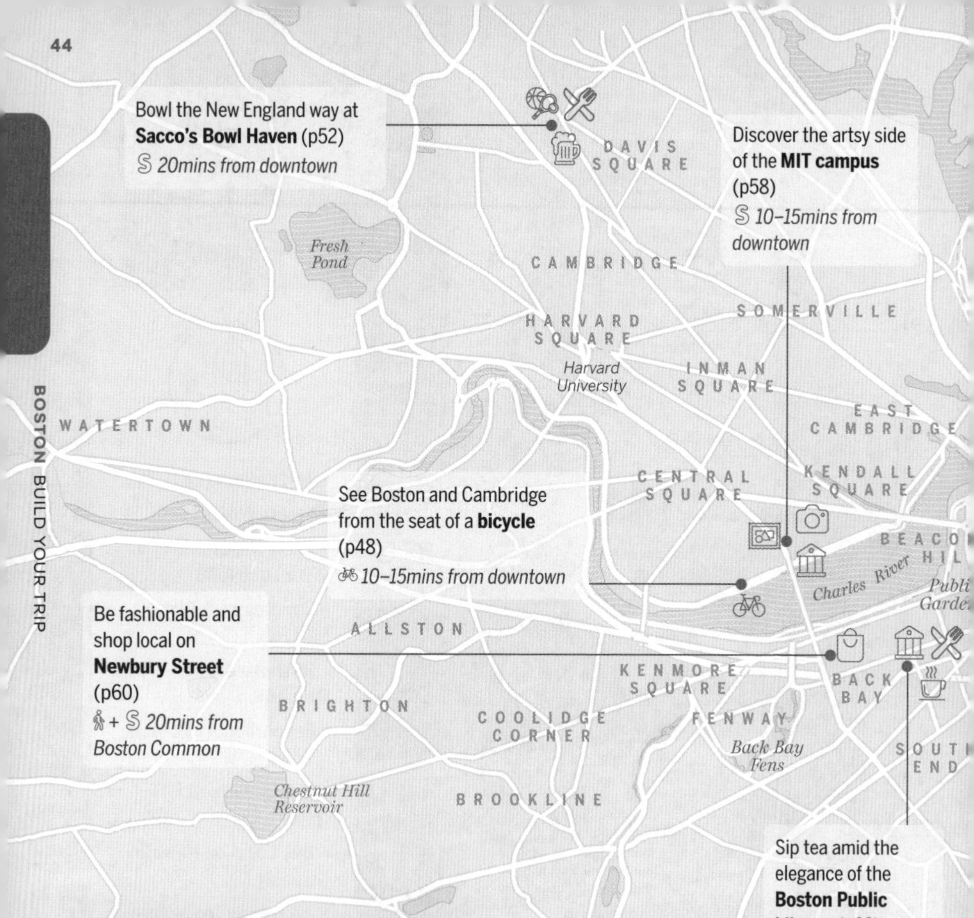

Bowl the New England way at **Sacco's Bowl Haven** (p52)
20mins from downtown

Discover the artsy side of the **MIT campus** (p58)
10–15mins from downtown

See Boston and Cambridge from the seat of a **bicycle** (p48)
10–15mins from downtown

Be fashionable and shop local on **Newbury Street** (p60)
+ 20mins from Boston Common

Sip tea amid the elegance of the **Boston Public Library** (p62)
+ 10–20mins from Boston Common

DAVIS SQUARE
Fresh Pond
CAMBRIDGE
HARVARD SQUARE
Harvard University
SOMERVILLE
INMAN SQUARE
WATERTOWN
EAST CAMBRIDGE
CENTRAL SQUARE
KENDALL SQUARE
BEACON HILL
Charles River
Public Garden
ALLSTON
KENMORE SQUARE
BACK BAY
BRIGHTON
COOLIDGE CORNER
FENWAY
Back Bay Fens
SOUTH END
Chestnut Hill Reservoir
BROOKLINE

BOSTON
Trip Builder

Can one city be all things to all people? Boston sure does try. This is where folks are as passionate about intellectual pursuits as they are about sports, where art and technology are intertwined, and where a fascinating history is matched by a progressive vibe.

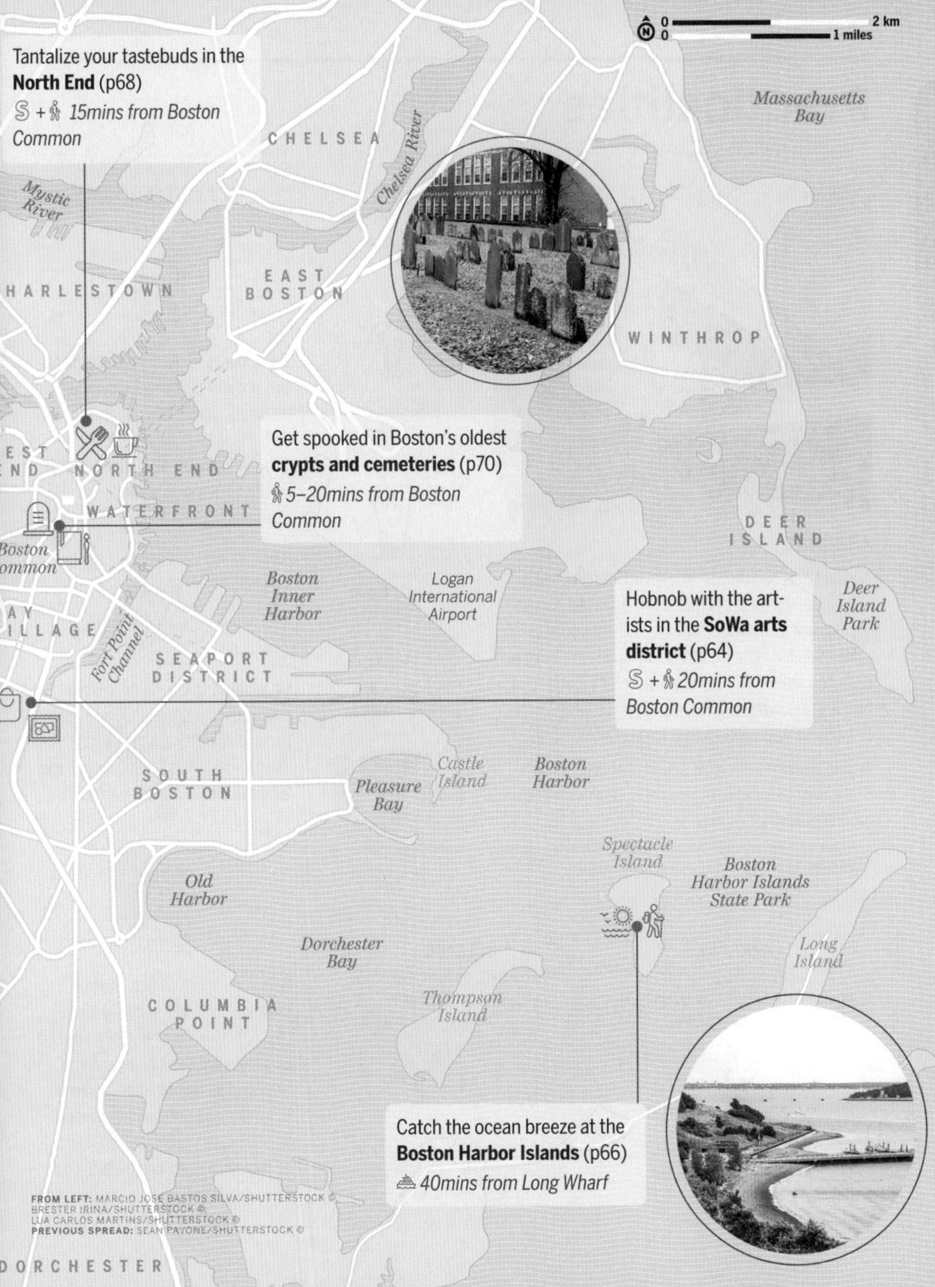

0 2 km
0 1 miles
Tantalize your tastebuds in the
North End (p68)
+ 15mins from Boston Common
CHELSEA
Chelsea River
Massachusetts Bay
Mystic River
CHARLESTOWN
EAST BOSTON
WINTHROP
Get spooked in Boston's oldest
crypts and cemeteries (p70)
5–20mins from Boston Common
WEST END
NORTH END
WATERFRONT
DEER ISLAND
Boston Common
Boston Inner Harbor
Logan International Airport
Deer Island Park
Hobnob with the art-
ists in the **SoWa arts district** (p64)
+ 20mins from Boston Common
BAY VILLAGE
Fort Point Channel
SEAPORT DISTRICT
SOUTH BOSTON
Castle Island
Pleasure Bay
Boston Harbor
Spectacle Island
Boston Harbor Islands State Park
Old Harbor
Dorchester Bay
Long Island
Thompson Island
COLUMBIA POINT
Catch the ocean breeze at the
Boston Harbor Islands (p66)
40mins from Long Wharf
DORCHESTER

Practicalities

2P2PLAY/SHUTTERSTOCK ©

ARRIVING

Airport You're likely to arrive at Boston Logan International Airport (pictured), located across the harbor in East Boston. From here you can take the silver line bus to South Station (free) or blue line subway to central Boston ($2.40). The bus and subway run from 5:30am to 12:30am. Otherwise you can catch a taxi for about $35.

Trains Services arrive at South Station or North Station, both located in central Boston with dedicated subway stops on-site.

HOW MUCH FOR A

Lobster roll $30

Craft beer $8–$10

Harvard sweatshirt $60

WHEN TO GO

APR–JUN
Sunny skies and mild temperatures; many events at local universities.

JUL–AUG
Busy tourist season with hot, humid weather.

SEP–OCT
Crisp temperatures, beautiful fall foliage and active student life.

NOV–MAR
Gray days with cold weather; fewer crowds and cheaper prices for hotels.

GETTING AROUND

T (Subway) The quickest way to get around is the subway, known as 'the T.' The T runs from 5:30am or 6am until 1:30am. Purchase CharlieTickets (one-way $2.40) at the vending machines at MBTA stations.

Bluebikes Boston's bike-share program has some 200 stations around the city. Buy a single 30-minute trip ($2.95) or get the 24-hour Adventure Pass ($10).

Bus A network of bus routes supplements the subway system ($1.70). The silver line is a special bus line that runs between the airport and South Station (free from the airport, but otherwise $2.40). Use your CharlieTicket or pay with cash on the bus (no change given).

EATING & DRINKING

Boston cuisine celebrates the bounty from local waters. Favorite local preparations include lobster rolls, oysters on the half-shell (pictured top right), and rich, creamy clam chowder. Italian immigrants and their descendants have turned the North End into a can't-miss destination for irresistible Italian-American cooking (especially cannoli; pictured bottom right), and Chinatown is packed with Asian eateries. Reservations are recommended for dinner. While Boston has its fair share of Irish pubs, it also has a dynamic craft-beer movement, with new microbreweries opening yearly.

Best craft beer
Trillium Brewing Co (p75)

Must-try lobster roll
Cusser's (p74)

PACKING LIST

- Comfortable walking shoes
- Reusable tote bag
- Reusable water bottle
- Umbrella and sunblock (the rumors about the weather are true)

CONNECT & FIND YOUR WAY

Wi-fi Wicked Free Wifi is Boston's free outdoor wi-fi service. Connect at parks and plazas around the city, including the Boston Common, City Hall Plaza and Quincy Market. Most restaurants, cafes and libraries also offer free wi-fi, as does Logan Airport.

Navigation Driving in Boston is challenging, due to the excess of traffic and one-way streets.

WHERE TO STAY

Boston offers a wide range of upscale accommodations, from intimate guesthouses to swanky hotels. Inexpensive accommodations are rarer, but prices drop significantly during low tourist periods.

Neighbourhood	Pro/Con
West End	Close to major sights; convenient transportation. Relatively affordable.
Downtown & Financial District	Close to major sights and waterfront; convenient transportation. Few affordable options.
Seaport District	Close to airport and waterfront; great dining and nightlife; city and harbor views. Few affordable options.
Back Bay & Fenway	Neighborhood charm; close to major sights; convenient transportation; great dining, shopping and nightlife.
South End & Chinatown	Neighborhood charm; great dining, shopping and nightlife. Relatively affordable.
Cambridge	Neighborhood charm; close to sights; convenient transportation; great dining, shopping and nightlife. Removed from city center.

MONEY

ATMs are widely available; credit cards are accepted at most hotels, restaurants and shops. Don't forget to tip your bartenders and servers (20% for good service), taxi drivers (15%) and housekeeping staff ($5 to $10).

01 Cycle the Charles RIVER LOOP

CYCLING | SCENERY | ARCHITECTURE

See Boston and Cambridge from the seat of a bike. Between the Charles River Dam and Watertown Sq, a paved, off-road cycling trail follows the Charles River, offering a glimpse of working waterfronts, spectacular cityscapes, inviting parklands and historic university campuses.

JON BILOUS/SHUTTERSTOCK ©

How to

Getting around By bicycle, of course! Get a one-day Adventure Pass from Bluebikes or rent more specialized vehicles from Urban AdvenTours.

When to go This ride is spectacular when the spring cherry blossoms burst and when the fall foliage is aflame, but it's a rewarding ride in any season.

Distance The round trip is 17 miles, but 10 bridges on the way offer ample opportunities to shorten the trip.

2P2PLAY/SHUTTERSTOCK ©

Boston on the Move

At the northeast end of the route, take a detour around **North Point Park** and **Paul Revere Park** to witness Boston on the move. The parks are connected by a long **footbridge** – an excellent vantage point to see trains chugging into North Station, cars roaring over the Zakim Bridge and boats plying the waters between harbor and river. Loop around the parks and back to Charles River Dam Rd to cross the river (near the Museum of Science).

SERGEY NOVIKOV/SHUTTERSTOCK ©

Riverside Ramble

The **Charles River Esplanade** is the centerpiece of the riverfront, with wonderful cycling and walking paths, picnic areas, playgrounds and lookout points. Also, beer. Climb up the **Longfellow Bridge** – lovingly known as

I Brake for Beer

From May to October, stop for refreshment at the Owl's Nest craft-beer gardens, operated by **Night Shift Brewing**, on the Esplanade or at Herter Park in Allston. Or, any time of year, walk from Paul Revere Park over the Charlestown Locks to their restaurant and 'innovation brewery' at **Lovejoy Wharf**.

Top left North Point Park. **Bottom left** Longfellow Bridge. **Top right** Cycling, Charles River Esplanade.

the 'Salt & Pepper' bridge – for a fabulous panorama of the Esplanade, the Back Bay and beyond. Artistic highlights include a sculpture of Arthur Fiedler, longtime conductor of the Boston Pops.

University Way

At the western end of the Esplanade, you'll get a quick glimpse of the **Boston University** campus, most evident from the students lounging on the 'BU Beach.' From here, the **Boston University Bridge** stretches over the Charles River, with a railway bridge below. This is a rare place where it's possible to ride a boat (or a bike!) under a train chugging under a car driving under a plane flying.

The sprawling campus of **MIT** (Massachusetts Institute of Technology) occupies the north side of the river between the Longfellow Bridge and the Boston University Bridge. You'll ride past several neoclassical landmarks – the **Walker Memorial** and the aptly named **Great Dome** – as well as many

How Long is the Mass Ave Bridge?

The Mass Ave Bridge – from Back Bay in Boston to MIT in Cambridge – is the longest bridge over the Charles River. Just how long is it? The graffiti-scrawled sidewalks measure the distance in 'smoots.' This obscure unit of measurement was invented in 1958 by those quirky kids at MIT. One smoot is approximately 5ft 7in, the height of Oliver Smoot, who was the shortest pledge of the Lambda Chi Alpha fraternity that year. And yes, his physical person was actually used for all the measurements.

So how long is the Mass Ave Bridge? 364.4 smoots plus one ear.

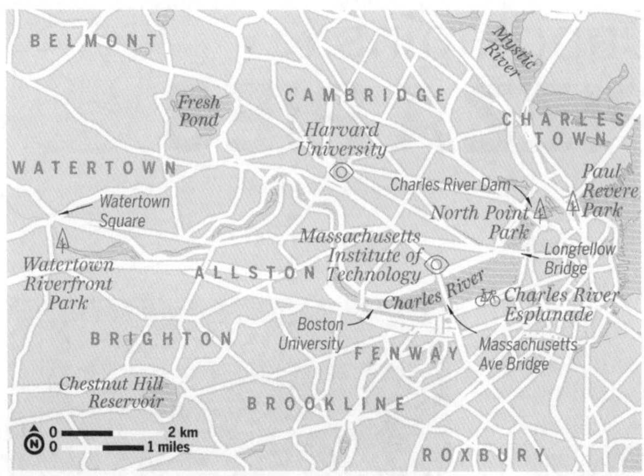

Left Mass Ave Bridge. **Below** Dunster House, Harvard.

modern buildings such as the red-brick, undulating **Baker House**, designed by Finnish architect Alvar Aalto.

A few miles further west, red-brick facades line the sidewalks and cupolas decorate the skyline on both sides of the river, as you pass through **Harvard University**. The business school occupies the south shore, dominated by the beautiful Georgian **Baker Library**. Harvard Stadium and other sports facilities are further along. The handsome buildings lined up along the north shore are the undergraduate residential houses, including **Eliot House** and **Dunster House**, both topped with cupolas. A few blocks from the river, the streets of **Harvard Square** bustle with student life.

Accessible Outdoors

The delightful **Watertown Riverfront Park** stretches along the north side of the Charles River, just east of Watertown Sq. Bike paths wind through the wooded area, but there is also a **Braille Trail** and lead ropes to guide the visually impaired (designed with input from the nearby Perkins School for the Blind). Ready to take a break? The musically inclined will have some fun sitting on – and playing – the marimba bench. (Yes, it is exactly what it 'sounds' like.)

02 Candlepins & PIZZA PIES

PIZZA | BEER | BOWLING

Somervillains have been bowling at Sacco's Bowl Haven since 1939, when the Sacco family operated 18 candlepin bowling alleys around the state. Nowadays, these old-fashioned New England lanes are few and far between. But folks still flock to Sacco's for the thin pins, the retro vibe and the fantastic flatbread pizza and craft beer.

TIM MA ©

How to

Getting there Take the red line to Davis.

When to go Any day of the week! Bowling starts at 10am, but the kitchen and bar don't open until noon.

Prices Bowling is $30 per lane per hour, plus $4 per person for shoe rental.

Top tip Reservations are recommended for bowling lanes on evenings and weekends.

Tenpin bowling is a beloved pastime, ingrained in American culture by *Laverne & Shirley* and *The Big Lebowski*. But candlepin bowling is something different altogether – a regional variation that originated in Worcester, Massachusetts, and took hold across New England (but nowhere else) in the mid-20th century.

Candlepin bowling catches non–New Englanders by surprise. The pins are tall, thin and straight, unlike the heavier, curvier pins used in tenpin bowling. The small handheld-size balls do not have finger holes. Because

Above Bowling, Sacco's. **Top right** Cocktail, Sacco's. **Bottom right** Flatbread pizza, Sacco's.

ⓘ Candlepin Basics

Check out the Massachusetts Bowling Association website *(masscandlepin.com)* for tips on candlepin form and etiquette, as well as a primer on how to score your game.

the pins are harder to knock down, each player gets three throws per box, or turn. Play a few strings and you'll soon discover that candlepin bowling requires a degree of strategy and finesse not normally associated with bowling.

Nowadays, as culture is becoming more uniform, many regionalisms are disappearing both in New England and around the country. Candlepin bowling is no exception – there are only a few candlepin bowling alleys left in the Boston area.

Fortunately, Sacco's is not going anywhere. Today, this Somerville institution is owned by American Flatbread, which brings a whole new level of enjoyment to candlepin bowling – namely, irresistible pizzas plus craft beer and cocktails. Honestly, the food and drinks are so good that you might come here to eat and drink, even if you didn't want to try out candlepin bowling.

But, trust us, you *do* want to try out candlepin bowling.

TIM MA ©

TIM MA ©

Birthplace of a Revolution

THE LOCAL HISTORY OF A NATIONAL BEGINNING

It started with a financial disagreement (of sorts), which grew into a revolution, which grew into a new nation. The American fight for independence from Britain began right here in Boston, when some local merchants got in a huff about unfair tax policies.

Left *The Destruction of Tea in Boston Harbor* by Nathaniel Currier. **Middle** *The Death of General Warren at the Battle of Bunker's Hill, June 17, 1775* by John Trumbull. **Right** Patriots' Day parade, Concord, MA.

IANDAGNALL COMPUTING/ALAMY STOCK PHOTO ©

Taxation Without Representation

In the 1760s, the British Parliament passed a series of acts placing greater financial burdens on the colonists. With each new tax, colonial resentment intensified, sparking vocal protests and violent mobs. Respectable lawyer John Adams defended these acts of defiance, citing the Magna Carta's principle of 'no taxation without representation.' To each act of rebellion, the British throne responded with increasingly severe measures, eventually dispatching Redcoat regiments known as 'regulars' to restore order and suspending all local political power.

Sons of Liberty

A clandestine network of patriots – the Sons of Liberty – stirred up public resistance to British policy. They were led by some well-known townsmen, including esteemed surgeon Dr Joseph Warren, upper-class merchant John Hancock, skilled silversmith Paul Revere and bankrupt brewer Sam Adams. In March 1770 a motley street gang provoked British regulars with slurs and snowballs until the troops fired into the crowd, killing five people. John Adams successfully defended the British troops, who were acting in self-defense. The Sons of Liberty, however, scored a propaganda coup with their depictions of the 'Boston Massacre.'

In 1773, the Parliament implemented a new tax on tea. When three tea-bearing vessels arrived in Boston Harbor, the Sons of Liberty raised the stakes. Disguised as Mohawk natives, they descended on the waterfront, boarded the ships and dumped 90,000lb of taxable tea into the

IANDAGNALL COMPUTING/ALAMY STOCK PHOTO ©

WANGKUN JIA/SHUTTERSTOCK ©

harbor. The king's retribution was swift: the port was blockaded and the city placed under military rule. British troops and warships arrived in Boston. Meanwhile, local townsfolk and yeoman farmers organized into citizen militias known as Minutemen. They drilled on town commons and stockpiled weapons in secret stores.

> Disguised as Mohawk natives, the Sons of Liberty descended on the waterfront, boarded the ships and dumped 90,000lb of taxable tea into the harbor.

Shot Heard Round the World

In April 1775 the British dispatched troops to seize a hidden stash of gunpowder. The Sons of Liberty got word of the troop movement, and William Dawes and Paul Revere galloped into the night to alert the Minutemen. At daybreak, imperial troops skirmished with Minutemen in Lexington and Concord. By midmorning, more militia had arrived and chased the bloodied Redcoats back to Boston in ignominious defeat. The inevitable had arrived: the War for Independence.

Boston figured prominently in the early phase of the American Revolution. In June 1775 Bostonians inflicted a blow to British morale at the Battle of Bunker Hill. The British eventually took the hill, but their losses were greater than expected. Britain's military occupation of the city continued until March 1776, when Washington mounted captured British cannons on Dorchester Heights and trained them on the British fleet in Boston Harbor. The British evacuated the city, trashing and looting as they went; Boston was liberated.

Patriots' Day

An official holiday in Massachusetts (as well as Maine), Patriots' Day commemorates the start of the Revolutionary War. On the third Monday in April, Bay Staters celebrate with historic reenactments, patriotic parades and pancake breakfasts. Big events take place in Concord and Lexington, but Boston has its own commemorations. On Sunday night, the Old North Church hosts a lantern-lighting ceremony, followed by a reading of Longfellow's poem. On Monday, a Patriots' Day Parade includes a wreath-laying ceremony at the graves of Paul Revere and William Dawes, followed by a reenactment of the riders' departures from Boston.

REVOLUTIONARY
Boston

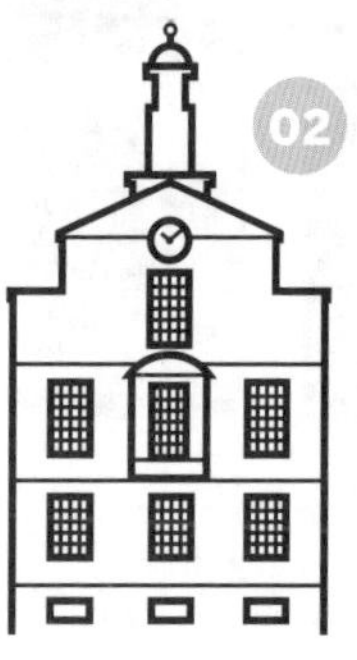

01 Freedom Trail

Guides lead informative tours of the Freedom Trail, a 2.4-mile walking tour of Boston's revolutionary sights.

02 Old State House

Site of the Boston Massacre in 1770 as well as the city's first reading of the Declaration of Independence in 1776.

03 Boston Massacre

Paul Revere's depiction of the 1770 Boston Massacre was effective propaganda in support of the Sons of Liberty.

04 Boston Massacre victims

The victims of the Boston Massacre are buried in a communal grave in the Granary Burying Ground.

05 Boston Tea Party

Bostonians reenact the 1773 protest when patriots, dressed up as Mohawks, dumped tea into the Boston Harbor.

06 Paul Revere

On April 18, 1775, Paul Revere rode from the North End to warn allies about the British advance on Concord.

07 Warren Tavern

Named for war hero Joseph Warren, this Charlestown bar opened in 1780. (Apparently Paul Revere was a regular.)

08 Sam Adams portrait

John Singleton Copley's painting in the Museum of Fine Arts depicts Sam Adams demanding the expulsion of British troops.

09 Bunker Hill Monument

The striking Charlestown landmark marks the site of the 1775 battle.

10 Longfellow House

After evacuation, General Washington set up headquarters in this beauty, once home to royal sympathizers.

11 Cambridge Common

Legend has it that George Washington took charge of the Continental Army here in 1775. Three cannons memorialize revolutionary heroes.

12 Independence Day

The annual fireworks display on the Esplanade is among the US' largest July 4th celebrations.

03 Arts Smarts AT MIT

ART | ARCHITECTURE | ACADEMIA

A recent building frenzy at MIT has resulted in some of the most architecturally intriguing structures you'll find on either side of the river. The university's progressive Percent-for-Art Program requires that a certain percentage of every building project budget be earmarked for art acquisitions, which explains the dozens of sculptures, murals and other striking displays around campus.

MARTIN WILLIAMS/ALAMY STOCK PHOTO ©

How to

Getting here Take the red line to Kendall.

Find the art Access a map of the public art with audio content *(listart.mit.edu/visit/public-art-map)*, or download an interactive map with thematic or geographic self-guided tours *(listart.oncell.com)*.

More info The List Visual Arts Center is MIT's contemporary art museum, offering cutting-edge exhibits on-site and student-led tours of the public art on campus.

JOHN HORNER ©, ARCHITECTS: HOWELER + YOON ARCHITECTURE

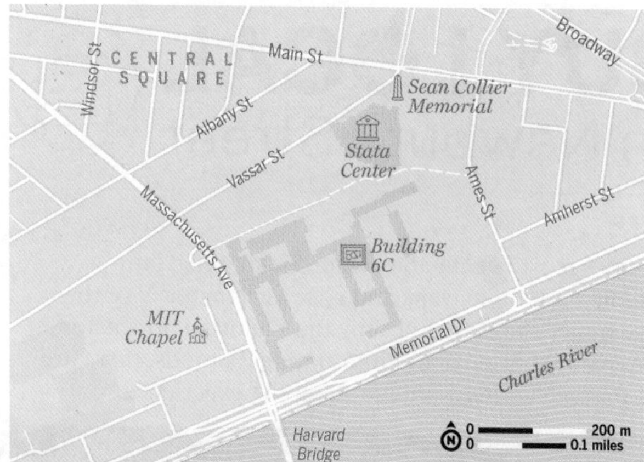

The MIT (Massachusetts Institute of Technology) campus is home to more than 50 architectural innovations and public art masterpieces, and that number continues to grow. (More than a dozen are creations of the 21st century.) Here are a few highlights.

Architectural anomaly Like something out of a Dr Seuss book, the **Stata Center** is composed of whimsical, colorful shapes and tilting metallic towers. Frank Gehry's signature idiosyncrasies – sloping walls, absence of doors – were a source of some controversy when the building opened, but it's a beloved and distinctive feature of the MIT campus.

In memoriam The **Sean Collier Memorial** was erected in 2015, on the site where the MIT police officer was killed by the Boston Marathon bombers. The sculpture is composed of 32 granite blocks which hold each other up, indicative of the theme 'strength through unity.'

Mystical MIT Upon first sight, you might not recognize Eero Saarinen's mysterious, windowless brick cylinder as a chapel. But the interior of the **MIT Chapel** offers an undeniably spiritual experience, with light streaming down from above, onto the spectacular shimmering altarpiece by Harry Bertoia.

Modern masterpiece Sol LeWitt's *Bars of Color within Squares* covers 5500 sq ft of the floor in **Building 6C**, which houses the physics department. Located in the atrium, the work is a surprising burst of shapes and colors, visible from many places around the building.

Top left Stata Center. **Bottom left** Sean Collier Memorial by J. Meejin Yoon

Unconventional Portraits

One of my favorite works on campus is Agnieszka Kurant's *The End of Signature* (2021), which visualizes the identity of the Cambridge and MIT communities through two massive signatures, rendered in neon and animated LED. Kurant used a machine learning system (artificial intelligence) that 'averaged' hundreds of individual signatures into one. I love how this work speaks to so many subjects at once: the act of collecting signatures for a common cause, a recognition of collective labor over ideas of individual genius, and the end of signature and handwriting in the digital age.

■ **Recommended by Natalie Bell,** *curator at the List Visual Arts Center @abellanatalie*

04 BUY LOCAL on Newbury Street

SHOPPING | FASHION | CAFES

Back Bay offers the city's most fashionable window-shopping, latte-drinking and people-watching. Fashion mavens and style aficionados love the high-end boutiques and bohemian shops that occupy the Victorian brownstones on Newbury St. Among the (many) national and international brands, there are still some Boston originals that make this a unique shopping experience.

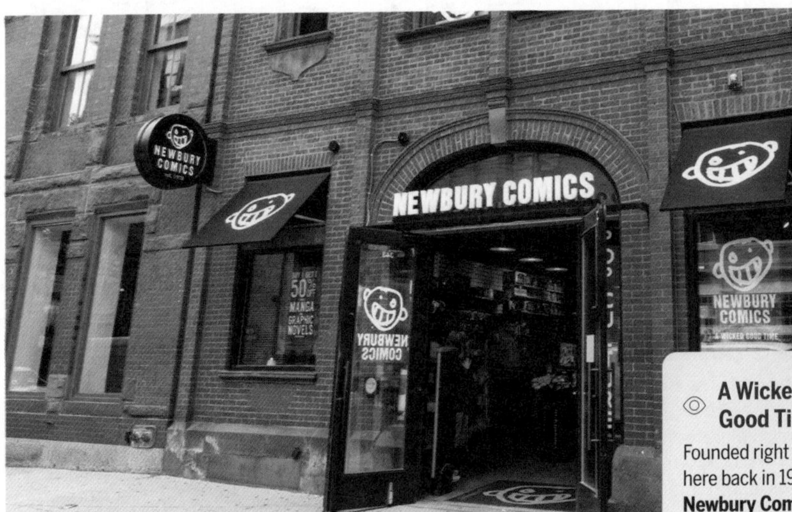

TORI SVIOKLA ©

Trip Notes

Getting here Take the green line to Copley or Hynes Convention Center, or orange line to Back Bay.

When to go Most shops are open from noon to 7pm daily.

Coffee break For a hot coffee or a sweet treat, stop at Bittersweet Shoppe or LA Burdick Chocolates.

Tax break There is no sales tax in Massachusetts on clothing up to $175. Automatic 6.5% discount!

A Wicked Good Time

Founded right here back in 1978, **Newbury Comics** has morphed from a comic-book store into a music store into a T-shirt, trading card and novelty store. While the concept and content have changed with the times, it's still a wicked good time for pop-culture junkies.

0 200 m
0 0.1 miles

Charles River

Harvard Bridge

04 The flattering, multifunctional styles at **Paridaez** are designed for women who work hard and play hard – all on the same day. Designed and manufactured in Massachusetts.

02 Don't walk, *run* to the **Tracksmith Trackhouse** for high-quality, purpose-designed running gear. This hub for the Boston amateur running community has weekly group outings and other events.

Beacon St

Gloucester St

Fairfield St

Marlborough St

Hereford St

Commonwealth Ave

Commonwealth Ave Mall

Bittersweet Shoppe

LA Burdick Chocolates (200m)

01 Get Boston's sweetest streetwear at **Johnny Cupcakes**. There are no pastries in this retro, frosting-scented bakery, just cool graphic T-shirts with a cupcake theme.

05 Get fitted at **Adelante Shoe Co** for custom-made shoes and boots. The smart leather footwear, handcrafted by fairly paid artisans in Guatemala, is shipped to your doorstep within three weeks.

Newbury St

BACK BAY

Boylston St

Newbury Comics

Massachusetts Turnpike

Massachusetts Ave

03 Do you like science? Stop by **Ministry of Supply**, founded by two MIT grads who aim to dress you up in clothes that are high-tech, planet-friendly and fashion-forward.

CLOCKWISE FROM LEFT: DAVID L. RYAN/THE BOSTON GLOBE VIA GETTY IMAGES ©, MICHAEL N. TODARO/GETTY IMAGES FOR AGENDA EMERGE ©, JORGE RIBAS/THE WASHINGTON POST VIA GETTY IMAGES ©

05 Afternoon Tea at the LIBRARY

ARCHITECTURE | ART | FOOD

Indulge your intellect and stimulate your senses when you visit the Boston Public Library, the esteemed 'shrine of letters' founded in 1852. Fronting Copley Sq, the original McKim building is a feast for the eyes – a veritable museum of exquisite art and architecture – with an elegant restaurant serving a feast for the mouth in the form of afternoon tea.

How to

Getting here Green line to Copley or orange line to Back Bay station.

When to go Tea is served Wednesday through Saturday; reservations required *(librarytea.com)*.

Self-guided tour Download the virtual booklet *Art & Architecture of the Central Library in Copley Square (apps.bpl.org/tourbooklet)*.

Don't miss The special collections hold countless treasures, including John Adams' personal library. Check the website *(bpl.org)* for details of exhibits showcasing the highlights.

Far left McKim lobby. Below Italianate courtyard. Near left Bates Hall Reading Room.

Charles Follen McKim's original Boston Public Library (BPL) building is a masterpiece of American Renaissance architecture, replete with stunning details and artistic gems. Minerva, goddess of wisdom, overlooks the entrance from the central keystone, hinting at what is inside.

First impressions are grand in the **McKim lobby**, where mosaic tiles adorn the ceiling. From there, a marble staircase leads past Pierre Puvis de Chavannes' inspirational murals and Augustus Saint-Gaudens' rough-hewn lions. The staircase terminates at the splendid **Bates Hall Reading Room**, where even the most mundane musings are elevated by the barrel-vaulted, 50ft coffered ceilings.

Nearby, the **Abbey Room** is named for the painter of the 1895 murals that recount Sir Galahad's quest for the Holy Grail. The 3rd-floor **Sargent Gallery** features John Singer Sargent's unfinished Judaic and Christian murals.

Back on the ground floor, the white-marble **Italianate courtyard** is surrounded by a covered arcade. The centerpiece fountain features a bronze sculpture of Bacchante, which scandalized Bostonians when it was first unveiled in 1897.

Overlooking the courtyard is the eponymous **restaurant**, where guests can top off their visit with traditional afternoon tea. Come dressed for the occasion and indulge in sandwiches, scones and sweets, accompanied by tea, of course, or tea-infused cocktails. It's all very sophisticated and civilized.

The Triumph of Religion

John Singer Sargent spent 29 years painting the expansive cycle of religious murals which are now the pièce de résistance of the BPL art collection. The murals trace the history of Western religion from the primitive worship of pagan gods to the foundation of the Law of Israel to the birth of Christ. Some scholars interpret that the sequence depicts a progression toward religious subjectivity and individualist spiritual pursuits. Others argue that the artist portrayed Christianity as more evolved than Judaism, which sparked controversy. The mural was never completed, due in part to the strong reaction from the Jewish community.

06 Get Creative IN SOWA

ART | FOOD | SHOPPING

The artistic community moved into the once-barren area south of Washington St, converted old warehouses into studios and galleries, and rebranded the place as 'SoWa.' And that's how Boston's innovative art and design district was born. Nowadays, it's a hotbed of creativity, packed with art venues, design showrooms and trendy dining.

How to

Getting here Take the orange line to Bay Bay station or Tufts Medical Center.

When to go Time your visit with SoWa First Fridays (5pm to 9pm, first Friday of the month) or with the SoWa Open Market (11am to 4pm on Sundays, from May to October).

Refuel Stop for lunch at Picco, or reserve for dinner at Myers + Chang or Brasserie.

The brick-and-beam buildings along Harrison Ave were originally used to manufacture goods ranging from canned food to pianos. Now these factories turn out paintings and sculptures instead. Housing about 70 artist studios and more than a dozen galleries, the **SoWa Artists Guild** is the epicenter of the South End art district. View the art and hobnob with the artists at the 'open studios' event held on the first Friday of every month. Or pop into the galleries to admire the art in a more formal setting.

Many artists also open their studios to visitors on Sundays (in season), when the **SoWa Open Market**

Top right Artist's stall, SoWa Open Market. **Bottom right** Farmers market stall, SoWa Open Market.

MICHAEL MOLONEY/SHUTTERSTOCK ©

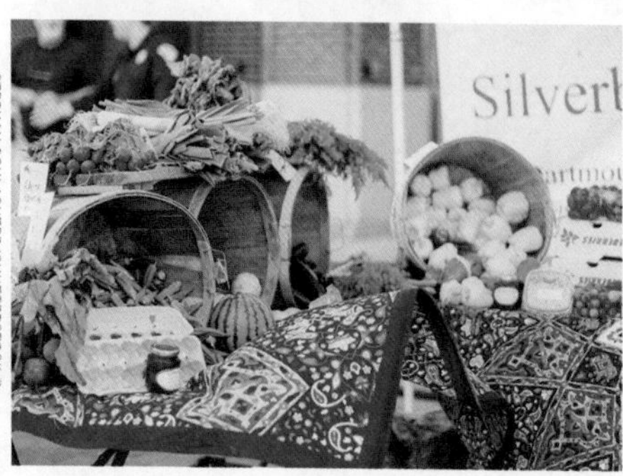

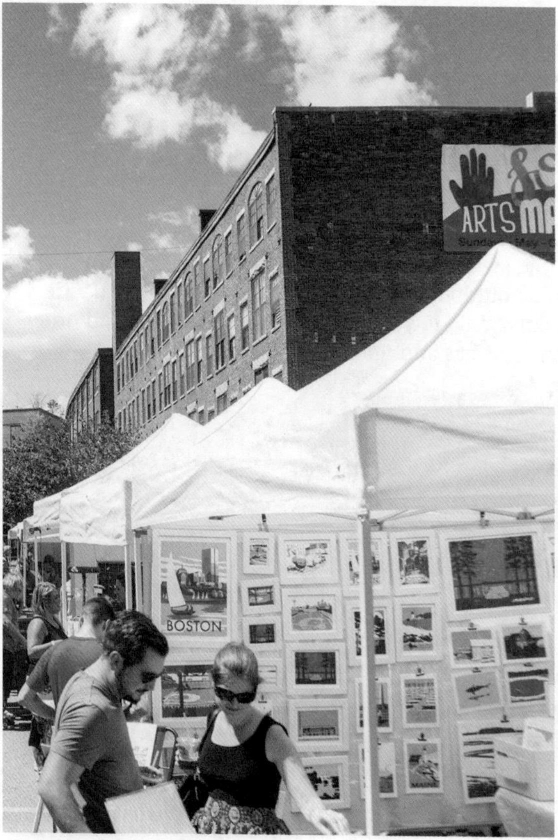

STEPHAN SCHLACHTER/SHUTTERSTOCK ©

Best of the South End

Best art Studios and galleries at 450 Harrison Ave

Best shops Olives & Grace; niche; Formaggio Kitchen

Best lunch stops Coppa Enoteca; anoush'ella; South End Buttery

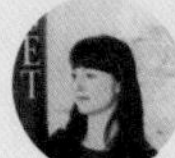

■ **Recommended by Jennifer Jean Okumura,** *painter and SoWa Artists Guild member @jennyjean*

takes over the nearby parking lots. More than 100 vendors set up shop under white tents, hawking arts and crafts, as well as edgier art, jewelry, homewares and homemade food and body products. There's also an indoor **Vintage Market**, a farmers market, food trucks and a beer garden. The whole affair is a fabulous opportunity for strolling, shopping and people-watching.

For a different side of the SoWa art scene, head two blocks north to **Underground at Ink Block**. What used to be an abandoned parking lot beneath the interstate is now an 8-acre playground and art space. A fantastic mural project has turned huge expanses of concrete wall space into a fabulous outdoor gallery for street art, with bold colorful pieces by a dozen local and national artists.

07 Hop the Harbor ISLANDS

HIKING | BEACHES | RUINS

Boston Harbor is sprinkled with 34 islands, many of which are open for trail walking, bird-watching, swimming, kayaking and camping. It's an unexpectedly fun and accessible outdoor adventure just a 40-minute boat ride from downtown Boston. Special events include live music, clam bakes and other family programs, especially on Georges and Spectacle Islands.

JOSEPH SOHM/SHUTTERSTOCK ©

How to

Getting here Boston Harbor Cruises runs seasonal ferries from Long Wharf to Georges and Spectacle Islands. There are shuttles to the smaller islands.

When to go The ferry runs on weekends from mid-May to mid-October, daily from the end of June to Labor Day.

Refuel There are concession stands on Georges and Spectacle Islands, but no food or water on the smaller islands – pack a picnic.

Top tip Don't try to visit more than two islands in a day: you'll spend all your time riding on or waiting for boats.

GREG KUSHMEREK/SHUTTERSTOCK ©

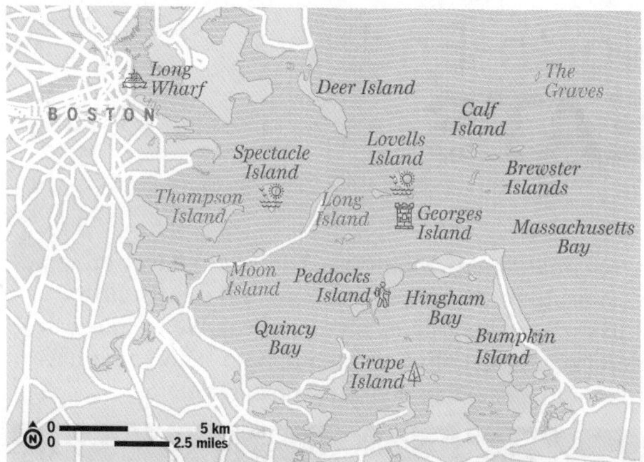

Exploring history More than a transportation hub, **Georges Island** is the site of Fort Warren, a 19th-century fort and Civil War prison. Guided tours are available and there is a small museum on-site, but the fort is largely abandoned, with many dark tunnels, creepy corners and magnificent lookouts to discover.

Lookout point A Harbor Islands hub, **Spectacle Island** has a large marina, a solar-powered visitor center and sandy, supervised beaches. Five miles of walking trails provide access to a 157ft peak, offering marvelous city views across the harbor.

Outer islands The outer islands are appealing for their relative remoteness and absence of crowds. One of the largest, **Peddocks Island** consists of four headlands connected by sandbars. Hiking trails wander through marsh, pond and coastal environs. Two deadly shipwrecks off **Lovells Island** bode badly for seafarers, but that doesn't seem to stop recreational boaters, swimmers and sunbathers from lounging on Lovells' long, rocky beach. European settlers used the island as a rabbit run, and descendant bunnies still run this place. True to its name, **Grape Island** is rich with fruity goodness. An arbor decked with cultivated grapes greets you opposite the boat dock, while the wild raspberries, bayberries and elderberries growing along the island's scrubby wooded trails attract abundant birdlife.

Top left Fort Warren, Georges Island. **Bottom left** View of Boston from Spectacle Island.

Peddocks Island

On Peddocks Island, there are few signs of the previous inhabitants, but it's clear why they were attracted to this 212-acre island and its rolling drumlins. Visitors can enjoy tree-covered hills, historic fort buildings from WWII, and views across the harbor of the Boston skyline and surrounding towns. A ferry pier and visitor center sit on the east side, and a long beach and mooring balls run along the west side.

■ **Insights from Alice Brown,** *Chief of Planning for the nonprofit organization Boston Harbor Now @BostonHarborNow*

08 North-End EATS

FOOD | CULTURE | CITY LIFE

The North End's warren of alleyways retains the Old World flavor brought by Italian immigrants, ever since they started settling here in the early 20th century. And when we say 'flavor,' we're not being metaphorical. We mean garlic, basil and oregano, sautéed in extra-virgin olive oil; rich tomato sauces that have simmered for hours; amaretto and anise; and delicious, creamy gelato.

JOSEPH SOHM/SHUTTERSTOCK ©

All Saints Way

'Mock all and sundry things, but leave the saints alone' – so goes an old Italian saying on the wall of a tiny North End alleyway and surrounded by thousands of images of saints. The **shrine** (4 Battery St; pictured above) is located behind a locked gate but is visible from the street.

Trip Notes

Getting here Take the green or orange line to Haymarket.

When to go Galleria Umberto closes its doors when the food runs out, which is often before 2:30pm. The place is not open on Sunday or during the month of July.

Suggested souvenir Rubio Aged Balsamic Vinegar is made by an artisanal producer in Modena, Italy, aged for 12 years, and sold exclusively at Salumeria Italiana grocery store.

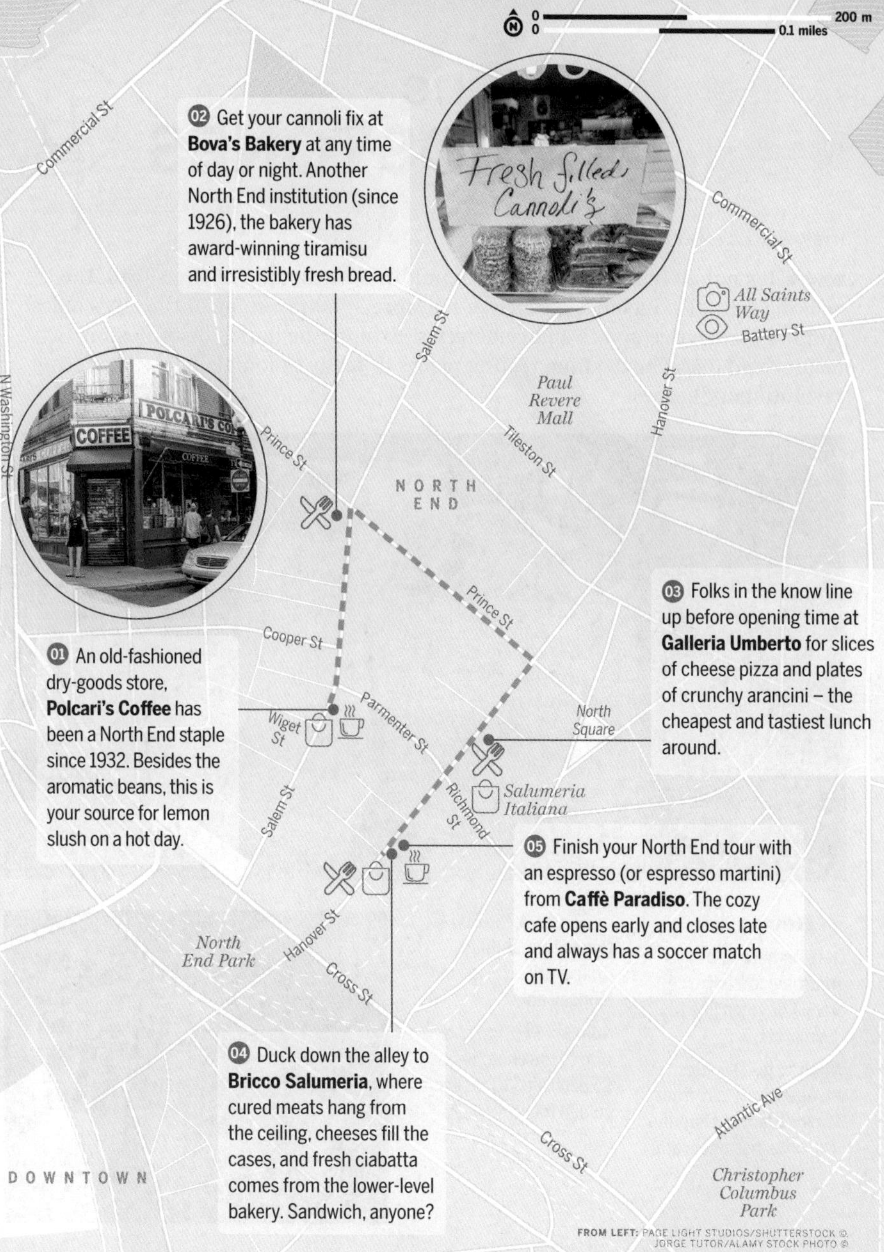

01 An old-fashioned dry-goods store, **Polcari's Coffee** has been a North End staple since 1932. Besides the aromatic beans, this is your source for lemon slush on a hot day.

02 Get your cannoli fix at **Bova's Bakery** at any time of day or night. Another North End institution (since 1926), the bakery has award-winning tiramisu and irresistibly fresh bread.

03 Folks in the know line up before opening time at **Galleria Umberto** for slices of cheese pizza and plates of crunchy arancini – the cheapest and tastiest lunch around.

04 Duck down the alley to **Bricco Salumeria**, where cured meats hang from the ceiling, cheeses fill the cases, and fresh ciabatta comes from the lower-level bakery. Sandwich, anyone?

05 Finish your North End tour with an espresso (or espresso martini) from **Caffè Paradiso**. The cozy cafe opens early and closes late and always has a soccer match on TV.

FROM LEFT: PAGE LIGHT STUDIOS/SHUTTERSTOCK ©, JORGE TUTOR/ALAMY STOCK PHOTO ©

09 Historic HEADSTONES

HISTORY | CEMETERIES | SPOOKINESS

It's not all monuments and old buildings along the Freedom Trail: the walking tour also includes a touch of macabre – mainly, some of the city's oldest and most evocative crypts and cemeteries. Explore the dark side of Boston history and discover the final resting places of many Colonial characters and revolutionary heroes.

NORMAN EGGERT/ALAMY STOCK PHOTO ©

How to

Getting here Red or green line to Park; orange or green line to Haymarket.

When to go The sites are open every day from 9am or 10am until 5pm. (The churches open later on Sunday.) The Bell & Bones Tour at King's Chapel is held Friday to Monday only.

Admission prices Admission to the churches is $5 each, or $10 for each guided tour.

CRAIG F. WALKER/THE BOSTON GLOBE VIA GETTY IMAGES ©

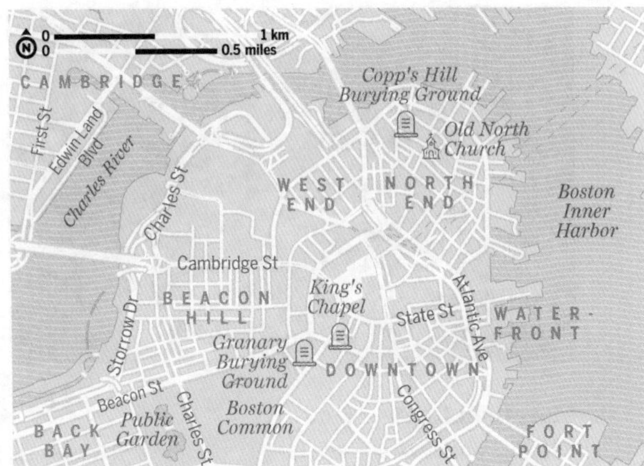

Granary Burying Ground Dating from 1660, this atmospheric atoll is crammed with historic headstones, many with evocative (and creepy) carvings. This is the final resting place of favorite revolutionary heroes, including Paul Revere, Samuel Adams, John Hancock and James Otis, as well as the five victims of the Boston Massacre.

King's Chapel This cemetery is the oldest in the city, with headstones that date back to the 1650s. Famous graves include John Winthrop, the first governor of the fledgling Massachusetts Bay Colony; William Dawes, who rode with Paul Revere; and Mary Chilton, the first European woman to set foot in Plymouth. Inside the chapel, there are 20 family tombs in the crypt, which you can visit on the guided Bell & Bones Tour.

Old North Church Boston's oldest church is famous for its steeple, where the sexton hung two lanterns to signal the route of advancing British soldiers. But the church holds plenty of history underground as well, with more than a thousand bodies entombed in the crypt below. Take the guided Crypt Tour to learn about the congregants buried here.

Copp's Hill Burying Ground Among the thousands of gravesites, this ancient cemetery contains the tomb of the Mather family – politically powerful and Puritan leaders and ministers during the Colonial period. Also buried here are more than a thousand free African Americans, many of whom lived in the North End.

Top left Headstones, King's Chapel Burying Ground. **Bottom left** Old North Church crypt.

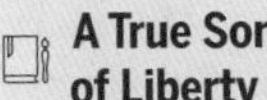

A True Son of Liberty

In Copp's Hill Burying Ground, look for the gravestone of Daniel Malcolm, whose epitaph lauds him as 'a true son of liberty, a friend to the public, an enemy of oppression, and one of the foremost in opposing the Revenue Acts on America.' British soldiers apparently took offense at this claim and used the headstone for target practice, as evident from the bullet marks. Turns out, Malcolm opposed the Revenue Acts so strongly that he smuggled 60 casks of wine without paying the duty – his only recorded revolutionary action.

Boston Marathon

THE WORLD'S OLDEST ANNUAL MARATHON

Patriots' Day means a lot of things to a lot of people. But since 1897, it means the Boston Marathon. Fifteen people ran that first race and only 12 finished; these days the Boston Marathon attracts some 30,000 participants and hundreds of thousands of spectators annually. (Learn more about Patriots' Day celebrations on p55.)

Left Wellesley College students' 'scream tunnel'. **Middle** Roberta Gibb. **Right** Runner holding a 'Boston Strong' sign.

KAYANA SZYMCZAK/GETTY IMAGES ©

Marathon Route

The 26.2-mile race starts in rural Hopkinton and winds its way through the western suburbs of Ashland, Natick, Wellesley, Newton and Brookline to Boston. Near the halfway mark, Wellesley College students traditionally form a 'scream tunnel,' offering eardrum-blowing screams of support to encourage the runners. Some of the marathon's most dramatic moments occur between mile 20 and 21, on Commonwealth Ave near Boston College. The course runs through the notorious Newton Hills to culminate at the aptly named Heartbreak Hill, rising a steep 80ft. Runners cruise up Beacon St, through Kenmore Sq (past cheering Red Sox fans), down Commonwealth Ave, turning right on Hereford St and left on Boylston St, and into a triumphant finish at Copley Sq. This final mile is among the most exciting places to be spectator.

Women Run This Town

Women began running in the Boston Marathon only in the 1960s. Roberta Gibb was the first woman to run in 1966, but she ran without properly registering, hiding in the bushes until the race started. The next year, Kathrine Switzer entered as 'KV Switzer.' When race officials realized a female was running the marathon, they tried to physically remove her from the course. The official rules were changed in 1971, and the next year eight women ran the Boston Marathon.

Marathon Celebrities

A famous father-and-son team, Rick and Dick Hoyt participated in the Boston Marathon for years. Rick suffers from cerebral palsy due to severe brain damage at birth.

PAUL CONNELL/THE BOSTON GLOBE VIA GETTY IMAGES ©

REUTERS/BRIAN SNYDER/ALAMY STOCK PHOTO ©

His father Dick was determined to give his son the chance to pursue his passions, including sports. With Dick pushing his son in a wheelchair, they competed in 72 marathons. In 2021, Dick died at the age of 80, and Rick has since announced his retirement – but not before completing the Boston Marathon 32 times.

Rosie Ruiz was the infamous Boston participant who in 1980 seemingly emerged from nowhere to win the women's division. It was determined that she did emerge from nowhere and had skipped most of the race. She was disqualified, but remains a favorite local villain.

Rosie Ruiz seemingly emerged from nowhere to win the women's division. It was determined that she did emerge from nowhere and had skipped most of the race.

Boston Strong

On Patriots' Day 2013, two bombs exploded near the finish line of the Boston Marathon, killing three and injuring hundreds. Many runners were unable to finish the race. The perpetrators were brothers Tamerlan and Dzhokhar Tsarnaev, residents of Cambridge. Tamerlan was later killed during a shootout with police; Dzhokhar was found guilty of some 30 federal offenses related to the attack. The tragedy was devastating, but Boston claimed countless heroes, especially the many victims that inspired others with their courage and fortitude throughout their recoveries. Locals commemorated the city's resilience with the motto 'Boston Strong' and a three-pillared memorial on Boylston St, where the bombs detonated.

Marathon Memories

The communities around Boston come out in full force to support this iconic race. These knowledgeable (and rambunctious) fans are great motivators: 'Get ya wahtah' coming from volunteers at the aid stations; Wellesley students screaming at the top of their lungs; 'You are at the top of Heartbreak Hill' signs. Chills ran through my spine taking that right turn on Hereford and left on Boylston for the grand finale. It's a truly magical moment.

■ **Insights from Sam Guo,** *amateur runner with 22 marathons under his belt (including three Bostons)* @gosamguo

Listings

BEST OF THE REST

History & Artistry

Boston Tea Party Ships & Museum

This unique museum in the Seaport District uses reenactments and multimedia to examine the 1773 protest. Bonus: here's your chance to dump tea into the harbor.

Isabella Stuart Gardner Museum

A splendid Venetian-style palazzo in Fenway houses Ms Gardner's exquisite art collection, especially Italian Renaissance and Dutch Golden Age paintings.

Harvard University

America's oldest college, Harvard University remains one of the country's most prestigious universities. The campus shows off some historic buildings around Harvard Yard, as well as impressive architecture and excellent museums.

John F Kennedy
Presidential Library & Museum

A fitting tribute to JFK's life and legacy, located south of the center at Columbia Point. The museum effectively uses audio and video to bring history into the present.

Greenway & Ocean Blue

Rose Kennedy Greenway

Where once a hulking overhead highway cut through the middle of Boston, now winds a 27-acre strip of landscaped gardens, fountain-lined greens and public art installations.

New England Aquarium Whale Watch

Set out from Long Wharf for the journey to Stellwagen Bank, a rich feeding ground for whales, dolphins and marine birds.

Baseball Pilgrimage

Fenway Park

Home of the Boston Red Sox since 1912, Fenway Park is the oldest operating baseball park in the country. Come to tour the park or see the Sox spank their opponents.

Seafood Delights

Cusser's $

Bringing a touch of elegance (and cocktails!) to the North Shore fast-food classics – namely roast-beef sandwiches, lobster rolls and clam chowder. Three locations in the West End, Back Bay and Fenway.

Legal Harborside $$

This casual restaurant and fish market in the Seaport District is a throwback to Legal's original outlet from 1904 (albeit with an updated menu). A+ for water views.

Neptune Oyster $$$

A North End favorite, this convivial oyster bar offers all kinds of local seafood served in all the ways – from traditional to tantalizing.

Rose Kennedy Greenway

Row 34 $$

Raw oysters and craft beer: what more do you want out of your Seaport dining experience? Okay, there are also delectably *cooked* seafood dishes, plus craft cocktails and a cool vibe.

Yankee Lobster $

An old-school waterfront seafood outlet, serving up fried-seafood platters and three kinds of lobster rolls. This is what the Seaport District used to look like.

International Appeal

Carmelina's $$

This understated, contemporary space in the North End serves up Sicilian dishes with a modern American twist – customers are crazy about the Crazy Alfredo and the Sunday Macaroni.

Puro Ceviche Bar $$

Choose between five types of ceviche, seven kinds of tacos and a slew of small plates, all served up with modern Latin American flare. Located in funky Back Bay basement digs.

Gourmet Dumpling House $

Known to locals as GDH, this unadorned eatery is a Chinatown go-to for fresh doughy Shanghai soup dumplings and crispy scallion pancakes.

Coppa Enoteca $$

This South End wine bar re-creates an Italian dining experience with authenticity and innovation, serving up cured meats, antipasti, pasta and other delicious small plates.

Cocktails & Craft Beer

Trillium Brewing Co $$

Boston's favorite microbrewery – not only for its excellent ales, but also for the fantastic Seaport taproom and rooftop deck (not to mention summer gardens on the Greenway).

ISRAEL PABON/SHUTTERSTOCK ©

Fenway Park

Bleacher Bar $$

Peek into Fenway Park, even if you can't get tickets to the game. This classy bar is tucked under the Fenway bleachers and offers a view onto center field.

Drink $$$

Drink kicked off the cocktail revival in Boston. They take the art of mixology seriously – and you will too, after you sample the concoctions in this sexy, subterranean space in the Seaport District.

Live Jive

Red Room @ Cafe 939

Students from the Berklee College of Music run this Back Bay joint, booking shows by interesting, eclectic up-and-coming musicians.

Club Passim

The folk music scene is alive and well in this little corner of Harvard Square, which continues to showcase top-notch indie, folk, blues and bluegrass musicians – just as it's done for 50-plus years.

Scan to find more things to do in Boston online

AROUND BOSTON

HISTORY | ART & ARCHITECTURE | LITERATURE

Experience Massachusetts online

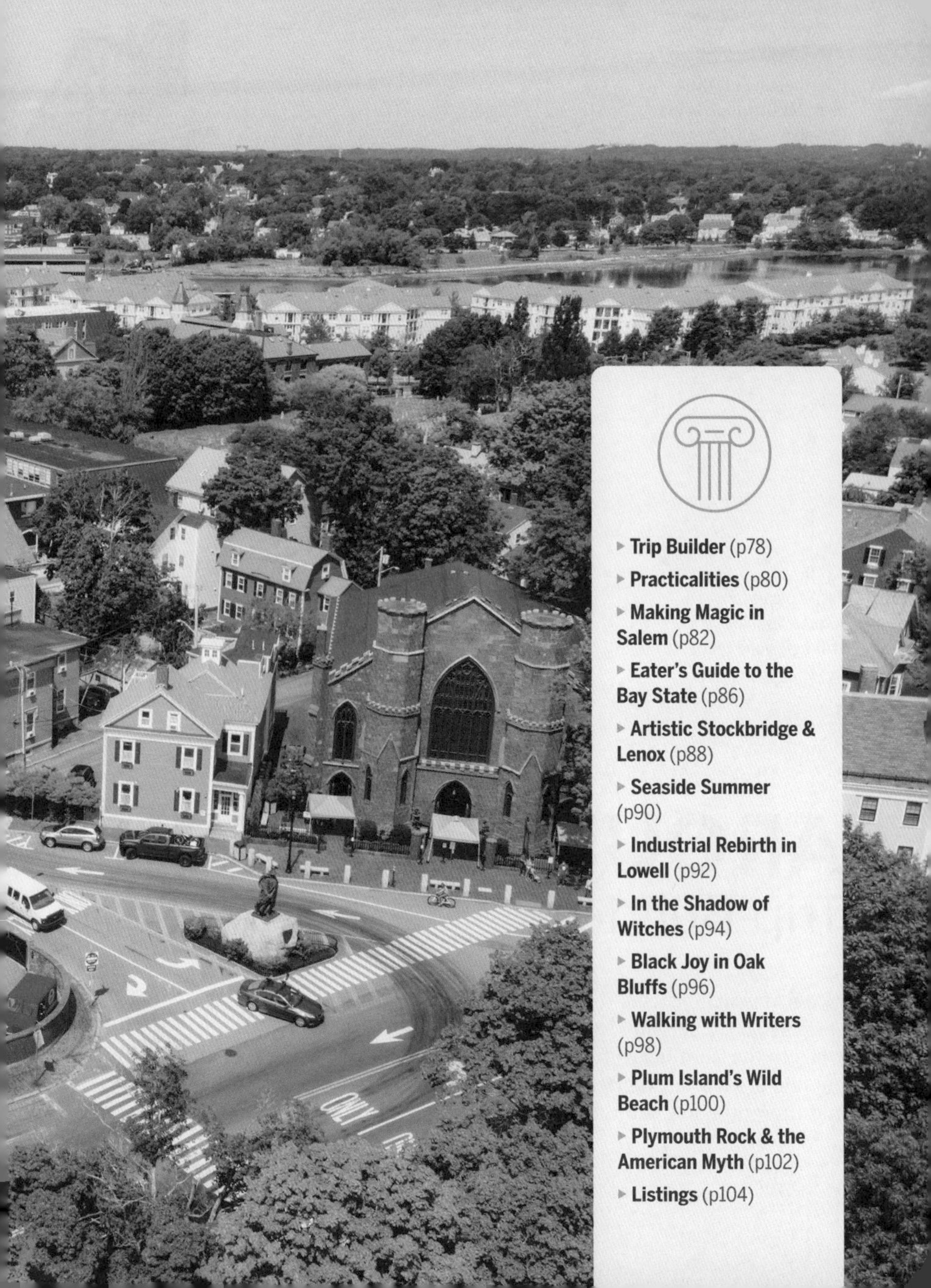

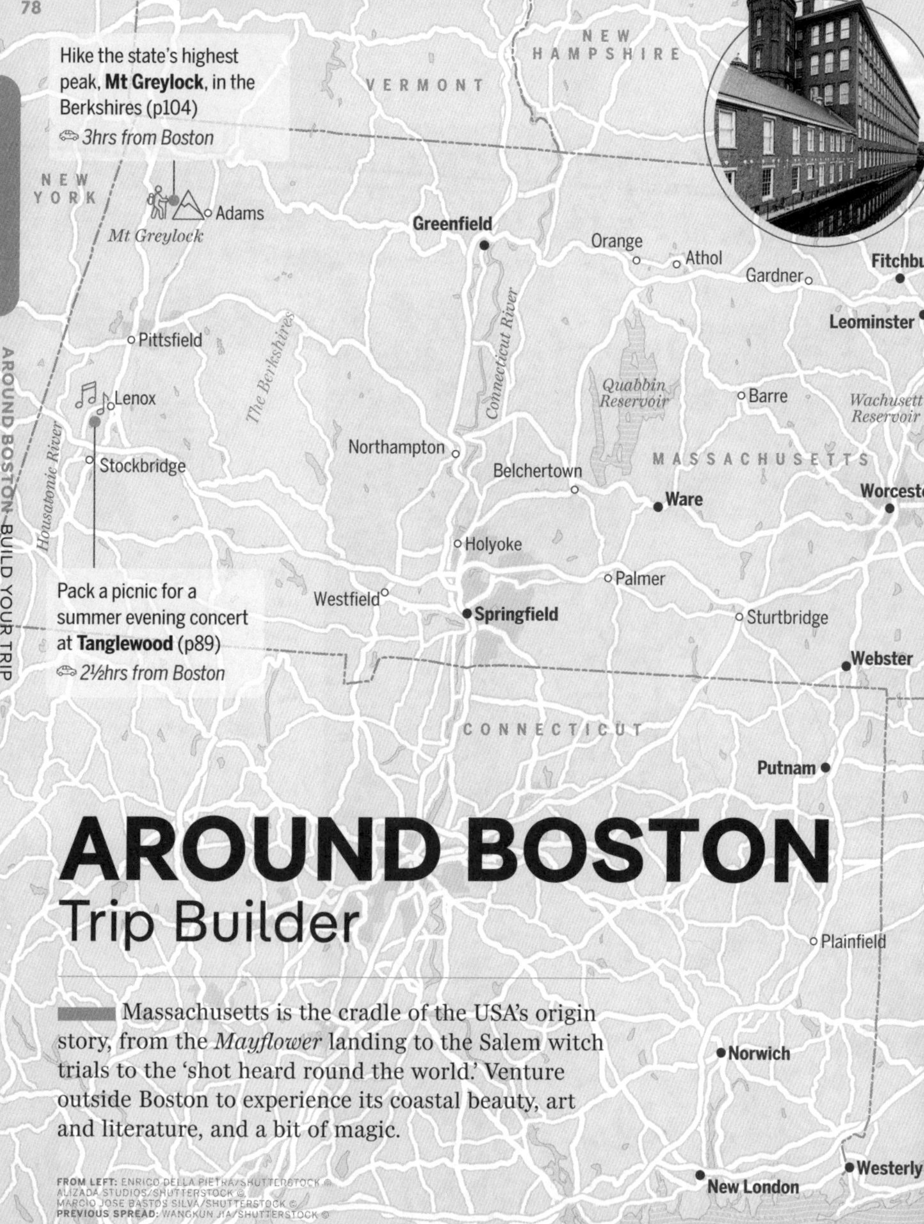

Hike the state's highest peak, **Mt Greylock**, in the Berkshires (p104)

3hrs from Boston

Pack a picnic for a summer evening concert at **Tanglewood** (p89)

2½hrs from Boston

AROUND BOSTON
Trip Builder

Massachusetts is the cradle of the USA's origin story, from the *Mayflower* landing to the Salem witch trials to the 'shot heard round the world.' Venture outside Boston to experience its coastal beauty, art and literature, and a bit of magic.

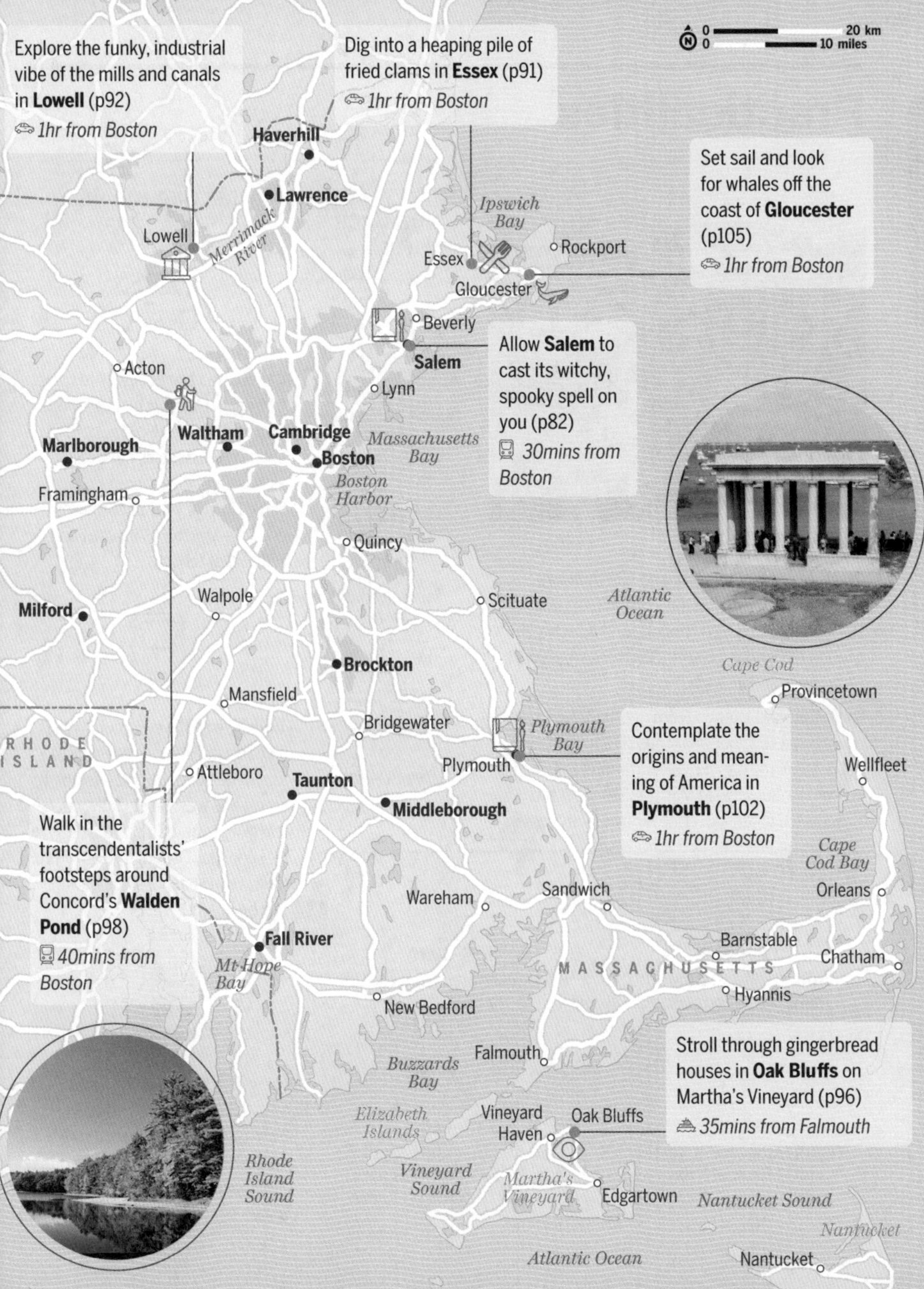
Explore the funky, industrial vibe of the mills and canals in Lowell (p92)
1hr from Boston
Dig into a heaping pile of fried clams in Essex (p91)
1hr from Boston
Set sail and look for whales off the coast of Gloucester (p105)
1hr from Boston
Allow Salem to cast its witchy, spooky spell on you (p82)
30mins from Boston
Contemplate the origins and meaning of America in Plymouth (p102)
1hr from Boston
Walk in the transcendentalists' footsteps around Concord's Walden Pond (p98)
40mins from Boston
Stroll through gingerbread houses in Oak Bluffs on Martha's Vineyard (p96)
35mins from Falmouth
0 20 km
0 10 miles
Haverhill
Lawrence
Lowell
Merrimack River
Ipswich Bay
Essex
Rockport
Gloucester
Beverly
Salem
Acton
Lynn
Waltham
Cambridge
Marlborough
Boston
Massachusetts Bay
Boston Harbor
Framingham
Quincy
Walpole
Milford
Scituate
Atlantic Ocean
Brockton
Cape Cod
Provincetown
Mansfield
Bridgewater
Plymouth Bay
RHODE ISLAND
Plymouth
Wellfleet
Attleboro
Taunton
Middleborough
Cape Cod Bay
Wareham
Sandwich
Orleans
Fall River
Barnstable
Chatham
Mt Hope Bay
MASSACHUSETTS
Hyannis
New Bedford
Falmouth
Buzzards Bay
Elizabeth Islands
Vineyard Haven
Oak Bluffs
Rhode Island Sound
Vineyard Sound
Martha's Vineyard
Edgartown
Nantucket Sound
Nantucket
Atlantic Ocean
Nantucket

Practicalities

THONGCHAI S/SHUTTERSTOCK ©

ARRIVING

Western Massachusetts and North Shore Take the train from Boston's South (pictured) or Back Bay Stations to Pittsfield, and from North Station to Concord, Lowell, Salem, Newburyport, Gloucester and Ipswich.

Cape Cod and islands From South Station, take a bus or, on summer weekends (Memorial Day to Labor Day), the CapeFLYER commuter rail. Ferries go from Woods Hole to Martha's Vineyard and Hyannis to Nantucket. Cape Air flies from Boston.

HOW MUCH FOR A

Fried-clam dinner $34

Tarot reading $40

Beach yoga $15

WHEN TO GO

JAN–MAR
Expect cold and snow with many attractions closed.

APR–JUN
Pack an umbrella and expect fewer crowds.

JUL–SEP
High season; warm weather, ideal for beach days.

OCT–DEC
Chilly weather and beautiful foliage. Expect the biggest crowds in Salem in October.

GETTING AROUND

Car A car is the best way to travel to Western Massachusetts, Cape Cod and smaller North Shore towns from Boston. Rent cars at locations throughout Boston. You can drive your car straight onto the Martha's Vineyard and Nantucket ferries.

Train The MBTA commuter rail is an easy and inexpensive way to reach metro Boston points north, south and west, especially when traveling from Boston to Salem ($8 one-way) during the autumn/Halloween season, since parking can be scarce.

Ferry The ferry is a scenic and overlooked option for traveling from Boston to Salem or Provincetown during warmer months. The seasonal (May to October) Salem ferry costs $25 round-trip.

EATING & DRINKING

Massachusetts is all about great seafood, like fried clams and lobster rolls (pictured top right), and it's best served 'in the rough' (think seafood shacks, picnic tables, salty air). Microbreweries and brewpubs offer hyper-local, one-of-a-kind brews that nod to the region, such as Notch Brewing's Salem Lager. An autumn visit isn't complete without a farm-stand apple cider doughnut (pictured bottom right), preferably hot and fresh out of the frier with a crunchy coating of sugar and cinnamon.

Best Essex fried-clam rivalry
Woodman's vs
JT Farnham's (p91)

Must-try hard apple cider
Far from the Tree,
Salem (p105)

WHERE TO STAY

True to its nickname, Massachusetts' cities and towns branch away from Boston like spokes from a hub. Although day trips from Boston are great, some places need deeper dives.

Town	Pro/Con
Salem	Staying in the heart of Salem is spooky fun, but October hotel reservations can be hard to get and should be made months in advance.
Stockbridge	Like a living Norman Rockwell painting, it's a quaint base for exploring the Berkshires, but foodies might be underwhelmed.
Oak Bluffs	The beachside 'gingerbread' town on Martha's Vineyard is busy in summer with crowds, but more like a ghost town in winter.
Gloucester	Beaches, food and art make this city so much more than fishing, but it's technically an island and epitomizes the old New England adage, 'can't get there from here.'

CONNECT

Wi-fi Widely available and free throughout the region at hotels, restaurants, coffee shops, museums, many stores and even on some public transportation. Phone signals can be spotty on beaches and in parts of the Berkshires.

WHAT'S THE DEAL WITH SCROD?

Scrod is on lots of menus, but not swimming in the ocean. 'Scrod' is the catch of the day, usually a whitefish like cod or haddock.

MONEY

Cards and mobile payments are widely accepted, but carry cash for smaller, seasonal businesses like in-the-rough seafood shacks and farm stands. On-site ATMs at these locations often have high fees.

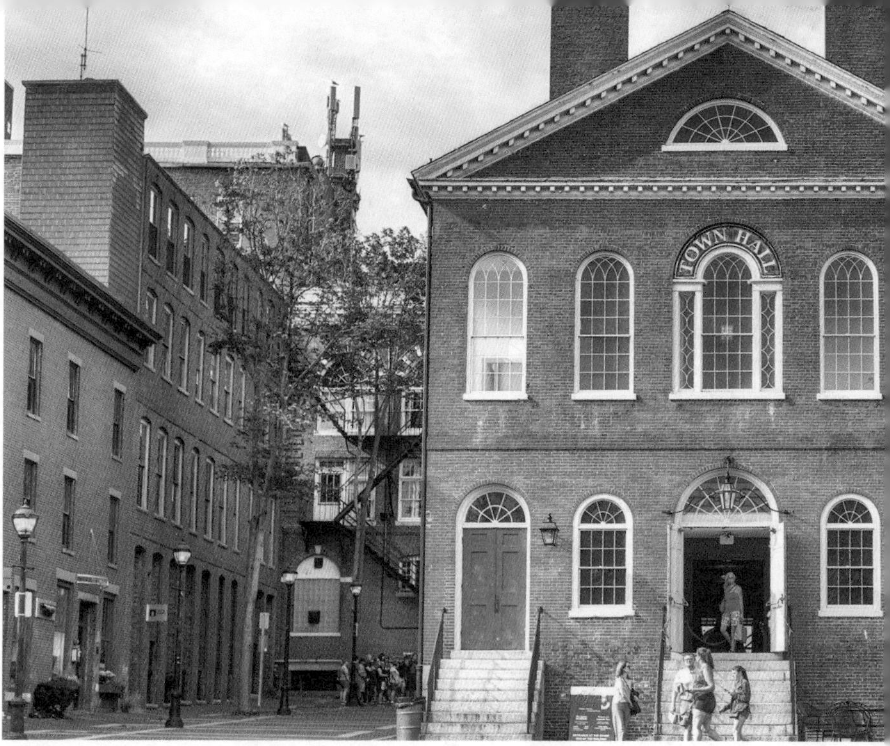

10 Making Magic IN SALEM

HISTORY | WITCHES | SHOPPING

The Puritans who executed their neighbors for witchcraft in 1692 would be shocked to see Salem today. The city has both capitalized on and learned from its past sins, resulting in an atmosphere that's radically welcoming, wickedly weird and fantastically fun.

DAN HANSCOM/SHUTTERSTOCK ©

How to

Getting here/around Downtown Salem is linked with the MBTA commuter rail station in Boston. Major sites are walkable.

When to go Spring, summer and fall are fantastic. It gets more crowded as Halloween nears. Expect fewer crowds, cold and snowy weather and closed attractions in the winter.

Haunted happenings October is a crowded, month-long Halloween party. Plan well in advance (up to a year) and check haunted happenings.org for an events calendar.

HEIDI BESEN/SHUTTERSTOCK ©

HEIDI BESEN/SHUTTERSTOCK ©

Cry Innocent & Pioneer Village

If you see a woman in a red bodice being arrested in the middle of Essex St, follow her and her jailer down the cobbled lane toward the **Old Town Hall**. *Cry Innocent: The People vs Bridget Bishop* is an immersive, interactive historical theater experience that invites the public to be jurors at Bridget Bishop's witchcraft trial. The arrest scene happens outside, and the rest of the performance happens indoors at the Old Town Hall. For another immersive experience, visit **Pioneer Village** which re-creates Salem in 1630. It was also used as a filming location for the movie *Hocus Pocus*.

The Witch House

The **Jonathan Corwin House**, known as the Witch House, is the only remaining structure

Witchy Souvenir

At the **Witchery** on Pickering Wharf, create the ultimate Salem souvenir: your own handmade broom. The broom-making workshops provide instruction and materials to choose from, like an ash or hickory handle, a bundle of broomcorn and extra adornments like crystals, dried flowers or bones to add a personal touch.

Top left Old Town Hall. **Bottom left** Jonathan Corwin House. **Top right** Ropes Mansion (p84).

in Salem with direct ties to the witch trials. Home to witch-trials judge Jonathan Corwin, the 17th-century house is suitably creepy looking, with a black exterior, gabled roof and diamond-paned windows. Inside, visitors can tour the house museum, which includes furniture, clothing, documents and folk healing methods from the time. During October, join storytellers there for nighttime tales of ghosts and the macabre.

The House of the Seven Gables

The 1668 **Turner-Ingersoll Mansion**, known as the House of the Seven Gables and the setting for Nathaniel Hawthorne's novel of the same name, is located at the edge of Salem Harbor and its grounds and interiors are open for visits and tours. If you're brave enough, climb the dark and steep 'secret staircase' up to the attic. Another real-life Salem building appears in Hawthorne's novel *The Scarlet Letter*: the **Custom House**,

A Magical Summer Weekend in Salem

Start the day with breakfast at the **Ugly Mug Diner**.

Enjoy the free garden behind the Georgian Colonial **Ropes Mansion** on Essex St.

Stroll down Chestnut St and other streets in the **McIntire Historic District** to see beautiful antique homes.

Have lunch at **Gulu-Gulu Cafe**. On Sundays, catch the afternoon drag show.

Visit **Charter Street Cemetery**, founded in 1637, adjacent to the Salem Witchcraft Memorial.

Take afternoon tea at **Jolie Tea Company**.

Do some shopping at places like **Sage** boutique and **Helios Floral**.

Grab dinner at **Settler**.

■ **Recommended by Erica Feldmann,** *founder of HausWitch Home + Healing @hauswitch*

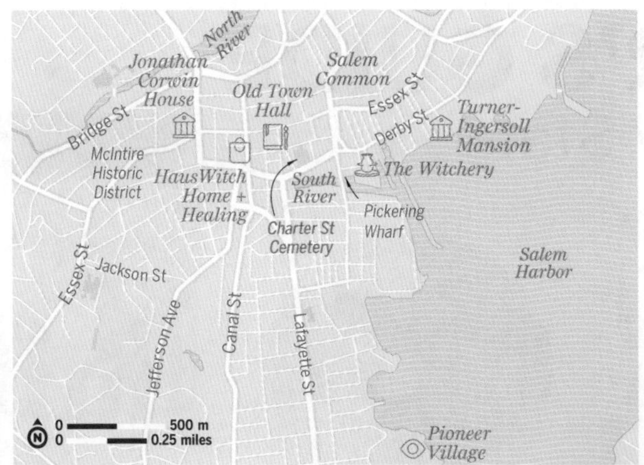

Left Historic architecture, Chestnut St.
Below The Coven's Cottage.

where he used to work as a surveyor. It is now part of the Salem Maritime National Historic Site.

Tools of the Trade

The Puritans whipped themselves into a hysteria trying to root out witchcraft, so it's a lovely irony that Salem is now home to such a flourishing witchcraft and magical community. Modern-day witches come from all walks of life and practice their craft in many different ways, but there are a few tools of the trade that many have in common, such as herbs, crystals, candles, incense and divination tools like tarot cards. Many shops in town cater to tourists, but many also offer tools and supplies (as well as tarot and other readings) for witchcraft practitioners.

Visit **HausWitch Home + Healing** for metaphysical home decor and gifts, spell kits, handcrafted wares and feminist energy. Find magical and metaphysical books, plus jewelry, gifts and tarot decks at **Pyramid Books**. For any herb you can think of (and lots you can't), **Artemisia Botanicals** is the place to be. For all the forest-witch vibes of your dreams, head to the **Coven's Cottage**.

EATER'S GUIDE
to the Bay State

01 Fried clams

A summer mainstay, battered and fried to a golden crisp. Fried-clam shacks dot the coast.

02 Apple cider doughnut

Visit a farm stand between the late summer and fall for freshly baked apple cider doughnuts.

03 Marshmallow Fluff

This sticky-sweet spread is a lunchbox staple thanks to the classic Fluffernutter (Fluff and peanut butter) sandwich.

04 Cranberries

Cranberry bogs cover southeastern Massachusetts. The tart fruit is popular year-round, but especially at Thanksgiving and Christmas.

05 Boiled dinner

Popular around St Patrick's Day, corned beef, cabbage and veggies are boiled in one pot and served with soda bread.

06 Wellfleet oysters

With their clean briny flavor and plump meats, these are favored among raw-bar connoisseurs.

07 Frappé

In Massachusetts, milkshakes are made with milk and syrup, whereas frappés also contain ice cream.

08 Cape Cod Chips

Salty kettle-cooked Cape Cod Chips are popular at restaurants and clam shacks, often served alongside fried seafood.

09 Baked beans

Redolent of molasses and salt pork, baked beans are served as breakfast sides or with hot dogs.

10 Roast-beef sandwich

Northern Massachusetts loves roast-beef sandwiches, said to be invented at Kelly's Roast Beef in Revere. Rivalries exist between restaurants.

11 Grape-Nuts ice cream

Find this old-school flavor at ice-cream stands statewide, made with vanilla-custard ice cream and Grape-Nuts cereal.

11 ARTISTIC Stockbridge & Lenox

ART | NATURE | MUSIC

The Berkshires have long been a haven for artists yearning to escape the city and get in touch with nature. Stockbridge and Lenox will nestle you right into that lifestyle, and although they might seem a little sleepy at first, it's easy to adjust to the slower pace and quiet appreciation of the gentle mountainous landscape through art and music.

T PHOTOGRAPHY/SHUTTERSTOCK ©

How to

Getting here/around Travel the two hours from Boston to Stockbridge by car to appreciate the scenery along the way.

When to go Visit in summer for Tanglewood, fall for fiery foliage, or spring for fewer crowds. Many attractions will be closed in the winter.

Historical digs Stay at the Red Lion Inn, in operation since 1773, to soak in claw-foot bathtubs, tour its historical art collection, and people-watch from a rocking chair on the front porch.

THERESA LAURIA/SHUTTERSTOCK ©

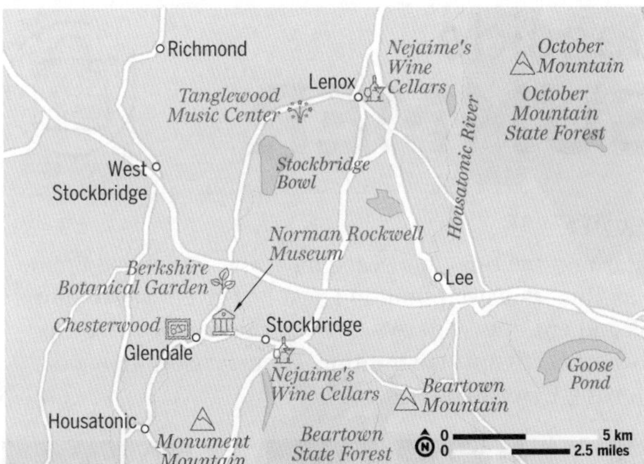

Top left Tanglewood Music Festival. **Bottom left** Berkshire Botanical Garden.

A perfect summer's night Here's the recipe for a perfect night at **Tanglewood**, the summer festival home of the Boston Symphony Orchestra and Boston Pops. Buy lawn tickets for a show at the open-air **Koussevitzky Music Shed**, where artists range from rock to folk to classical. Stop at **Nejaime's Wine Cellars** in Stockbridge or Lenox to pick up picnic provisions and a bottle of wine. Curate your own or choose from one of their ready-made baskets (complete with plates and cutlery) like the six-course 'French Country for Two.' Pack a picnic blanket and chairs (or rent chairs or cushions when you arrive). Park for free, set up your spread and toast to the music.

So much more than flowers The 24-acre **Berkshire Botanical Garden** is not just a living museum of gardens, greenhouses, woodlands, herbs and topiaries. It also leans into the region's affinity for art and music, hosting nature-inspired art exhibitions in its **Anna and Frederick Henry Leonhardt Galleries** and a 'Music Mondays' series from July to September that features evening concerts in the gardens. Picnics and lawn chairs are encouraged.

Creativity alive The summer home of Lincoln Memorial sculptor Daniel Chester French, **Chesterwood** has 10 buildings across its 122 acres, but the standout is the sculpting studio. Overlooking **Monument Mountain**, it has a 26ft-high ceiling tall enough to accommodate large-scale equestrian statues.

Art Imitating Life

Stockbridge's people and places feature prominently in many iconic works by illustrator Norman Rockwell, who called the town home for 25 years. Here are four things at the **Norman Rockwell Museum** not to miss:

Rockwell's *Four Freedoms*, inspired by Franklin D Roosevelt's vision for universal freedoms throughout the world.

Stockbridge Main Street at Christmas, Rockwell's panoramic painting of the snowy town center which still looks much the same today.

The gallery features each of Rockwell's 323 *Saturday Evening Post* covers.

There's also the art studio that Rockwell called his 'best studio yet.' It's open from Memorial Day to Columbus Day.

■ **Tips from Stephanie Haboush Plunkett,** *chief curator of the Norman Rockwell Museum @NRockwellMuseum*

12 Seaside SUMMER

SEAFOOD | ANTIQUES | ARCHITECTURE

Salt marshes, mudflats and the tidal landscape have always defined life in Ipswich and Essex, where an illustrious shipbuilding past has given way to new claims to fame: fried clams and antiques. These towns are perfect for moseying on a warm summer's day, whether it's antique hunting, clam-shack-hopping or floating down the gently flowing Essex River.

JAMES KIRKIKIS/SHUTTERSTOCK ©

How to

Getting here There's an Ipswich MBTA commuter train from Boston, but a car is easier if you're planning to do some serious antiquing.

When to go Beaches and boats call for warm weather, since ocean breeze can make the temperature drop even on the hottest days. Plus, it's peak clam season in the summer months.

Clam-shack lingo A 'plate' of seafood usually comes with multiple sides, whereas a 'boat' is a smaller portion that comes with fries.

EVERYDAY ARTISTRY PHOTOGRAPHY/ALAMY STOCK PHOTO ©

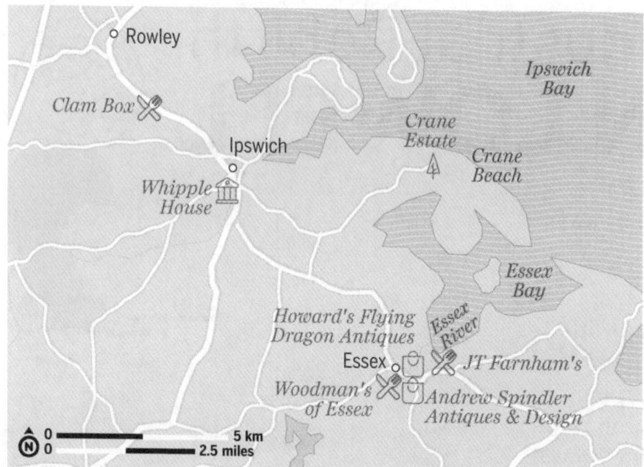

Antiques of all varieties Essex' Main St is lined with antique shops filled with highly curated and refined pieces – like **Andrew Spindler Antiques & Design** – and rusty gold, like **Howard's Flying Dragon Antiques**. Next door in Ipswich, the antiques are a little different. Ipswich has more First Period houses (built from about 1625 to 1720) than any other town in the US, thanks in part to a rough economy. Ipswich's port was too small for big trade ships, so while sea captains in Salem and Newburyport spent their maritime wealth building fancy new Federal-style brick mansions, folks in Ipswich had to settle for their old, pitched-roof and wooden-shingle houses, says Ipswich town historian Gordon Harris. Bad for them, good for us. Ipswich is like a time capsule.

Clam wars Local lore says **Woodman's of Essex** invented the fried clam in 1916, sparking both a culinary craze and a friendly rivalry between other nearby clam shacks. Judge for yourself by sampling fried clams at three beloved spots. The iconic Woodman's of Essex is touristy and always busy. **JT Farnham's**, also in Essex and right on the edge of the Great Marsh, is smaller and cash-only. **Clam Box** is in Ipswich – look for the roof shaped like a takeout container and line out the door all summer. Order at the counter and opt for full belly clams, rather than clam strips, for the full experience.

Top left Howard's Flying Dragon Antiques. **Bottom left** Crane Estate

By the Sea

Visit **Crane Beach** in Ipswich to experience its soft white sand and gentle waves.

Paddle down the Essex River and its winding creeks with outfitters like **Foote Brothers Canoe & Kayak Rental**.

Cruise the Essex River with **Essex River Cruises & Charters**.

Get a closer look at First Period houses on a walking tour with Ipswich town historian Gordon Harris, or buy a ticket from the **Ipswich Museum** to tour the 1677 **Whipple House** (Memorial Day to October).

See how the other half lived at the 1920s **Crane Estate** and its Great House in Ipswich, a 56,881-sq-ft Tudor Revival mansion surrounded by landscaped gardens and sweeping ocean vistas.

13 Industrial Rebirth IN LOWELL

ARCHITECTURE | HISTORY | CANALS

Two hundred years ago, Lowell was whirring and clattering with industry. Powered by the mighty Merrimack River, brick textile mills – and the mill girls and immigrants working inside them – made Lowell one of the country's industrial powerhouses. Lowell's manufacturing golden age might be long over, but the mill buildings remain, reimagined and reborn.

Lowell National Historical Park
Merrimack River
Merrimack Riverwalk
Northern Canal Walkway
Suffolk Mill
Boott Cotton Mills Museum
Mill No. 5
South Common
0 1 km
0 0.5 miles

How to

Getting here/around Take the MBTA commuter rail northwest from Boston to Lowell. Downtown Lowell and its waterway paths are very walkable.

When to go Spring, summer and fall for walking around downtown, the river and boating.

Welcome to Lowell Lowell's immigrant heritage endures. Today, the city is home to the second-largest Cambodian population in the US, so don't sleep on the food.

Lowell's industrial boomtown past is impossible to ignore, with its imposing brick mill buildings, smokestacks, locks and canals still giving the city its distinctive gritty character. Here's how to explore Lowell's mills, three ways.

From the past Visit the **Boott Cotton Mills Museum** at **Lowell National Historical Park** to see ongoing exhibits including the incredible Weave Room, which is filled with more than 80 working cotton looms that fill the space with the sights, sounds and smells of working in the mills. Take a ranger-guided walking tour of the still-

Top right Boott Cotton Mills Museum. **Bottom right** Lowell National Historical Park.

TRAVELVIEW/SHUTTERSTOCK ©

WANGKUN JIA/SHUTTERSTOCK ©

Music in the City

The **Lowell Folk Festival** is the country's longest-running free folk festival. Visit downtown Lowell during the last full weekend of July to experience music, food, folk crafts and street performers.

working water turbine at the **Suffolk Mill**.

From the present The restored (c 1873) **Mill No. 5** calls itself 'an indoor street-scape,' and that's apt. There's a vintage, salvaged vibe inside the mill, where you'll find a weekly indoor farmers market, a quirky independent movie theater (ask about Weirdo Wednesdays), a coffee shop and soda fountain, boutique shops, a revolving vendor bazaar and other odd delights.

From the water From May through the end of September, take a national park boat tour of Lowell's canals to get an up-close look at this complex system. Appreciate the water on foot by traipsing the **Northern Canal Walkway** or strolling along the **Merrimack Riverwalk** and the 'Mile of Mills' on the Merrimack River.

■ **Recommended by Kevin Coffee,** *chief of interpretation and education at Lowell National Historical Park @LowellNPS*

14 In the Shadow of WITCHES

HISTORY | WITCH TRIALS | ROAD TRIP

While many of the Salem witch trials happened in Salem, most of the accused witches (and their accusers) lived in surrounding towns, and for more than 400 years these memories have lingered in quiet pockets of Essex County. Take a day-long road trip away from Salem's crowds to explore lonely witch-trial sites.

G.MUSHINSKY/SHUTTERSTOCK ©

Trip Notes

Getting here/around Renting a car lets you make stops at any beaches, shops, cemeteries, small museums or eateries that catch your eye.

Funerary art Many Colonial cemeteries with ties to the Salem witch trials display haunting funerary art carved into the tombstones, like winged skulls called 'death's heads,' skulls and crossbones, and winged-cherub 'soul effigies.'

Hub towns Marblehead, Danvers, Topsfield, North Andover

*This itinerary was recommended by **Richard Trask**, the Danvers town archivist and a witch-trial expert*

Low-Tide Treasure

You don't need a boat to explore Marblehead's **Crowninshield Island**. Arrive an hour before dead low tide (the tide's lowest point) to walk across the dry channel to explore the 5-acre island's sandy beach, loop trail and woodlands. Leave within one hour after dead low tide or you'll be swimming back to shore.

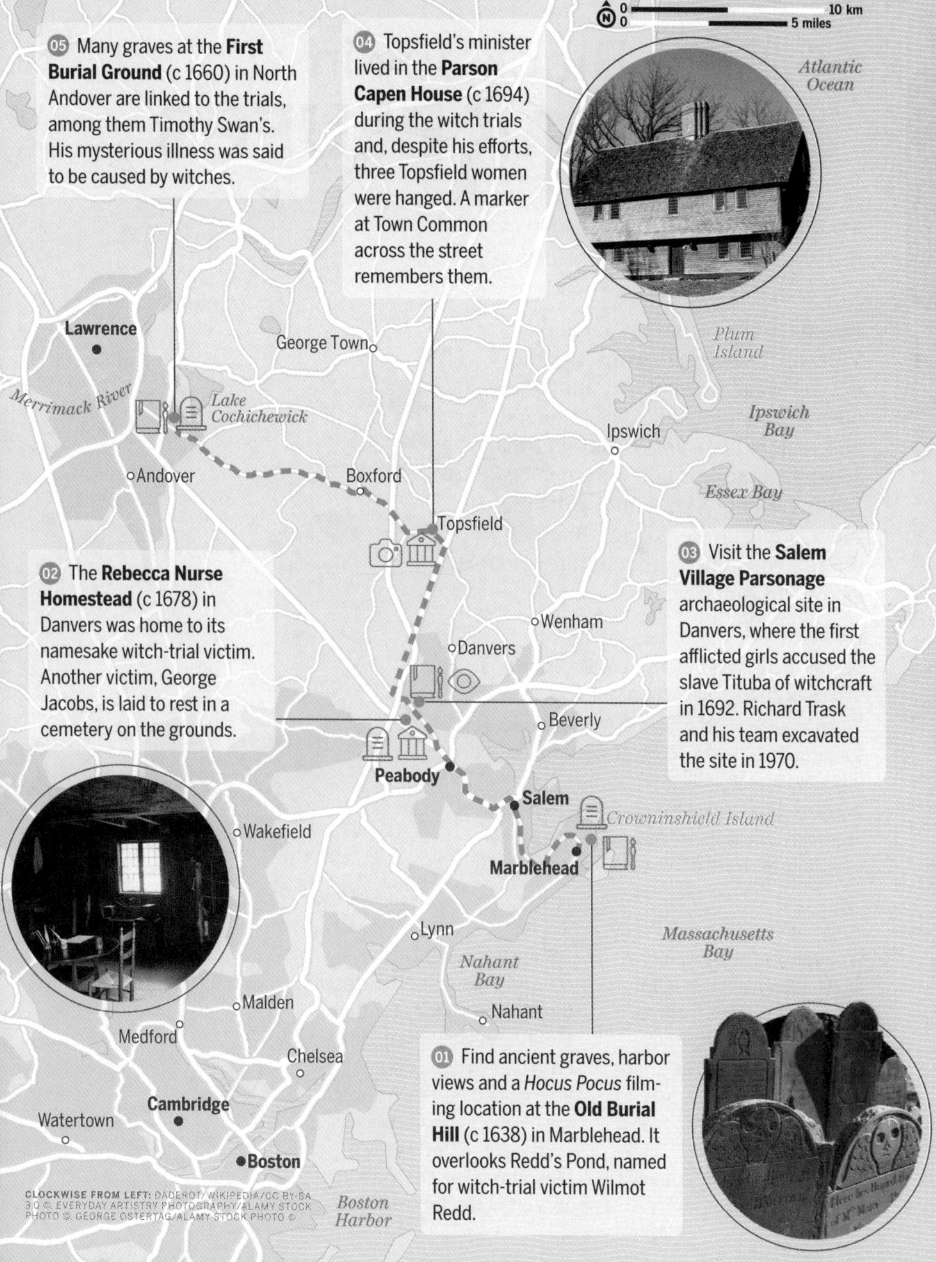

CLOCKWISE FROM LEFT: DADEROT/WIKIPEDIA/CC BY-SA 3.0 ©, EVERYDAY ARTISTRY PHOTOGRAPHY/ALAMY STOCK PHOTO ©, GEORGE OSTERTAG/ALAMY STOCK PHOTO ©

15 Black Joy in OAK BLUFFS

BEACHES | CULTURE | BLACK HERITAGE

On the island of Martha's Vineyard, where the word 'summer' is a verb, the town of Oak Bluffs has been a haven for Black vacationers and residents for more than 125 years. Journalist, author and longtime Oak Bluffs resident Skip Finley calls the town 'a place where being Black doesn't consume as much time or effort as over in America.'

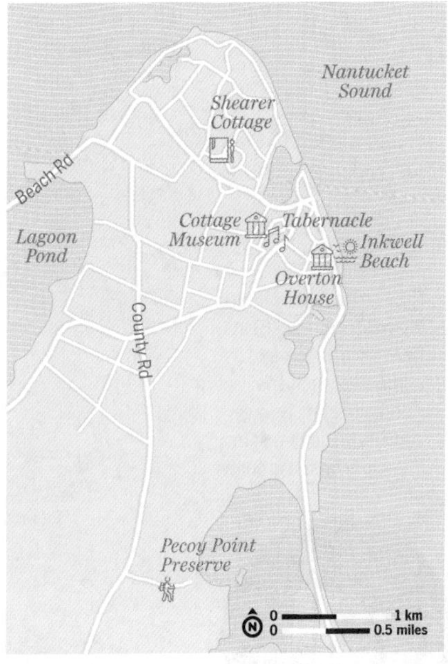

How to

Getting here Travel by ferry from Woods Hole on Cape Cod to Oak Bluffs year-round.

When to go Summer is perfect for beach days, but spring and fall are also lovely. Things are quiet and often closed in the winter.

Public transit Explore the island's six towns via year-round public transit bus and paratransit services from the Martha's Vineyard Transit Authority.

Whether you're 'up island' or 'down island,' each of Martha's Vineyard's six towns offers something different, from Chilmark's fishing-village vibe to the sailing hub of Edgartown to the natural wonder of Aquinnah's Gay Head Cliffs. But for pure charm, nothing beats Oak Bluffs.

Stroll through the candy-colored gingerbread houses at the **Martha's Vineyard Camp Meeting Association**, either on your own or on a summertime guided tour. Learn about the neighborhood's religious origins at the **Cottage Museum** or experience a concert at the **Tabernacle**.

Top right Martha's Vineyard Camp Meeting Association. **Bottom right** Flying Horses Carousel.

DANITA DELIMONT/ALAMY STOCK PHOTO ©

MICHAEL GORDON/SHUTTERSTOCK ©

Beach Day

Oak Bluffs' **Inkwell Beach** is a beloved spot for the Black community. Start your day there with the local Polar Bears club at 7:30am for a swim from July 4 to Labor Day.

Take a spin on the **Flying Horses Carousel**, the country's oldest-operating platform carousel. While riding on the antique horses, try your luck at grabbing the brass ring to win a free ride.

One of Skip Finley's favorite spots in Oak Bluffs is **Pecoy Point Preserve**, a stunning 17-acre landscape perfect for hiking, biking, picnicking, boating and swimming along the shores of the tidal, salt-water **Sengekontacket Pond** (known locally as Sengie).

The **African American Heritage Trail of Martha's Vineyard** has several stops in Oak Bluffs, including **Shearer Cottage**, the island's first Black-owned guesthouse which still welcomes visitors, and **Overton House**, known as the 'Summer White House' of the Civil Rights movement.

Rub shoulders with Holly-wood stars to celebrate Black filmmakers and watch feature, documentary and short films at the **Martha's Vineyard African American Film Festival** every August.

16 Walking with WRITERS

LITERATURE | HIKING | HISTORY

There must be something in the air west of Boston because it's been fertile ground for some of the country's most beloved writers, like Louisa May Alcott, Emily Dickinson and Henry David Thoreau. Catch some of that creativity yourself by visiting their homes, walking through the landscapes that inspired them and even visiting their final resting places.

ANTONY SOUTER/ALAMY STOCK PHOTO ©

How to

Getting here/around Take the MBTA commuter rail from Boston to Concord. A car is best for points further west.

When to go Hiking in fall is extra pretty thanks to the foliage. In the summer add a dip in Walden Pond to your hike.

Author's Ridge Pay your respects or leave pens, notes and trinkets on the graves of writers like Ralph Waldo Emerson, Louisa May Alcott, Henry David Thoreau and Nathaniel Hawthorne at Concord's Sleepy Hollow Cemetery.

SHANSHAN0312/SHUTTERSTOCK ©

Some incredible women writers, from Anne Bradstreet to Phillis Wheatley to Sylvia Plath, have hailed from Massachusetts. Visit three of their homes on a scenic 134-mile road trip through Western Massachusetts.

Start in Concord at **Orchard House**, where Louisa May Alcott wrote and set her classic story of sisterhood, *Little Women*. Visit year-round to tour the house and see the bedroom and desk where Alcott wrote her most famous novel; drawings covering the walls and woodwork by Alcott's sister, May (the model for Amy March); and a trunk full of homemade costumes for the Alcott sisters' theatrical performances.

Head west to Amherst to visit the newly renovated **Emily Dickinson Museum**, comprised of two historic houses belonging to the Dickinson family including the Homestead, where Emily was born and lived. Explore the buildings on a 60-minute guided tour, which includes an intimate look inside Emily's bedroom, and walk the grounds with an audio tour that's free with museum admission.

Continue west to Lenox and **The Mount**, Edith Wharton's palatial estate. Explore the vast grounds and elegantly landscaped gardens year-round or take the seasonal tours inside the house museum (including spooky ghost tours). Artists- and writers-in-residence programs and special events like NightWood, a holiday light-and-music installation, make The Mount feel less like a monument to the past and more like a celebration of the present.

Top left Orchard House. **Bottom left** The Mount.

Walking Concord

Here's a perfect summer walk through Concord:

Spend the morning at Orchard House.

Walk about a mile, passing the Concord Museum, to **Ralph Waldo Emerson House**.

Follow trail markers along the wooded 1.7-mile **Emerson–Thoreau Amble** to Walden Pond and visit a re-creation of Thoreau's house.

Loop around the 1.9-mile **Walden Pond Path**, stopping for a swim anywhere, including a sandy beach with lifeguards on duty over the summer.

Head back to town for an ice cream and a visit to **North Bridge**, where the 'shot heard round the world' was fired in 1775, starting the American Revolution.

Recommended by Vanessa Zoltan, *author and pilgrimage guide based in Massachusetts @vanessamzoltan*

Plum Island's WILD BEACH

WILDLIFE | HIKING | BEACH

Plum Island, a barrier island north of Cape Ann, is perfect for those who crave a bit of wildness with their beachgoing. It has a lot packed onto it for an 11-mile spit of always-shifting sand – from a luxury hotel, restaurants, homes and a lighthouse at one end, to protected dunes, wild marshlands and a tiny state park at the other.

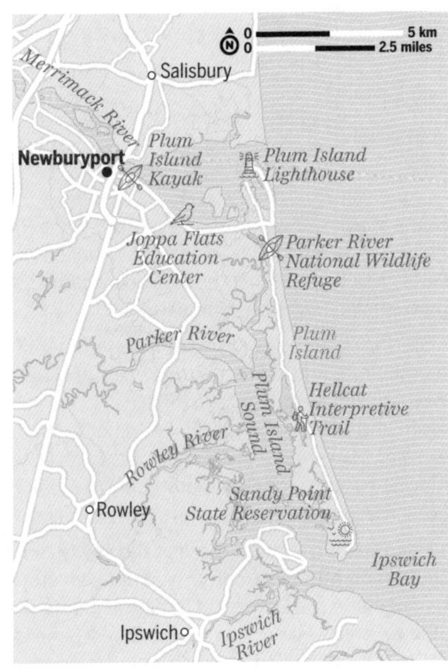

How to

Getting here Take Plum Island Turnpike from downtown Newburyport over a drawbridge onto the island. Local buses also service the island.

When to go Late summer for the beach and restaurants; summer and winter for birding.

Pack bug spray In early summer, Plum Island is overrun with biting flies called greenheads that leave painful welts on their victim's skin. Locals know that they disappear with the first full moon after July.

Like the shifting dunes themselves, Plum Island is always changing: it's been home to hotels, restaurants, beachfront mansions, shingled shacks, a polio camp, an airport and a national wildlife refuge, among other things. All the while, you're at nature's mercy: you might see a new sandy shoal forming on the north side of the island, creating a low-tide playground; huge swaths of the wildlife-refuge beach is closed from April 1 until whenever the piping plovers fledge and fly off; and in July, greenheads rule, unless the wind is coming off the ocean that day. Plum Island is temperamental, but it's also wild and free. Here's how to spend a weekend:

Stay at **Blue – Inn on The Beach**. Have breakfast at **Mad Martha's Island Cafe** and a lobster roll at **Bob Lobster** (p105).

Visit the historic **Plum Island Lighthouse** and explore the 1.4-mile **Hellcat**

DEWSNUGGETS/SHUTTERSTOCK ©

Interpretive Trail through freshwater marsh and maritime woodlands.

Take a morning or evening yoga class on the beach. National park passes are valid for **Parker River National Wildlife Refuge** admission.

Try to get an early parking spot at **Sandy Point State Reservation** (or cycle there down the unpaved road).

Go bird-watching solo or with Mass Audubon's **Joppa Flats Education Center**.

Paddle through the Parker River National Wildlife Refuge, Plum Island Sound and other waterways with **Plum Island Kayak**.

Bird-Watching 101

Plum Island's bird-watching is spectacular all year:

Spring Tropical migrating birds

Late summer Shorebirds, tree swallows

Fall Migrating ducks

Winter Loons, snowy owls, other raptors

Tips from David Moon, *community science and coastal resilience manager, Mass Audubon North Shore @MassAudubon*

Above Snowy Owl, Park River National Wildlife Refuge.

SUCHAN/SHUTTERSTOCK ©

Plymouth Rock & the American Myth

UNPACK AMERICA'S ORIGIN STORY IN PLYMOUTH

The story of the Pilgrims landing the *Mayflower* on Plymouth Rock in 1620 looms large in American mythology. But seeing the rock itself is kind of a letdown and its pedigree as the true first landing site is fuzzy. It's also a prime example of history being written by the winners.

Left Plymouth Rock. **Middle** Pilgrims landing, 1620. **Right** *Mayflower II.*

Many cultures have an origin myth, and America's is as familiar as baseball and apple pie. It goes something like this. In 1620, the Pilgrims arrived at Plymouth Rock in Massachusetts in search of religious freedom. During a hard winter spent mostly on their ship, the *Mayflower,* half of them died. But in spring, they were greeted by friendly indigenous people who taught them how to fish and cultivate crops, and in 1621 they celebrated the first Thanksgiving with members of the Wampanoag tribe.

It's a tale that encapsulates so many American values – religious and personal freedom, pulling yourself up by your bootstraps, equality and liberty – and it's been told and retold for generations. It's no wonder, then, that roughly one million people a year visit **Pilgrim Memorial State Park** and the famous Plymouth Rock.

But as far as tourist attractions go, **Plymouth Rock** is a controversial one. First, it's housed in a sunken pit on a bed of dirt and surrounded by a fence. Second, there's its questionable origin story: It wasn't identified as *the rock* until 1741 – 121 years after the *Mayflower* landing. And then there's what it represents: looking at Plymouth Rock might remind you of perseverance, freedom and the American dream or colonialism, betrayal and genocide.

Finally, we must ask about the American origin myth itself. Why is this rock celebrated as the bedrock of America? Why not rocks in Saint Augustine, Santa Fe or Jamestown, all of which had earlier European settlements? That's to say nothing of the vast communities and cultures that were already established on this land thousands of years before the Pilgrims ever set sail.

NORTH WIND PICTURE ARCHIVES/ALAMY STOCK PHOTO ©

QUIGGYT4/SHUTTERSTOCK ©

To celebrate those other places and people with equal fervor and reverence would be to unravel important parts of the American myth. And we've seen, especially in recent years, how hard that is to do.

That's not to say Plymouth isn't worth visiting or that the town isn't actively grappling with its complex history. Seeing Plymouth Rock might be anticlimactic, but **Plimoth Patuxet Museums** (formerly called Plimoth Plantation) is a fascinating living history museum. It re-creates and interprets historic Patuxet (home to the native Wampanoag communities) and Plymouth Colony in the 1600s, and features a working reconstruction of the Plimoth Grist Mill (c 1636). There's also the *Mayflower II*, a full-scale reproduction of the *Mayflower*. More pilgrim-related sites are found throughout the town, including monuments, statues and even a sarcophagus at Coles Hill – where the English colonists and the Wampanoag people signed a peace treaty in 1621 – containing the remains of some of the pilgrims.

> Why is this rock celebrated as the bedrock of America? Why not rocks in Saint Augustine, Santa Fe or Jamestown, all of which had earlier European settlements?

Ultimately, visiting Plymouth is a reminder that the past is always more complicated than we want it to be. And perhaps it isn't the past at all, but something our future depends on.

Coles Hill

Overlooking Plymouth Rock and Plymouth Bay, Coles Hill is another symbol of Plymouth's complicated legacy. Now a National Historic Landmark, it's where the Pilgrims buried *Mayflower* passengers who died during their first Massachusetts winter in 1620–21. A sarcophagus on the site contains what historians believe to be the remains of other *Mayflower* settlers, which were discovered during the 18th and 19th centuries. But Coles Hill is also a place of reckoning. Since 1970, indigenous people have gathered here on Thanksgiving for the National Day of Mourning, which remembers the evils and injustices that European settlers committed against Native American people. A town plaque commemorates the annual event.

Listings

BEST OF THE REST

Immersive History

Old Sturbridge Village

Chat with costumed historians at this living history museum, which re-creates an early 19th-century New England village with 40 historically furnished antique buildings, gardens, trails and heritage breed animals.

Battleship Cove

Battleship Cove in Fall River is a 'fleet' museum that's literally on the water. It's home to a Maritime Museum, plus historical vessels like naval ships, aircraft and a submarine.

Amazing Museums

Hammond Castle Museum

An eccentric inventor built a medieval-style castle in Gloucester and filled it with art – now it's a museum. Seasonal events, like candlelight and spiritualism tours, add to the weird ambience.

Peabody Essex Museum

This Salem institution is renowned for its American, Asian and maritime art. Its historic house collection includes the 200-year-old Yin Yu Tang, transported from China and reassembled in Salem.

The Amazing World of Dr Seuss Museum

Dr Seuss is one of Springfield's favorite sons. His namesake museum has art, hands-on exhibits, interactive elements like the Giant Marble Maze, and a re-creation of the artist's studio.

New England Botanic Garden at Tower Hill

This 171-acre garden museum in Boylston has more than a dozen formal gardens, woodlands, a visitors center, special events, greenhouses, an apple orchard and more to explore.

Hikes & Walks

Bish Bash Falls

Take a moderate hike to Massachusetts' highest waterfall at Bish Bash Falls State Park in the town of Mt Washington on the New York border.

Mt Greylock

Hike or drive (seasonally) to the 3491ft summit of Mt Greylock, Massachusetts' highest point, where there's a quarter-mile wheelchair-accessible loop. There's also primitive hike-in camping at Mount Greylock State Reservation.

Great Island Trail

The Cape Cod National Seashore's Great Island Trail is up to 8.8 miles round-trip, depending on your route.

Halibut Point State Park

With views extending into Maine, hiking Halibut Point State Park, a former granite quarry in Rockport, will take you to the very edge of the Massachusetts North Shore.

Old Sturbridge Village

Seafood in the Rough

Lobster Pool $$

The only thing that rivals the lobster rolls, fried-fish boats and other seafood dishes at this casual, BYOB Rockport restaurant are the incredible views over Ipswich Bay.

Bob Lobster $$

After a day on Plum Island, order a classic lobster roll or try one of the chef's specialty creations like the one topped with slow-braised short rib and bacon onion jam.

PJ's Family Restaurant $$

The red-and-white awnings and menu packed with fried clams, lobster rolls and other seafood-shack faves are a sure sign that you've arrived at this family-owned Wellfleet institution.

Fun Breweries

Northampton Brewery $

A rooftop bar and community events make the locally (and humanely) raised food and sustainably brewed, house-made beer even better.

Jack's Abby $$

Find a beer garden, beer hall, brewery tours, food and award-winning lagers – including year-round brews like the Shipping Out of Boston amber lager or Smoke & Dagger black lager – in Framingham.

Mighty Squirrel $

Expect beers packed with a ton of personality, like the Cloud Candy IPA with juicy tropical-fruit flavors, plus local food trucks, live music and trivia at this Waltham taproom.

Far from the Tree $

Sip lovingly made craft ciders, try your hand at trivia and enjoy local food pop-ups inside or on the patio not far from downtown Salem.

LYDIA MAY/SHUTTERSTOCK ©

Humpback whale, Cape Ann

On the Water

Schooner Fame

Set sail across Salem Sound on a replica of the 1812 privateer *Fame* from May to October. Learn about the War of 1812 and Salem history on daytime or sunset sails.

Cape Ann Whale Watch

Spot humpback whales, harbor seals, dolphins and other marine life off the coast of Gloucester at the Stellwagen Bank National Marine Sanctuary. Peak whale-watching months are April to October.

Zoar Outdoor

Adventurers will love whitewater rafting, kayaking and ziplining their way through the Berkshires and Lowell on full or half-day trips for different skill levels. Lodging is available, too.

Pirate Adventures

Hunting for treasure, singing sea shanties and storytelling are core elements of this interactive pirate voyage in Hyannis on Cape Cod, which is geared toward families with kids.

Scan to find more things to do in Massachusetts online

RHODE ISLAND

OUTDOORS | DINING | ARTS

RHODE ISLAND
Trip Builder

Topping the 147-sq-mile Narragansett Bay, Providence is Rhode Island's cultural and culinary hub. Sailing capital Newport is awash in Colonial and Gilded Age history, while quintessential New England villages dot the countryside. Summer means beach days in South County.

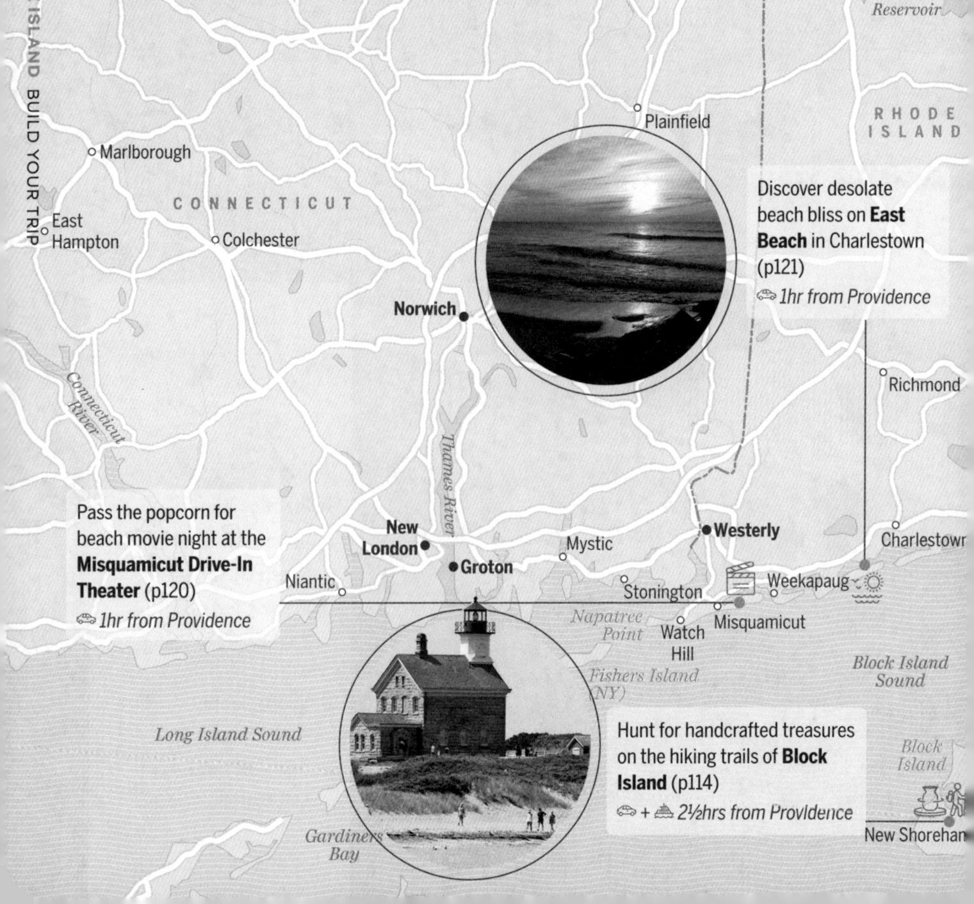
Take a tour of monumental murals in downtown **Providence** (p112)
Downtown Providence
Scituate Reservoir
RHODE ISLAND
Plainfield
Marlborough
CONNECTICUT
East Hampton
Colchester
Discover desolate beach bliss on **East Beach** in Charlestown (p121)
1hr from Providence
Norwich
Richmond
Connecticut River
Thames River
Pass the popcorn for beach movie night at the **Misquamicut Drive-In Theater** (p120)
1hr from Providence
New London
Groton
Niantic
Mystic
Westerly
Charlestown
Stonington
Weekapaug
Napatree Point
Watch Hill
Misquamicut
Fishers Island (NY)
Block Island Sound
Long Island Sound
Hunt for handcrafted treasures on the hiking trails of **Block Island** (p114)
+ 2½hrs from Providence
Block Island
New Shoreham
Gardiners Bay

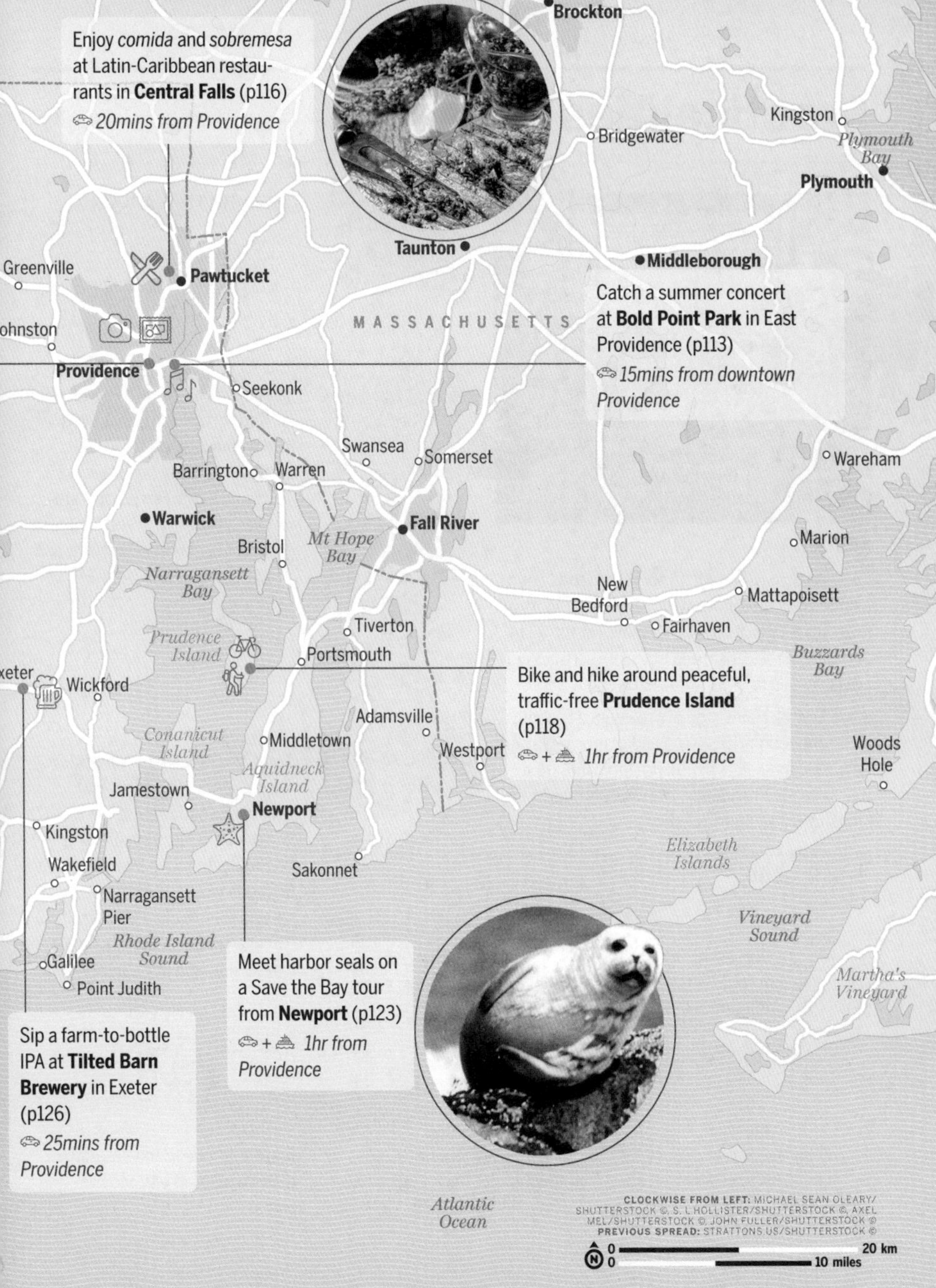
Enjoy *comida* and *sobremesa* at Latin-Caribbean restaurants in **Central Falls** (p116)
20mins from Providence
Brockton
Bridgewater
Kingston
Plymouth Bay
Plymouth
Taunton
Middleborough
Greenville
Pawtucket
Catch a summer concert at **Bold Point Park** in East Providence (p113)
15mins from downtown Providence
MASSACHUSETTS
ohnston
Providence
Seekonk
Swansea
Somerset
Wareham
Barrington
Warren
Warwick
Fall River
Bristol
Mt Hope Bay
Marion
Narragansett Bay
New Bedford
Mattapoisett
Fairhaven
Tiverton
Prudence Island
Portsmouth
Buzzards Bay
xeter
Wickford
Bike and hike around peaceful, traffic-free **Prudence Island** (p118)
+ 1hr from Providence
Adamsville
Conanicut Island
Middletown
Westport
Woods Hole
Aquidneck Island
Jamestown
Newport
Kingston
Wakefield
Sakonnet
Elizabeth Islands
Narragansett Pier
Rhode Island Sound
Vineyard Sound
Galilee
Point Judith
Meet harbor seals on a Save the Bay tour from **Newport** (p123)
+ 1hr from Providence
Martha's Vineyard
Sip a farm-to-bottle IPA at **Tilted Barn Brewery** in Exeter (p126)
25mins from Providence
Atlantic Ocean
0 20 km
0 10 miles

Practicalities

ARRIVING

TF Green International Airport (*pvdairport.com*; pictured) Located in Warwick, 20 minutes south of Providence. Rental cars, taxis, public buses ($2 to downtown Providence) and rideshare services are available. Cab fare to Providence is about $40.

Train Amtrak trains stop at Providence Station, with connections to Boston and points north and New York and points south. Boston commuter trains stop in Providence, Warwick and North Kingstown (Wickford Junction).

HOW MUCH FOR A

Beer at Narragansett Brewery
$7.50

Clam cakes and chowder
$10

Providence Bruins game ticket
$20

WHEN TO GO

JAN–MAR
Low season; cold, wet weather is better for indoor activities.

APR–JUN
Spring flowers presage sunny days; great for hiking and biking.

JUL–SEP
Busy beach and outdoor event season with reliably warm days.

OCT–DEC
Cooler weather brings spectacular fall foliage and holiday cheer.

GETTING AROUND

Car A car is essential for venturing beyond downtown Providence or Newport. Most destinations can be reached via three connected interstate highways: I-95, I-195 and I-295. Ferries operate between Providence and Newport (seasonal), plus Narragansett and Block Island.

Train and bus MBTA commuter rail stations in Providence, TF Green International Airport and Wickford are more useful for getting to Boston than intercity travel in Rhode Island. RIPTA offers bus service throughout Rhode Island (other than Block Island), but it can be slow and infrequent.

Bicycle Rhode Island has more than 60 miles of off-road bike paths.

EATING & DRINKING

Restaurant dinner service generally ends around 9pm on weeknights, perhaps 10pm on weekends. Kitchens at bars tend to stay open later, but late-night dining options are limited. Must-try foods include quahog chowder (pictured top right), fried calamari (pictured bottom right), hot wieners and Del's lemonade. Graduates of Providence's Johnson & Wales University's culinary school enhance the local dining scene. The state is known for its Italian food (especially in the Federal Hill neighborhood), seafood, Portuguese, and – increasingly – Latin-Caribbean cuisine.

Best meal with a view
Roof deck, Matunuck Oyster Bar (p120)

Must-try Latin American meal
Sharks Peruvian Cuisine, Central Falls (p116)

CONNECT & FIND YOUR WAY

Wi-fi Free wi-fi is available at public libraries, bookstores, coffee shops and restaurants.

Navigation The website visitrhodeisland.com has information on air, bus, bike, ferry and train travel.

JAMESTOWN–NEWPORT FERRY

The seasonal (May to October) Jamestown–Newport ferry is a traffic-beating way to visit Newport, making stops downtown, at Fort Adams, the Ann St pier, Rose Island and Jamestown.

WHERE TO STAY

Rhode Island is small enough that you can get almost anywhere in an hour or less; stay close to what interests you most, and drive to the rest.

Place	Pro/Con
Downtown Providence	Walk from brand and boutique hotels to dining, museums, the Riverwalk and the historic East Side.
Warwick	Local charm is lacking, but more affordable rates and a central location make airport area hotels a good base.
Newport	Rhode Island's best mix of lodgings includes hundreds of inns and B&Bs, plus waterfront and Gilded Age hotels.
Watch Hill	The small-town charm of a seaside village mixed with some of Rhode Island's most elegant hotels and resorts.
Block Island	Grand Victorian-era hotels, small inns and B&Bs come to life in summer, but prepare to pay for the experience.

MONEY

Credit cards and, increasingly, mobile payments are accepted nearly everywhere. Cash tips are appreciated. Restaurant Week events offer good deals on dining.

18 Creative CAPITAL

ARTS | CULTURE | MUSIC

Home to the Rhode Island School of Design (RISD) and the first art club in the US to admit women as members, Providence has a diverse and lively arts scene that operates both underground and plastered on the walls of some of the city's most prominent buildings.

RANDY DUCHAINE/ALAMY STOCK PHOTO ©

How to

Getting here Four major highways converge in Providence, including I-95, I-195, Rte 6 and Rte 146. Amtrak and MBTA commuter trains stop at Providence Station. TF Green International Airport is 20 minutes away.

When to go Festivals are seasonal, but Providence's art galleries, exhibits and museums are open year-round.

Big Nazo Performance art is part of Providence's creative milieu: you may encounter wandering bands of bizarre and grotesque puppets from Big Nazo Labs *(bignazo.com)* on city streets.

QUIGGYT4/SHUTTERSTOCK ©

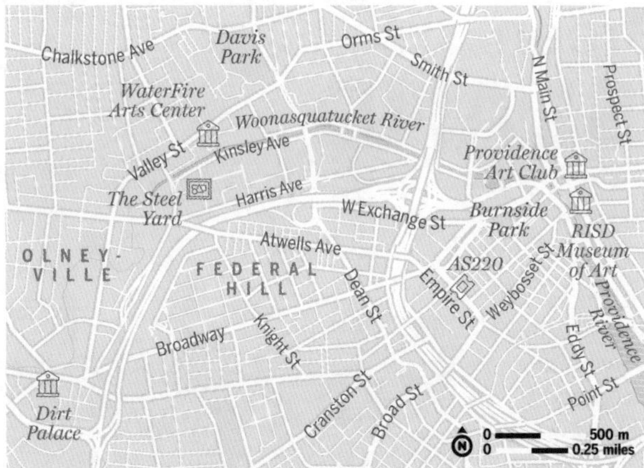

Providence Art Club Women helped found this College Hill institution in 1880. Galleries are open to the public; the Thomas St complex includes the **Fleur de Lys Building**, an architectural landmark.

The Steel Yard and the Dirt Palace The Steel Yard is a working foundry where artists fabricate public art and offer classes on blacksmithing and welding; events include a fiery Steel Pour. Founded by feminist artists, the Dirt Palace has residential studios, galleries and exhibition spaces.

Massive murals Building-sized murals in downtown Providence depict scenes rural and urban, concrete and abstract. Contributors include street artists like Shepard Fairey, best known for his Barack Obama *Hope* poster. The **Avenue Concept** app has a self-guided walking tour.

WaterFire Barnaby Evans' immersive art installation, with flaming wood braziers in Providence's rivers, is staged from May to November. The **WaterFire Arts Center** has permanent exhibition space and hosts Wilbury Theater Group performances.

RISD Museum of Art Eclectic exhibitions include collections of European, Asian and ancient Greek and Roman art.

AS220 Downtown art incubator is a performance space, restaurant and bar. Local artists exhibit unjuried works in galleries; the AS220 Main Stage hosts live music, comedy and poetry readings, with plays at a black box theater.

Top left The Steel Yard.
Bottom left Fleur de Lys Building

Providence's Music Scene

Talking Heads met in Providence as RISD students, Deer Tick launched their career here, and the city continues to have a vibrant live music scene. In addition to big venues like **The Strand**, **The Vets** and the **Providence Performing Arts Center**, the **Columbus Theatre** and **The Met** (in Pawtucket, but close to Providence) attract national touring acts, while local bands perform at smaller clubs like **Fete Music Hall**, **Dusk**, **The Parlour**, **Alchemy** and AS220. **Bold Point Park** in East Providence hosts an outdoor waterfront concert series.

■ Recommended by Umberto Crenca, *artist and founder of AS220 @as220*

19 Green ISLAND

NATURE | OUTDOORS | ACTIVE

One of the 'Last Great Places' named by the Nature Conservancy, Block Island blends the appeal of a vibrant beach destination with an ecofriendly vibe: over 40% of the island has been set aside for preservation. Powered by the wind and interwoven with hiking trails, Block Island can put you in touch with nature and still serve you sunset cocktails at day's end.

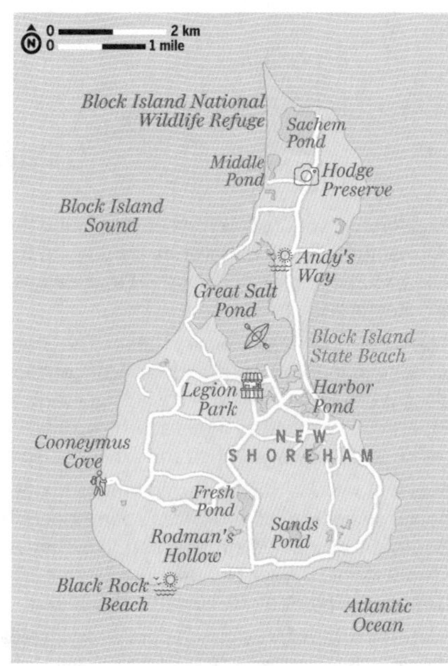

How to

Getting here Ferries operate year-round from Point Judith to Block Island, seasonally from Newport. Commercial flights connect via Westerly.

When to go Nature trails are open year-round; other attractions may close in the winter. April to October are the best months to visit.

Trailhead taxis Cabs can take you to and from trails.

Green beds The Sea Breeze Inn and the Darius Inn offer lodging with a commitment to sustainability.

Greenway trails The Nature Conservancy maintains a 28-mile network of hiking trails on Block Island – some easy meadow walks passing through farmland, others more strenuous hikes involving steep climbs and scrambles over uneven ground, but often rewarded with beautiful coastal views.

The Glass Float project Glass artist Eben Horton creates and hides more than 500 glass orbs each year along the trails and beaches on Block Island; devoted seekers are dubbed 'orbivores.'

Wind power About 4 miles from the Block Island coast is the first commercial offshore wind farm in the US. Five turbines produce 30MW of electricity, providing green energy to the entire island. **Fish the World** offers tours.

Eco-kayaking Naturalist Corrie Heinz of **Pond and Beyond Kayak** in New Harbor leads two-hour paddling tours of the **Great Salt Pond** touching on island history, aquaculture (including

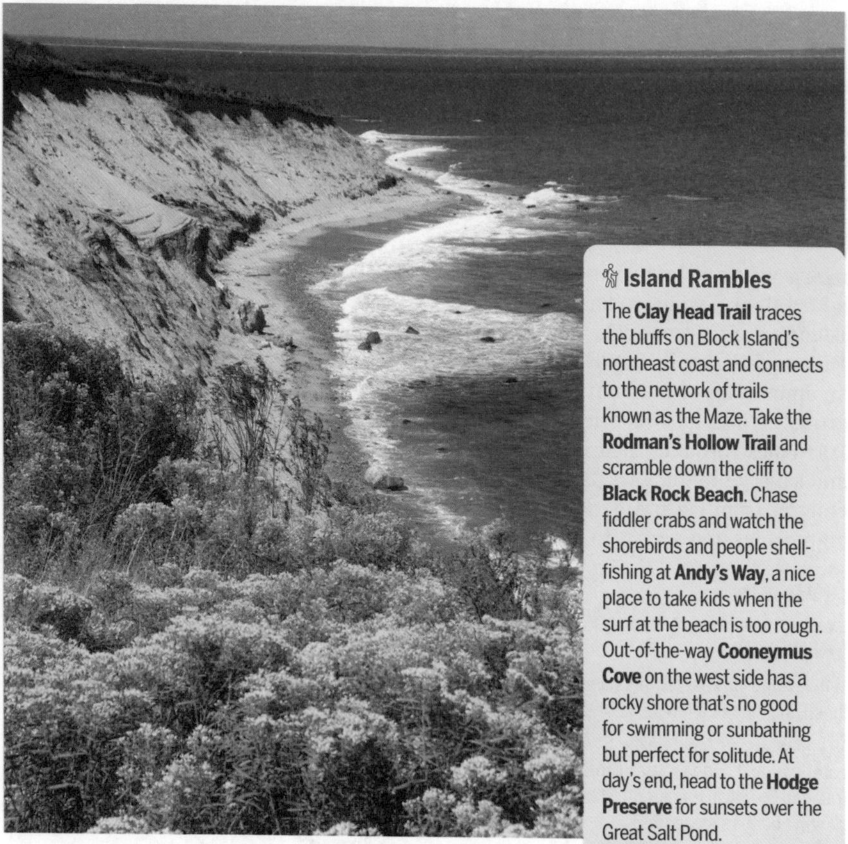

AGEFOTOSTOCK/ALAMY STOCK PHOTO ©

Island Rambles

The **Clay Head Trail** traces the bluffs on Block Island's northeast coast and connects to the network of trails known as the Maze. Take the **Rodman's Hollow Trail** and scramble down the cliff to **Black Rock Beach**. Chase fiddler crabs and watch the shorebirds and people shell-fishing at **Andy's Way**, a nice place to take kids when the surf at the beach is too rough. Out-of-the-way **Cooneymus Cove** on the west side has a rocky shore that's no good for swimming or sunbathing but perfect for solitude. At day's end, head to the **Hodge Preserve** for sunsets over the Great Salt Pond.

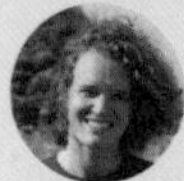

■ **Recommended by Charlotte Herring,** *Block Island coordinator, The Nature Conservancy @tncrhodeisland*

a visit to an oyster farm), wildlife and environmental preservation.

Farmers market Block Island's small community of farmers and artists gather at **Legion Park** on Saturday mornings from June to October to sell local produce, shellfish, flowers and arts and crafts.

Bike the Block Nearly all of Block Island is comfortably within reach by bicycle (if not without some hills), and a well-marked bike trail makes for a healthy and environmentally friendly day of pedaling to lighthouses, beaches and hiking trails.

Above Clay Head.

20 Melting POT

FOOD | CULTURE | NEIGHBORHOODS

Waves of immigrants have added their distinctive flavor to Rhode Island's dining scene. The Federal Hill neighborhood in Providence has an abundance of Italian restaurants, grocery stores and bakeries. The Portuguese brought their love of seafood and sausage to the East Bay. Now, émigrés from Latin America are adding empanadas and arepas to the mix.

Chalkstone Ave
Central Falls
Los Andes
Smith St
N Main St
Woonasquatucket River
Costantino's Venda Ravioli
Scialo Bros Bakery
Atwells Ave
Dean St
Joe Marzilli's Old Canteen
Providence River
Broadway
Broad St
Broad St
Johnny's Chimis Place
La Tia
0 1 km
0 0.5 miles

How to

Getting here Take Exit 30 on I-95 to reach downtown Central Falls.

When to go Most restaurants are open daily for lunch and dinner; a few serve breakfast, too.

Stanleyburgers Amid Dexter St's multicultural eateries you'll find Stanley's Famous Hamburgers, founded by Polish immigrant Stanley F Kryla and slinging burgers since 1932.

Dexter St dine around Latin American immigrants make up a significant portion of Central Falls' population, breathing culinary vitality into this old mill town. Fanning out from the city center, Dexter St and Broad St are lined with Colombian, Guatemalan, Peruvian and Mexican restaurants, bakeries and fruit parlors; menus are usually bilingual. **Sharks Peruvian Cuisine** does an excellent *pulpo a la parrilla* (grilled octopus with sautéed vegetables).

Broad St food trucks Street-food lovers flock to South Providence's main drag at night, where brightly lit food trucks such as **La Tia** and

Top right *Pulpo a la parrilla.*
Bottom right Scialo Bros Bakery.

VALERY_VOLKOV/SHUTTERSTOCK ©

PORT MANGO/SHUTTERSTOCK ©

Best Eats in Central Falls

Try **El Paisa** (598 Dexter St) for Colombian whole fish dinners and **La Herradura** (716 Dexter St) for *barbacoa* tacos. **La Sorpresa** (723 Broad St) makes *chicharrón* and sweets like *pan de queso*.

■ **Recommended by David Dadekian,** *founder of Eat Drink RI @eatdrinkri*

Johnny's Chimis Place serve Dominican food like tostadas, *chicharrón* (fried pork skins) and, of course, chimichurri.

On the Hill Federal Hill, a short walk from downtown, is the heart of Providence's Italian community with its La Pigna arch over Atwells Ave, the fountain courtyard of De Pasquale Sq, and established eateries like **Joe Marzilli's Old Canteen**, **Scialo Bros Bakery** and **Costantino's Venda Ravioli** grocery store. But demographic shifts have seen a few taquerias open on the Hill, and further west on Atwells Ave you'll find more Latin American restaurants.

Los Andes A Peruvian powerhouse on the Rhode Island dining scene, this Providence restaurant consistently ranks among the state's best. Chef-owner Cesin Curi's menu includes parrilla-grilled meats, paella and melt-in-your-mouth ceviche.

The Bay's the Thing

RHODE ISLAND'S WATERY HEART

No state is quite as defined by a natural feature as Rhode Island is by Narragansett Bay. The Ocean State wraps around New England's largest estuary: Providence straddles the tidal rivers at its head, while Newport faces the open ocean at its mouth.

ELBERT BAEZ/SHUTTERSTOCK ©

Left Rose Island. **Middle** Roger Williams. **Right** Beavertail Lighthouse.

When Giovanni da Verrazzano sailed into Narragansett Bay in 1524, he found the land on either side of the bay occupied by members of the Narragansett and Wampanoag tribes, who made their summer camps along the shores and reaped an abundance of fish and shellfish from its waters. Centuries later, Rhode Islanders still turn to the bay for the spring striped bass run and pull quahog clams out of the shallows.

The native names of the bay islands are sometimes overlooked. 'Jamestown' is actually the small town on **Conanicut Island**, for example, not the name of the island itself. Newport, Portsmouth and Middletown all share **Aquidneck Island**, the largest in the bay. Bridges to both islands were built only within the past century. No such span has ever reached the bay's second-biggest landmass, **Prudence Island**, which thus remains a sleepy backwater; many Rhode Islanders go their whole lives without visiting.

Rhode Island founder Roger Williams, a Puritan minister, gave Prudence its virtuous name along with those of several others nearby: Patience, Hope and, more ominously, Despair. These smaller islands are inhabited primarily by birds and deer, like the majority of the islands in the bay.

A sail on Narragansett Bay reveals a placid environment, with rocky shores guarded by picturesque lighthouses and small coves dotted with sailboats and fishing boats. That hasn't always been the case, however. A Colonial farm once occupied **Patience Island**, but it was burned by the British (who occupied Newport from 1776 to 1779 during

EVERETT COLLECTION/SHUTTERSTOCK ©

WANGKUN JIA/SHUTTERSTOCK ©

the Revolutionary War). **Dutch Island** was named for the Dutch East India Company trading post that was established here in 1636.

Newport visitors are often surprised to learn of the city's former reputation as a rough-and-tumble Navy town; tourism didn't really kick in until after the Atlantic destroyer fleet departed in the late 1970s. The Navy made its presence felt all over the bay, establishing a seaplane base on the north end of **Gould Island** and testing torpedos off the south end. **Rose Island**, where visitors can stay overnight in a historic lighthouse, includes the ruins of an 18th-century fort and ammunition bunkers from WWII.

The best way to view most of these islands is from the water, as the military and the state environmental protection agency restrict access to some.

The best way to view most of these islands is from the water: the military still restricts access to some, while the state environmental agency has declared others off-limits to protect wildlife and keep people from stumbling into old cisterns and other ruins.

Besides, there's plenty to see in Narragansett Bay from the deck of a boat: the forbidding walls of **Fort Adams**, built in the mid-1800s to protect the bay from attacks by sea; the delicate span of the **Mount Hope Bridge**; and 17 lighthouses, including sturdy **Beavertail Lighthouse** standing watch over the crashing surf at the south end of Conanicut. One lighthouse is harder to spot: only the base remains of Whale Rock Light, toppled in the great hurricane of 1938.

Dear Prudence

Rhode Island founders Roger Williams and John Winthrop divided Prudence Island between themselves in 1637, and not a lot has changed since. The Division Wall still stands, marking the path of one of dozens of hiking trails on the island, more than 80% of which is preservation land. The only way to get here is by ferry from Bristol. Pack a lunch: there's just a single store and no restaurants. But with only 200 year-round residents, Prudence Island's roads are blissfully free of traffic – perfect for pedaling through cool forests, sparse pine barrens and to hidden beaches.

21 South County SUMMERS

BEACH | OUTDOORS | SEAFOOD

The Atlantic shore of Rhode Island has some of the best beaches on the East Coast. While sunning in the sand is ingrained in local culture – many Providence residents have beach homes even though the drive down from city to shore is well under an hour – the beach is just the beginning of a summer day in South County.

MALEO PHOTOGRAPHY/SHUTTERSTOCK ©

How to

Getting here US Rte 1 accesses the entire South County shoreline.

When to go Best beach weather is June to late September.

Beach passes State beaches like East Matunuck, Scarborough and Misquamicut are open to residents and nonresidents alike. Parking passes cost $6 to $20 daily, but you can bike or walk in for free.

Drive-in movies Misquamicut Drive-In Theater shows classic summer films like *Jaws* (weekends May to October), and hosts live concerts.

ALLARD ONE/SHUTTERSTOCK ©

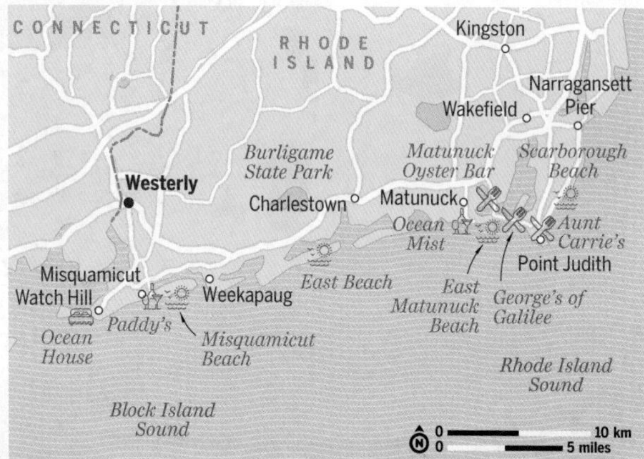

Quahogs These native clams are used to make chowder and clam cakes; locals (and visitors with a shellfishing license) can rake for quahogs at low tide alongside **Galilee Escape Rd** in Narragansett to supply their own clam bake.

If you prefer that someone else catch and cook your meal, set course for nearby **George's of Galilee** for local seafood served seaside. **Aunt Carrie's** has been a traditional stop for fish and chips after a day at Scarborough or Roger W Wheeler State Beach since 1920. **Matunuck Oyster Bar** hauls in shellfish from its own oyster farm on Potter Pond behind the restaurant; arrange for a tour before dinner.

East Beach This state beach has one of the most desolate stretches of shoreline in Rhode Island; it's also a rare beach that allows 4WD vehicles on the sand and camping within sound of the crashing waves. Misquamicut has the opposite atmosphere, with rowdy beach bars like **Paddy's** and a carousel, arcade and kiddie rides at **Atlantic Beach Park**.

Watch Hill At the southwestern point of Rhode Island, Watch Hill has been an upscale beach colony since the Victorian age, and the grand **Ocean House** hotel has been restored even beyond its former glory. The **Weekapaug Inn** is more off the beaten path but equally genteel; an on-staff naturalist leads kayak tours of Quonochontaug Pond.

Top left Quahogs. **Bottom left** Ocean House.

The Ocean Mist

The Ocean Mist beach bar hangs above the waves in Matunuck and has local and national bands playing; don't miss the free Sunday Funday shows. At intermission, breathe in the ocean air on the wraparound deck, where alfresco breakfast Benedicts and surprisingly good Mexican food are also served.

22 Seas the DAY

OUTDOORS | SAILING | HISTORY

Founded in 1636, Newport has always been a sailing town. Merchant ships, privateers and pirates set forth from Newport Harbor during the City by the Sea's earliest days. The Navy arrived in the 19th century; later came America's Cup yacht racing and the annual Newport to Bermuda race.

ALLAN WOOD PHOTOGRAPHY/SHUTTERSTOCK ©

DARRYL BROOKS/SHUTTERSTOCK ©

All Hands Aboard

Experiencing Newport from the sea can be as simple as taking an excursion on an America's Cup winning yacht *(12meteryachtcharters.com)*, a former Narragansett Bay rum runner *(cruisenewport.com)*, or an 80ft schooner *(sail-newport.com)*. **Sail Newport** *(sailnewport.org)* offers lessons and sailboat rentals if you want to try your hand at the tiller.

Stripers & Seals

Experienced anglers can charter a fishing boat out of Newport Harbor in pursuit of striped bass, sea bass, bluefish and other native species. If you're a novice, **Fish'n Tales Adventures** runs introductory fishing and lobstering trips; you keep what you catch. Harbor seals also call Narragansett Bay home – meet them on a **Save the Bay** tour.

How to

Getting here Rte 138 is the main highway to downtown Newport, connecting to I-95 to the west and I-195 to the east. Jamestown–Newport and Providence–Newport ferries run during summer.

When to go Peak sailing season is May to September.

Parking Parking in Newport is scarce: the biggest public lot is behind the Gateway Visitors Center.

What to wear Sunscreen, sunglasses and a waterproof jacket are boating essentials.

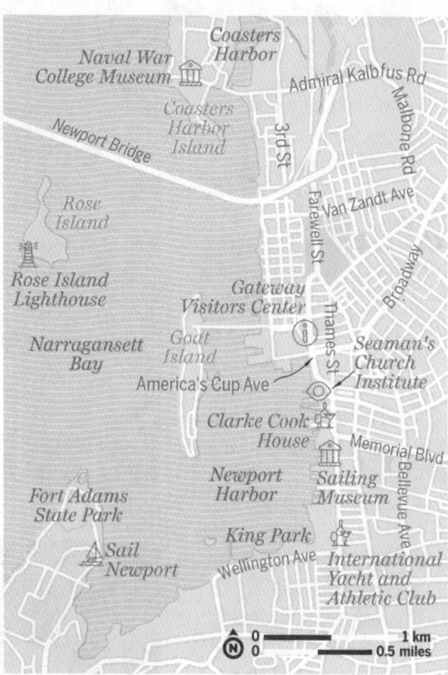

Top left Sailing, Newport Bay.
Bottom left Fishing boat, Newport.

Drink Like a Sailor

You can share fish stories with sailors at almost any Newport bar or restaurant in the summer, but the bar at the **International Yacht and Athletic Club** (IYAC) is the undisputed home port for Newport mariners after a long day on the water. The Candy Store at the **Clarke Cook House** is where Dennis Conner and crew hung out during their America's Cup run in the 1970s and '80s.

Museums & Lighthouses

Newport's new **Sailing Museum** in the historic Armory Building on Thames St is home to the National Sailing Hall of Fame as well as the America's Cup Hall of Fame.

Located in the former Newport Asylum for the Poor, the **Naval War College Museum** documents the centuries-long association of the US Navy in Newport and Narragansett Bay, naval history, and the story of the War College itself. The college and the museum

Ida Lewis

Lime Rock lighthouse keeper Ida Lewis saved at least 18 people from drowning in the waters of Narragansett Bay – her first when she was just 12 years old, the last when she was 63. Called 'the bravest woman in America' in the 19th century, Lewis is remembered in many ways in Newport: the **Ida Lewis Yacht Club**, located in the former Lime Rock lighthouse, is named in her honor (its pennant has 18 stars representing all of Lewis' rescues); the US Coast Guard buoy tender *Ida Lewis* is based in nearby Middletown; and Lewis' grave, with a headstone engraved with an anchor and oars, can be visited in Newport's **Common Burying Ground**.

Showboats

Held in mid-September, the **Newport International Boat Show** is one of the largest in-water boat shows in the country. Dreaming of an even bigger boat? The **Newport Charter Yacht Show**, held in June, includes dockside tours of palatial mega-yachts, some more than 200ft long.

RAKSYBH/SHUTTERSTOCK ©

are located on an active Navy base, so while admission is free, visitors need to clear a background check first.

Play lightkeeper for a day (or week) at the 1870 **Rose Island Lighthouse** in Newport Harbor. Guest rooms on the 18-acre island include the original keeper's apartment, the foghorn building, and barracks of the never-completed Fort Hamilton.

Seamen's Church

The Seamen's Church Institute is a bit of a relic in Newport's touristy core: founded in 1919, it still operates as a safe haven for struggling sailors, including lodging and affordable meals for mariners. The guest rooms are popular with sailing crew members, and the 39ft cafe is open to the public and serves breakfast and lunch. The **Chapel of the Sea**, with its hand-painted walls depicting saints and nautical themes, offers a moment of quiet contemplation amid the summer hustle outside; ask to see the Institute's **Discovery Deck**, an interactive exhibit on Newport's maritime history.

FAR LEFT: EMILY RIDDELL/ALAMY STOCK PHOTO ©
LEFT: JOHN VAN DECKER/ALAMY STOCK PHOTO ©

Left Ida Lewis Yacht Club. **Top** Clarke Cooke House. **Right** Seaman's Church Institute.

Listings

BEST OF THE REST

Wines & Brews

Whalers Brewing Company $$

An old mill building in South Kingstown stocked with games that's pet- and family-friendly; lots of beer on tap, but food is BYO. Try a pint of Rise, an award-winning American pale ale.

Tilted Barn Brewery $$

Farm-to-bottle brewery in Exeter raises its own hops for lip-puckering IPAs. The two-story barn and outdoor patio with Adirondack chairs add country charm to tastings.

Carolyn's Sakonnet Vineyards $$

The perfect end to a head-clearing coastal drive to Little Compton ends with a glass of wine at Carolyn's, where the owner appends inspirational themes to each vintage.

Taproot Brewing Company $$

Can't decide between beer and wine? The Taproot brewery is co-located with Newport Vineyards; sit by the vines to enjoy live music during the warmer months.

Sons of Liberty $$

Patriotic-themed whiskeys sold by the bottle or cocktails at the bar. Single-malt Uprising and Battle Cry malt whiskies are distilled from stout beer and Belgian wheat, respectively. Located in South Kingstown.

Unique Eats

Olneyville New York System $

Tiny wieners smothered with onions and meat sauce and sprinkled with celery salt are lined up on a grill man's arm for your dining pleasure – particularly popular after midnight. Located in Providence.

Evelyn's Drive-In $$

Be bold and try the lobster chow mein at this no-frills roadside seafood shack in Tiverton, or stick to the standards like lobster rolls.

Delekta Pharmacy $

Only in Rhode Island is a milkshake called a 'cabinet' and coffee the flavor of choice; this Warren gift shop is the undisputed champion of the frozen caffeinated treat.

DePetrillo's Pizza & Bakery $

Whether you call it 'bakery pizza,' 'party pizza' or 'pizza strips,' Rhode Island's cheese-less, Sicilian-style pizza is a strangely alluring savory snack.

Kids' Stuff

Roger Williams Park Zoo

Rainforest and African animal habitats are fun to stroll through, but the zoo shines with an interactive barnyard, accessible play area, wetlands walk and zipline.

Biomes Marine Biology Center

The hands-on aquarium focuses on the marine life of Narragansett Bay and the Atlantic Ocean.

LEE SNIDER PHOTO IMAGES/SHUTTERSTOCK ©

Green Animals Topiary Gardens

The kid-oriented educational program includes tortoise, shark and horseshoe crab feedings.

Rail Explorers

A 6-mile coastal tour on the tracks of the former Newport and Narragansett Bay Railroad is a fun workout: riders use pedal power to propel two- and four-passenger rail cars.

Green Animals Topiary Gardens

Wander the grounds of this Portsmouth country estate to meet a menagerie of topiary animals and other designs lovingly trimmed from ornamental bushes.

Guide Time

La Gondola

Climb aboard an authentic Venetian gondola and be serenaded with Italian love songs during this tour of Providence's downtown rivers; slip under a series of arched bridges to reach Waterplace Park.

Rhode Island Red Food Tours

Foodie tours of Providence and Newport touch on architecture, culinary traditions and history between a half-dozen stops to meet chefs and sample local food and drink.

Newport Classic Car Tours

If you're going all Gilded Age in Newport, pair your mansion visit and rooftop cocktails at the Vanderbilt hotel with an Ocean Drive tour in a 1924 Studebaker convertible or a 1929 Model A Ford.

Experience Rhode Island

There's not much in Rhode Island that's more than an hour's drive, and this tour company gives a pretty good overview of the state with its Rhode Island in a Day tour.

Old Slater Mill

Get Historical

Old Slater Mill

Circa 1793 Blackstone River textile mill that's considered the birthplace of the American Industrial Revolution. Tours include still-operating looms and the waterfall and raceway that powered them.

General Nathanael Greene Homestead

George Washington's best general is remembered for his military exploits in the Carolinas, but he grew up in this Quaker homestead in Rhode Island, where he founded the still-active Kentish Guards.

Coggeshall Farm Museum

Living history museum that explores how tenant farmers worked coastal salt-marsh farms in the 1790s, with costumed interpreters and pens and pastures inhabited by heritage-breed livestock.

Scan to find more things to do in Rhode Island online

CONNECTICUT
HISTORY | DIVERSITY | ART
Experience Connecticut online

WELCOME
MYSTIC SEAPORT ENTRANCE
WHEN THIS YOU SEE
REMEMBER ME
THE PHOTOGRAPHY OF
EVERETT SCHOLFIELD AND GEORGE TINGLEY
NOW ON EXHIBIT
R.J. SCHAEFER BUILDING

CONNECTICUT
Trip Builder

Settled by the Dutch way before the *Mayflower*, Connecticut tells its long and proud past in museums and historic homes. With 618 miles of coastline, there's no shortage of seaside communities. Inland, you'll find everything from amusement parks to casinos.

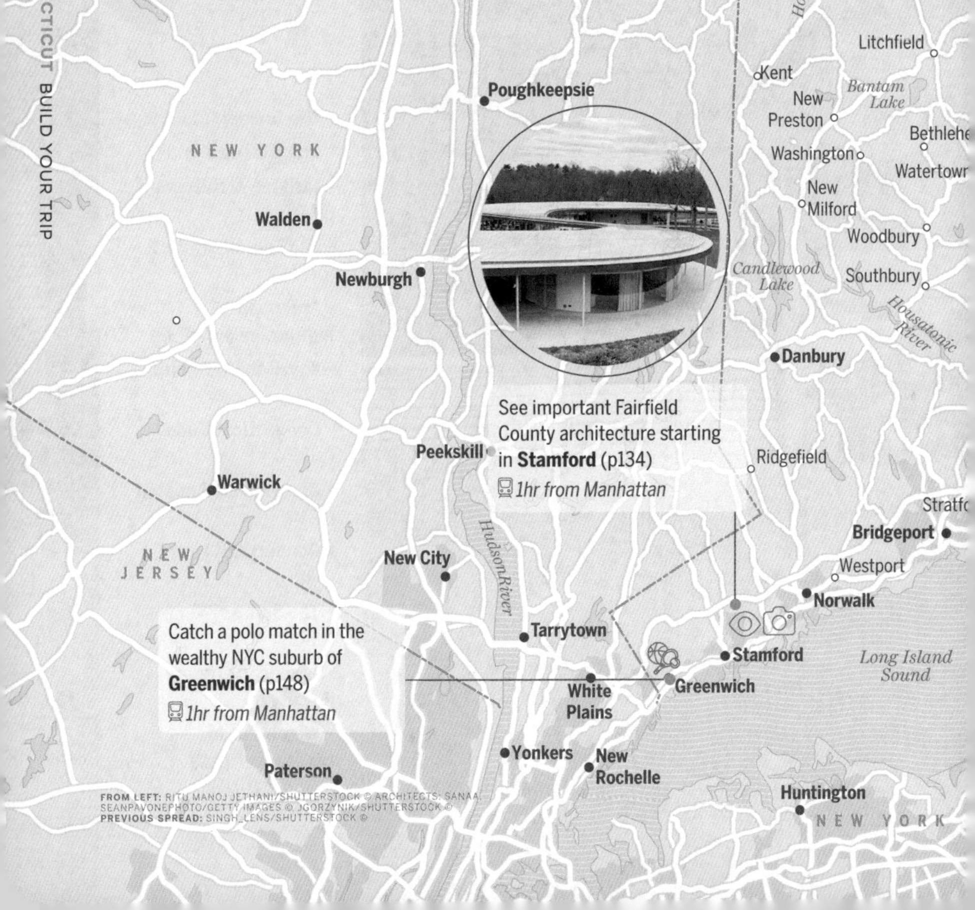

See important Fairfield County architecture starting in **Stamford** (p134)
1hr from Manhattan

Catch a polo match in the wealthy NYC suburb of **Greenwich** (p148)
1hr from Manhattan

Great Barrington
Canaan
Salisbury
Norfo
Millerton
Housatonic River
Cornwall
Torringto
Litchfield
Kent
Bantam Lake
New Preston
Bethlehe
Washington
Watertowr
New Milford
Woodbury
Candlewood Lake
Southbury
Housatonic River
Danbury
Poughkeepsie
NEW YORK
Walden
Newburgh
Peekskill
Ridgefield
Warwick
Stratfo
Bridgeport
Westport
NEW JERSEY
New City
Hudson River
Norwalk
Tarrytown
Stamford
Long Island Sound
Greenwich
White Plains
Yonkers
New Rochelle
Paterson
Huntington
NEW YORK

Tour the **Hartford** homes of neighbors Mark Twain and Harriet Beecher Stowe (p150)
45mins from New Haven
0 20 km
0 10 miles
MASSACHUSETTS
Sturtbridge
Springfield
Webster
Union
Stafford
Granby
Connecticut River
Enfield
Woodstock
Winsted
Windsor Locks
Putnam
New Hartford
Simsbury
Rockville
Lift a pint at a Connecticut brewery, starting in **Manchester** (p142)
15mins from Hartford
Avon
Storrs
Collinsville
Burlington
Hartford
Manchester
Andover
Farmington
New Britain
Willimantic
Plainfield
Rocky Hill
Hebron
Bristol
Marlborough
Lebanon
See real dinosaur footprints and life-size statues, beginning in **Rocky Hill** (p152)
15mins from Hartford
CONNECTICUT
Portland
Colchester
Waterbury
Middletown
Meriden
Norwich
Naugatuck
Higganum
Salem
East Haddam
Montville
Wallingford
Uncasville
Thames River
Connecticut River
Chester
Charlestown
North Haven
Seymour
New London
Westerly
Essex
Groton
Mystic
Waterford
Stonington
Old Saybrook
helton
New Haven
Guilford
Madison
Old Lyme
Niantic
Noank
Block Island Sound
Saybrook Point
Fishers Island (NY)
Stony Creek
Clinton
Explore the state's maritime history in the pretty seaside town of **Mystic** (p136)
1hr from New Haven
Orient
Gardiners Island
Spend a day kayaking around the scenic **Thimble Islands** (p140)
20mins from New Haven
Greenport
Gardiners Bay
Southold
Shelter Island
earn about the *mistad* across the tate, starting in **New Haven** (p144)
45mins from artford
Montauk
Sag Harbor
East Hampton
Great Peconic Bay
Riverhead
Bridgehampton
Southampton
Long Island
Hampton Bays
Atlantic Ocean

Practicalities

MYSTIC STOCK PHOTOGRAPHY/SHUTTERSTOCK ©

ARRIVING

Air Bradley International Airport is the state's busiest. TF Green International Airport in Providence, Rhode Island, is near Connecticut's northern border. NYC's airports LaGuardia and JFK are about an hour from Greenwich; Westchester County Airport is right on the states' border.

Train Amtrak has 12 Connecticut stops including New Haven, Hartford and Mystic. Commuter rail lines Metro-North and Shore Line East connect many communities.

HOW MUCH FOR A

Lobster roll
$21

Craft beer
$7

Large plain pizza
$24

GETTING AROUND

Car It's most convenient to drive around the state. Routes are well marked, gas stations are plentiful, and parking garages and lots are marked with signs. In some areas with paid parking you'll need quarters or an app.

Train Amtrak and commuter train stations are often near enough to attractions to walk, but many have taxi stands if needed.

Walking Hartford's downtown is very walkable, as are parts of New Haven and towns like Mystic and Stonington.

WHEN TO GO

JAN–MAR
Beautiful blankets of snow, but also expect icy road conditions.

APR–MAY
Rain, mud, blooming gardens and comfortable temperatures.

JUN–AUG
Roads are busy, especially on weekends with travel to beaches.

SEP–DEC
Peak leaf-peeping in October; magical holiday decorations in December.

EATING & DRINKING

The Connecticut style of lobster roll (pictured top right) is hot and buttered versus a cold salad prepared with mayonnaise. Try locally sourced Copps Island oysters and Arethusa Farm's world-renowned cheese. New Haven is known for pizza, with Frank Pepe's (pictured bottom right) and Sally's Apizza leading the way; both can be found in and beyond the city. Louis' Lunch in New Haven claims to have made the first hamburger in 1900. Drop in for a burger cooked in the seasoned cast-iron vertical broiler (in use for more than a century), and don't ask for ketchup.

Best ice cream
Mystic Drawbridge Ice Cream (p137)

Must-try pizza
Frank Pepe's white-clam pie

CONNECT & FIND YOUR WAY

Wi-fi Coverage can be spotty in rural areas so if you're planning a drive in the woods, download a map of your route.

Navigation Major highways, especially I-95, are known for heavy traffic, so use the Waze app to navigate around slowdowns.

MONEY

The further you get from Fairfield County, the lower the prices. Look for deals like the Connecticut Art Trail Passport and hotel packages. Museums often offer free days, and Groupon has Connecticut discounts.

WHERE TO STAY

Unless there's a compelling reason to stay in cities like New Haven and Hartford, it's more pleasant to book accommodations elsewhere as the state is known for its charming inns.

Town	Pro/Con
Greenwich	Upscale dining and shopping near Fairfield County's cultural attractions; it's pricey though.
Farmington	A pretty town with its own attractions near Hartford, though not exactly hopping.
Kent	Art and design stores and a waterfall; near other cute towns, lakes and breweries.
Litchfield	Something for everyone from hiking to spirit tasting, though fairly quiet.
Ledyard	Ledyard and Uncasville are draws for casinos with dining, entertainment and shopping; not places to go for a quiet getaway.
Mystic	Popular, especially in summer, so book in advance.

CAR SAFETY

If you're driving, use common sense: lock your car, don't leave valuables in plain sight, and don't leave the car running when you're not in it.

23 STRIKING Architecture

ARCHITECTURE | HISTORY | LANDSCAPES

Since Lower Fairfield County is a wealthy New York City suburb, you would be forgiven for thinking that mansions are the only architectural eye candy here. However, in a span of 15 miles there are four notable structures that are both very different and very striking.

Design Must-See

A favorite of mine, the Glass House (pictured) is a must-see for anyone interested in the history of 20th-century design. The enigmatic collection of buildings and artworks on this curated, bucolic estate challenges our conception of architecture in a way that only Philip Johnson could.

Recommended by Connecticut architect David Scott Parker FAIA, *Trustee of the National Trust for Historic Preservation @dsparkerarchitects*

Trip Notes

Getting here/around Several of these buildings are near Metro-North train stations but the most efficient way to tour them is by car.

When to go Generally, the Fish Church is open for Sunday service year-round, the Glass House and Lockwood-Mathews Mansion close in winter, and Grace Farms is closed Mondays. Check the websites for advance tickets.

Top tip Allow several hours for the Glass House: there are numerous buildings and tours start and end at the visitor center in New Canaan. This pretty town is a good place for lunch.

04 Undulating down a soft slope, a building called The River at **Grace Farms** seamlessly blends into the surrounding meadows, trails and pond in a design by Pritzker Prize–winning firm SANAA.

02 America's first mansion will look familiar if you've seen either of the *Stepford Wives* movies. A mix of architectural styles, the **Lockwood-Mathews Mansion Museum** is a 62-room stunner with no shortage of gilt, frescoes or marble.

03 The home of one of the world's most famous architects, Philip Johnson, the **Glass House** is set on 49 beautiful acres with 14 buildings including an art and sculpture gallery.

01 Inspired by the great cathedrals of Europe, the **Fish Church** impressively uses 20,000 pieces of stained glass to convey what it's like to be inside a giant jewel box.

0 — 10 km
0 — 5 miles

NEW YORK

New Canaan

Westport

Norwalk

South Norwalk

CONNECTICUT

Stamford

Long Island Sound

Greenwich

TOP: ALEXANDER FRIEDMAN/SHUTTERSTOCK ©
BOTTOM: RANDY DUCHAINE/ALAMY STOCK PHOTO ©
OPPOSITE: RITU MANOJ JETHANI/SHUTTERSTOCK ©

24 The Lure of MYSTIC

BOATING | AQUARIUM | DINING

The one place most people have heard of in Connecticut is Mystic due to its two powerhouse attractions – the pretty waterfront downtown, and the film *Mystic Pizza*. Mystic was a center for Colonial shipbuilding, and its identity is rooted in the water: sailing, seafood, nautical art and fashion. There are more than enough options to keep people of all ages occupied for days.

How to

Getting here/around Mystic is on the water, close to the Rhode Island border, off I-95. There's an Amtrak stop near the center of town.

When to go Although many businesses are open year-round, you'll find the most activity in the summer.

Nearby You'll be happy you spent a couple of hours in idyllic Stonington Borough or tried lobster at Abbott's or clams at Costello's in tiny Noank.

Boat buffs could spend all day at the **Mystic Seaport Museum**, a re-created 19th-century seafaring village with lots of child-focused experiences. Penguins, seals and (controversially) beluga whales draw crowds to the **Mystic Aquarium**. If visiting both, consider purchasing the Mystic Pass.

Pop into the boutiques and galleries along West Main St. Take a river cruise, hop into a kayak, or join a unique tour in a two-person speedboat. Explore the natural history exhibits, trails and events at the **Denison Pequotsepos Nature Center**. Or head to **Enders Island**, a religious

Top left Main St, Mystic. **Bottom left** Painted turtle, Denison Pequotsepos Nature Center.

IAN G DAGNALL/ALAMY STOCK PHOTO ©

Whale Tale

Look for distinctly painted whale statues, each with a signature color and design. The one outside Bank Square Books, painted by local artist Pamela Zagarenski, is covered with whales. You're whale-come to see for yourself!

■ **Tip from Annie Philbrick,** *owner of Bank Square Books*

@banksquarebooks

retreat that welcomes all to wander its beautiful grounds.

If you've seen *Mystic Pizza* or read *Esquire's* roundup of the 40 best new restaurants in the US (Nana's Bakery & Pizza), you'll know that there are some notable pizza places in Mystic. Seafood lovers won't want to miss **Oyster Club** and **Treehouse**, its beautiful outdoor space. The sales line 'Beer, Burgers and Bourbon' of its sister restaurant, **Engine Room**, says it all, and a boisterous good time will be had at the waterfront **Red 36**. You'll find the state's best lobster omelet at **Kitchen Little**, which is only open for breakfast and lunch. As for dessert, it would be sacrilege to walk past **Mystic Drawbridge Ice Cream** without getting a scoop. The roadside stand **Sea Swirl** has been serving clams and ice cream for generations.

GEORGE OSTERTAG/ALAMY STOCK PHOTO ©

STAN TESS/ALAMY STOCK PHOTO ©

American Impressionism

BUCOLIC LANDSCAPES WHERE ART WAS CREATED

In the late 1800s, when American artists returned from Paris and started making French Impressionism their own, many of them lived, painted and taught in Connecticut art colonies. Today, you can tour these sites, view art made on the premises, and walk the bucolic landscapes that the artists captured more than a century ago.

Left Florence Griswold Museum **Middle** Weir Farm. **Right** Hill-Stead Museum.

French Impressionists first exhibited their radical new technique in Paris in 1874. Their rapid brushstrokes resulted in blurred subjects and shocked audiences accustomed to realistic academic painting styles. Approximately a decade later, Impressionism was growing in appreciation among critics and art audiences, and American artists sought European instruction to meet patron demand. Connecticut artists were at the forefront of this new way of capturing a changing world.

The East Coast was both a center for wealthy patrons and for art schools like New York City's Art Students League. When the railroad reached Connecticut in 1888, new opportunities became available for city-dwelling artists wishing to paint bucolic landscapes en plein air like their French counterparts and to collaborate and experiment with other like-minded painters.

Connecticut's first American Impressionist art colony was formed in a harborside boarding house near the train station in Cos Cob, a part of Greenwich. Now known as the **Bush-Holley House** and part of the Greenwich Historical Society, it was a gathering place for artists and writers known as the Cos Cob Art Colony.

Beginning in 1891, John Henry Twachtman, who lived elsewhere in Greenwich, and Julian Alden Weir taught summer classes at the Holley House for members of the Art Students League. Other leading American Impressionist artists who were part of the Cos Cob Art Colony from the early 1890s until the 1920s include Childe Hassam, Theodore Robinson, and Elmer MacRae, who married the proprietors' daughter.

NANCY KENNEDY/SHUTTERSTOCK ©

SHANSHAN0312/SHUTTERSTOCK ©

On the Lieutenant River up the coast in Old Lyme, a yellow Georgian home surrounded by lovely gardens was the setting for Miss Florence's boarding house. Landscape artist Henry Ward Ranger arrived in 1899 and other artists including Hassam, Willard Metcalf, Matilda Browne and William Chadwick followed, forming the Lyme Art Colony.

For more than three decades, artists were inspired by the blooming gardens, flowing river and nearby clapboard churches and farmhouses of what's now the **Florence Griswold Museum**, affectionately called the FloGris.

> Now a national park site, Weir Farm's 60 wooded acres in Wilton cost Julian Alden Weir $10 and a painting.

Now a national park site, Weir Farm's 60 wooded acres in Wilton cost Julian Alden Weir $10 and a painting. Artistic royalty, his father taught drawing at West Point and his brother was director of the Yale School of Fine Arts. After studying art at New York's National Academy of Design and the École des Beaux-Arts in Paris, Weir's work, particularly his landscapes, became critically acclaimed.

Although not a boarding house like the Holley House and FloGris, **Weir Farm** hosted artists over the years such as Hassam, Twachtman and John Singer Sargent. Weir helped found the Society of American Artists, was president of the National Academy of Design, and joined the Metropolitan Museum of Art's board of directors. Weir Farm is closed November through April.

Connecticut Art Trail

The three sites listed here and 19 other museums are on the Connecticut Art Trail, whose passport is the best bargain in the state: $35 to visit them all. The highest-profile participating museum is Hartford's **Wadsworth Atheneum** whose enormous holdings span the centuries. The **Bruce Museum** in Greenwich, the **New Britain Museum of American Art**, and Waterbury's **Mattatuck Museum** display American Impressionist paintings. A great place for kids, the **Stamford Museum & Nature Center** has farm animals and a well-designed playground, and Farmington's **Hill-Stead Museum** is an elegant house museum with an impressive collection of French Impressionist paintings.

25 Kayak the THIMBLES

KAYAKING | ADVENTURE | ISLANDS

Halfway up the Connecticut coast, the Thimble Islands dot the shoreline. Approximately two dozen islands in this picturesque private archipelago have homes perched atop rocky foundations, allowing stunning 360-degree water views. Narrated ferry tours run in season and you can also rent a kayak, canoe or stand-up paddleboard for a beautiful day on the water.

JEREMY GRAHAM/ALAMY STOCK PHOTO ©

How to

Getting here/around Take Exit 56 off I-95 and wind your way through the blink-and-you-miss-it charming borough of Stony Creek to the marina.

When to go The season generally runs May to September.

Top tip Unless you are invited by a homeowner or end up at the Stewart B McKinney National Wildlife Refuge on the furthest island from shore, Outer Island, these pint-sized islands that have been a summer refuge for the wealthy for generations are off-limits for landing.

PHUCTECHNOLOGY/SHUTTERSTOCK ©

If you want to feel like you're in Maine without the five-hour drive, head to **Stony Creek** and hop in a kayak for a paddle around the Thimble Islands. If you don't have your own kayak, a few area outfitters rent them and offer tours.

Meandering around these lovely little islands you'll see their homes up close, but remember that they are private property. Some are simple and others grand, on stilts or sprawling, with tennis courts and meticulously landscaped grounds.

Consider the difficulties of living on an island. Think about how the homes were built, every concrete pour and light fixture having to be delivered by boat. Living on an island presents challenges for grocery shopping, contractor calls and visits with friends. You can't take an Uber home or order pizza delivery. What you do get is serenity, privacy and membership in a very small club of Thimble Island homeowners. There is ferry service for locals but most have their own boats.

For a good overview of the islands, plan on being in the water about three hours and come prepared. Check tide charts and be aware of currents and wind. Wear layers and sunscreen, avoid marked channels, and dodge the wakes of motorized boats. Bring a chart and a compass, lunch and a waterproof bag, but most of all, be wary of rocks.

Far left Governor Island.
Bottom left Thimble Island homes.
Near left Kayaking, Stony Creek.

Paddle Tips

The easiest route to **Outer Island** from the Stony Creek launch is to paddle toward **Rogers Island** – the big island just offshore – then stay left and keep cutting left past **Potato**, **Governor** and **Kidd** islands. This should take novices 1½ to two hours depending on wind speed and tide, and someone more experienced between 40 minutes and an hour.

This area has more than islands and more than one season. There are tidal rivers and marshlands, and foliage in fall when there's a lot less marine traffic. Depending on the water temperature, we usually operate through October 31.

■ **Recommended by Rob Haesche,** *owner of Thimble Island Kayak Rental @thimbleislandkayakrental*

26 Connecticut SUDS

BREWERIES | FOOD | CULTURE

Connecticut's craft breweries run the gamut from waterside hotspots to closet-sized passion projects. This selection spans the state and leads to quaffs like the cleverly named I'll be a Monkey's Dunkel (a Dunkelweizen from Elicit) and Charter Oak's Stubborn Yankee Lager.

Trip Notes

Getting here/around The state's main thoroughfare, I-95, connects many of these spots.

When to go Some breweries are closed at the beginning of the week, so plan to drop in from Wednesday to Sunday.

Top tip Find a brewery near you or create your own beer itinerary at ctbeer.com.

100-Plus Reasons for a Rideshare

With more than 100 breweries, Connecticut offers lots of stops to travelers who value tasting experiences. Some that might not be on your radar that locals adore are **Tox Brewing Company** in New London, **Nod Hill Brewery** in Ridgefield, and **Great Falls Brewing Company** and **Norbrook Farm Brewery** in the state's northwest.

Insights from Kevin Mardorf, *CTBeer.com founder @CTBeer*

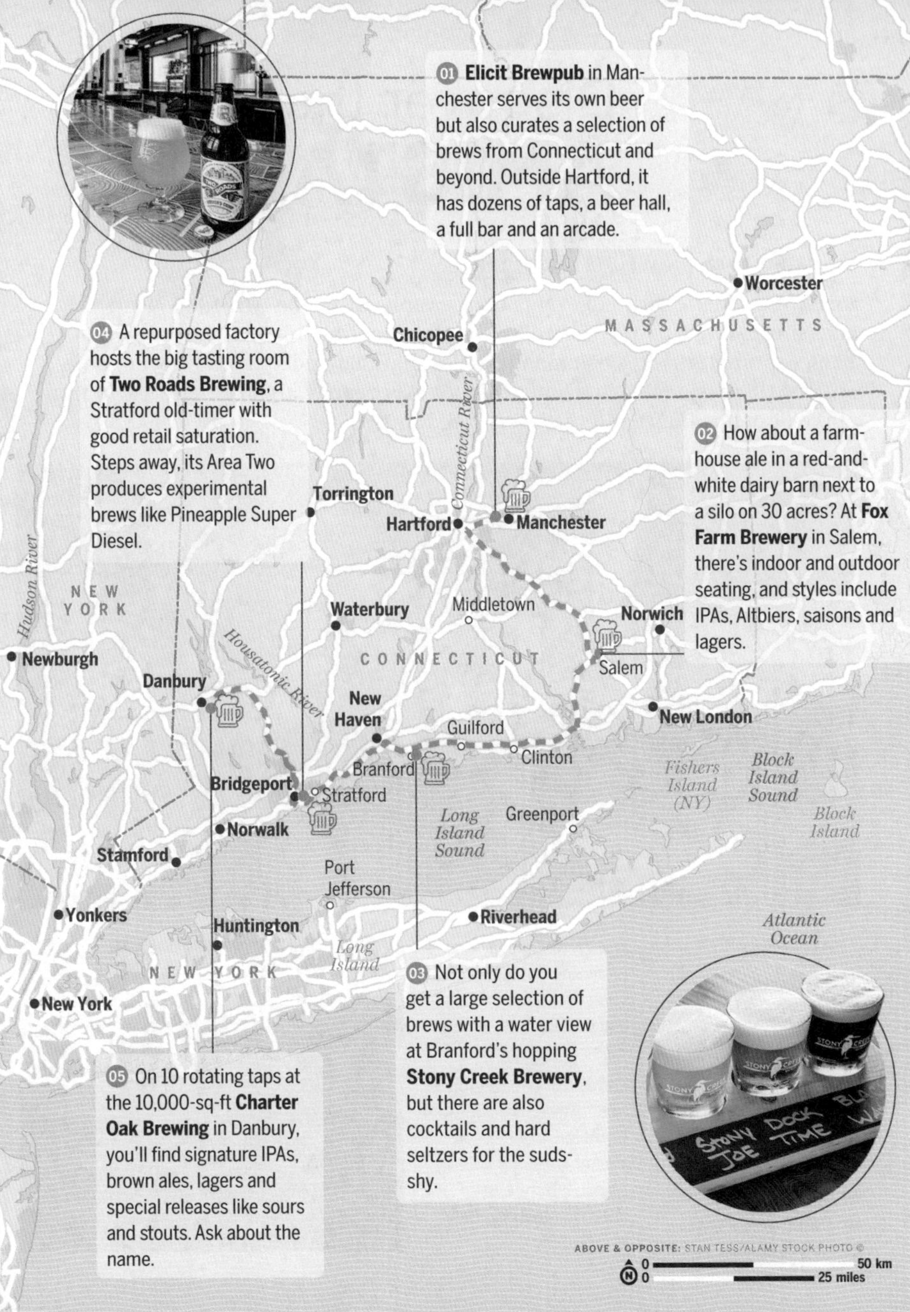

ABOVE & OPPOSITE: STAN TESS/ALAMY STOCK PHOTO ©

Discover the AMISTAD

BLACK HISTORY | MUSEUMS | CULTURE

A dramatic series of events that was pivotal in the struggle toward abolishing slavery in the United States played out mainly in Connecticut. In 1839, captured Africans commandeered a ship that ended up in New London. Former US president John Quincy Adams successfully argued their case in front of the Supreme Court and they were freed in 1841.

RANDY DUCHAINE/ALAMY STOCK PHOTO ©

How to

Getting here/around New Haven and New London are on I-95; I-91 leads to Hartford and its suburb of Farmington. Trains and buses are readily available. These sights are in walkable downtown areas.

When to go Most sights are closed on Mondays: the New Haven Museum is open Wednesday to Saturday, the Custom House Thursday to Sunday, and the Old State House Tuesday to Saturday.

More info For background, watch Steven Spielberg's 1997 film, *Amistad*. For a list of *Amistad*-related sites in the state, see ctfreedomtrail.org/trail/amistad/sites.

ANASTASIA MILLS HEALY/LONELY PLANET ©

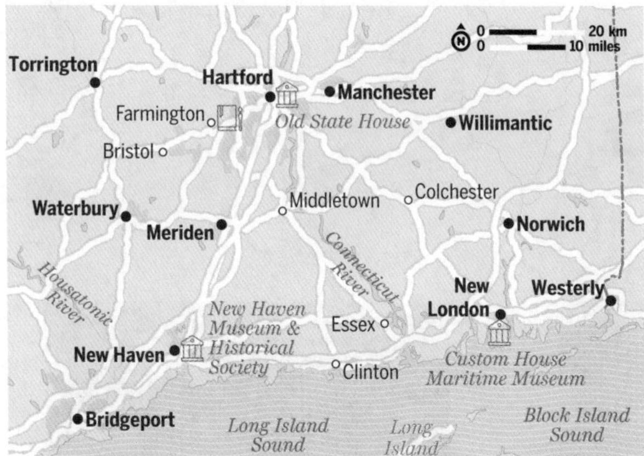

It was a complicated case with rival international stakeholders, diplomatic deception, and issues of states' rights versus federal intervention. Although abolitionists throughout America banded together to raise awareness and funds for the captives' defense and repatriation, Connecticut citizens were on the front lines. There are numerous sites in the state that interpret and memorialize the events of the *Amistad*. Here are some major ones.

The best-known *Amistad*-related holding of the **New Haven Museum & Historical Society** is a portrait of the Mende revolt leader Sengbe Pieh, aka Joseph Cinque. There's an Amistad Memorial on the former site of the jail where the captives were held, and a replica of the schooner is a traveling classroom whose home port is Long Wharf.

The *Amistad* was moored in New London and its cargo auctioned here. An exhibition at the **Custom House Maritime Museum** tells the pivotal role the city played.

One of the captives' trials took place in the **Old State House** in Hartford (p155), which has exhibits relating to the *Amistad* and a wonderful museum of Connecticut history.

When the Mende were freed, the town of **Farmington** hosted and educated them until funds were raised for their passage back to Sierra Leone.

Top left New Haven Museum & Historical Society. **Bottom left** Old State House.

Delving Deeper

Did you know there were four children among the *Amistad* captives kidnapped from Africa in 1839 to be sold into the slave trade? One captive, Margu, later returned to the US to become the first African to graduate from an American college. *The Amistad Story: Cinque Lives Here* exhibit at the New Haven Museum features significant materials from the *Amistad* incident, including the famous portrait of Sengbe Pieh (Joseph Cinque), the leader of the revolt; a painting of the schooner *La Amistad*, and a letter from John Quincy Adams, who argued successfully on behalf of the Africans before the US Supreme Court.

■ **Insights from Khalil Quotop,** *director of education at the New Haven Museum @newhavenmuseum*

PHOTO CREDIT: DEFINING STUDIOS©

Connecticut **FIRSTS**

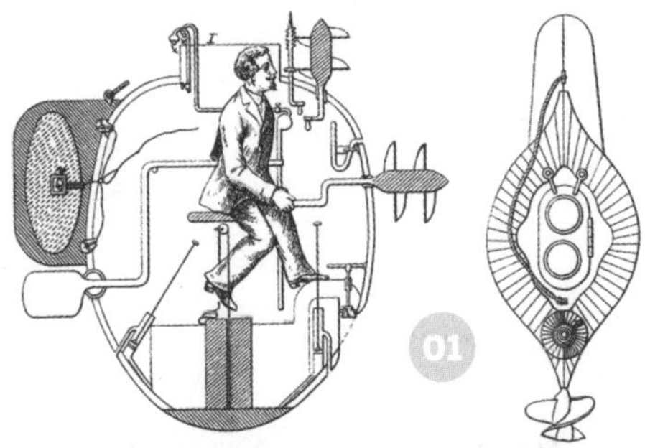

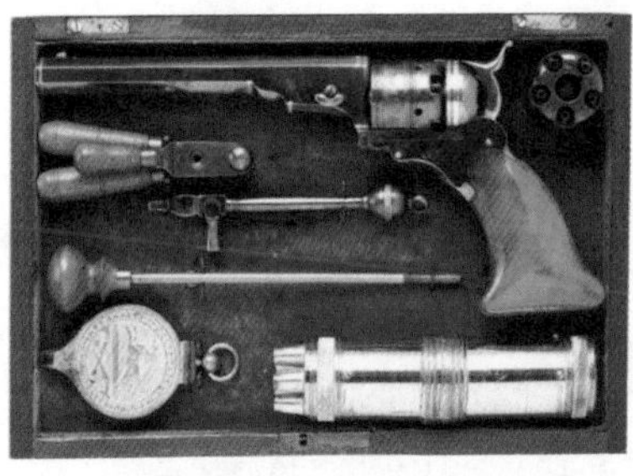

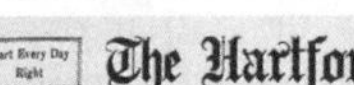

The Hartford Courant

139 Die, More Than 225 Hurt In Circus Fire
Five Arrested On Manslaughter Charges
U.S. Troops Menace Heights Above La Haye

Panic And Blaze Trap Hundreds

05

01 Submarine

You can find replicas of David Bushnell's human-powered 1776 submarine in Essex and Groton.

02 Helicopter

Igor Sikorsky designed and flew the world's first practical helicopter in Stratford in 1939.

03 Revolver

Hartford native Samuel Colt patented the revolver in 1836 and manufactured weapons in his hometown for decades.

04 Dictionary

In 1806, Noah Webster published the first American dictionary; you can visit his house in West Hartford.

05 Newspaper

The *Hartford Courant* has been continuously published since October 29, 1764.

06 Frisbee

When Yale students in the 1920s discovered that empty pie tins from Bridgeport's Frisbie Pie Company caught air, a craze was born.

07 Wiffle ball

David Mullany crafted the first Wiffle ball for his son in 1953; since then the Shelton company has produced millions of them.

08 Art museum

The Wadsworth Atheneum, the US' first public art museum, was founded in Hartford in 1842.

09 Cotton gin

Yale grad Eli Whitney invented the cotton gin in 1794 and created the first modern factory in Hamden; you can visit the site today.

10 Sewing machine

Elias Howe patented a sewing machine in 1846 and manufactured them in a Bridgeport factory.

28 The Sport OF KINGS

POLO | SPORTS | OUTDOORS

One of the wealthiest communities in the United States, Greenwich has attracted celebrities and scions of industry over the centuries. All the indicators of wealth are here including private schools, private country clubs and private yacht clubs, but entry to a sport played by royalty and attended by the elite can be had for as little as $40 per car.

ANASTASIA MILLS HEALY/LONELY PLANET ©

How to

Getting here Greenwich is the first town over the New York border. The best route to Conyers Farm is the North St exit of the Merritt Pkwy (Rte 15). Get a taxi or rideshare from the Metro-North train station.

When to go High-goal polo is played on Sunday afternoons in June, July and September. If it's been raining, be prepared for a cancellation due to the muddy field.

Sun cover If you're sensitive to the sun, study the map before buying tickets to find seats in the shade or bring a hat and sunscreen.

Conyers Farm With a spectacular backcountry setting, the **Greenwich Polo Club** is in Conyers Farm – a 1500-acre development where 1% reside in estates valued in the double-digit millions. The club and its team White Birch were founded by the paper tycoon Peter Brant, one of the world's top art collectors.

Polo basics Two teams of four players try to hit a ball into the opposing team's goal. It's a rousing and exhausting game with highly trained horses galloping across a 300yd field; for perspective, a football field is

Above Greenwich Polo Club. **Top right** Polo match, Greenwich Polo Club. **Bottom right** Spectators, Greenwich Polo Club.

Museum Gem

In a beautiful converted barn on the polo grounds, the **Brant Foundation Art Study Center** is a small, free, by-appointment-only contemporary art museum that sometimes hosts open-house events on match days.

100yd. The match is divided into periods called chukkers and at the halfway mark, spectators are invited to walk on the field and stomp the divots (loose pieces of turf that has been torn up by the horses' hooves). This is an ideal opportunity to check out everyone's fashion.

Making the most of the day Gates open at 1pm; matches start at 3pm and last close to two hours. Food and drinks are available but many spectators bring picnics; binoculars are also useful. Children and leashed dogs are welcome and although there is no dress code, people often dress up. If you opt for East Lawn seating, it's a long walk from the parking area across the field. This means you should pack lightly and be aware that crossing to the West Lawn, where the bathrooms and refreshments are, is restricted during play.

29 American Literary ROYALTY

LITERATURE | MUSEUMS | CULTURE

Many people have heard of Mark Twain and Harriet Beecher Stowe, but most don't know that they lived right next door to each other in Hartford and that both National Historic Landmark homes offer tours. The two writers and their homes are very different; tours shed light on the authors, their work and their times.

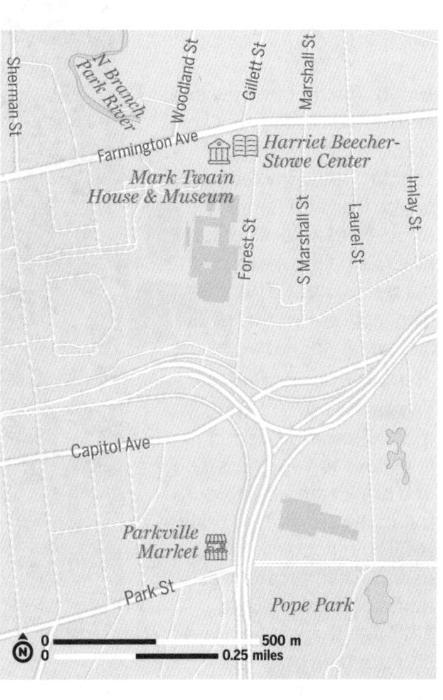

How to

Getting here The homes are next to each other off I-84; each has a parking lot. There are many trains and buses in the capital, or cabs and rideshares.

When to go The Twain House is closed on Tuesdays January to March; the Stowe Center is open Thursday to Saturday. Book a tour for both houses in advance.

Themed tours Go behind the scenes of Twain's house with his butler or take a family tour about slavery and social justice at the Stowe Center. For the context, visit the museum at the Twain House before the tour.

Mark Twain House & Museum In keeping with his larger-than-life persona, Samuel Clemens aka Mark Twain (1835–1910) built a 25-room High Victorian Gothic home and employed a Tiffany & Co–affiliated design firm to decorate it with motifs influenced by exotic travels. One of America's most celebrated authors, Twain lived here with his family from 1874 to 1891. He wrote *The Adventures of Tom Sawyer*, *The Prince and the Pauper*, and *The Adventures of Huckleberry Finn* in his 3rd-floor office, which doubled as a billiard room. Leave time to see objects like Twain's

Top right Harriet Beecher Stowe Center. **Bottom right** Mark Twain's office and billiard room.

TRAVELVIEW/SHUTTERSTOCK ©

HEMIS/ALAMY STOCK PHOTO ©

Lunch Idea

One of my favorite spots in Hartford is the new **Parkville Market**, the state's first food hall. With 22 vendors boasting global flavors, this visually stunning destination truly offers something for everyone.

Recommended by Stephanie Webster, *editor in chief of* CTbites *@ctbites*

glasses and failed printing invention in the museum, which runs a 23-minute Twain documentary on a loop.

Harriet Beecher Stowe Center Although separated in age by a generation, Twain and Harriet Beecher Stowe (1811–96) ran in the same circles and socialized. They were neighbors for almost two decades; hers was the more demure of the two homes. It's hard to overestimate the popularity of *Uncle Tom's Cabin*, Stowe's anti-slavery novel published in 1852 before she moved to Hartford. In her lifetime, the only book to outsell it was the Bible. Stowe Center visitors learn about the author and her books in the context of slavery, racism and sexism past and present. Inspiring takeaways are that words matter and that one person can make a difference.

30 Watch Out for DINOSAURS

HISTORY | KIDS | PARK

Connecticut was one of the earliest US colonies and indigenous people lived here way before then, so historical sites are expected. What's not as anticipated are remnants of a history before humans. In 1966, a construction crew uncovered 2600 dinosaur footprints on a Rocky Hill site that's now a state park. In Montville, 50 life-sized dinosaurs tower over trails at a family attraction.

GEORGE OSTERTAG/ALAMY STOCK PHOTO ©

How to

Getting here/around Dinosaur State Park is 10 miles south of Hartford, a few minutes off I-91. Nature's Art Village is 41 miles south of the park, and not far from I-95 and New London on Rte 85.

When to go Dinosaur State Park is open year-round but some activities are only offered May to October. Dinosaur Place is open April to October but it's part of a year-round complex called Nature's Art Village.

Special events Check their websites for special events like an Easter egg hunt (Dinosaur Place) and animal presentations (Dinosaur State Park).

ANASTASIA MILLS HEALY/LONELY PLANET ©

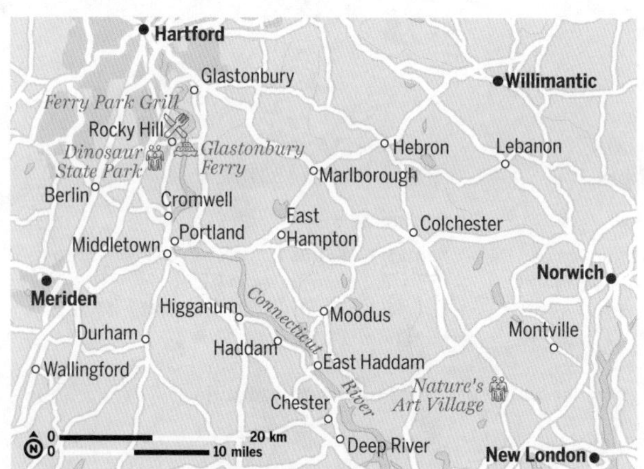

Top left Dinosaur footprint, Dinosaur State Park. **Bottom left** Dinosaur Place.

About 200 million years ago, Rocky Hill was a dinosaur hotspot. Under **Dinosaur State Park's** geodesic dome at one of the world's largest dinosaur trackways, look down into the mudflats to see real dinosaur footprints and models of Dilophosaurus and Anchisaurus; and gaze up for Dimorphodon, a carnivorous flying reptile with a 4ft wingspan. Interactive exhibits teach and test dino knowledge, small live animals such as frogs and ferrets are displayed, and there's also geocaching, track casting, and gem and fossil mining available. Two miles of trails wind through the grounds, and an arboretum includes specimens of the cedar of Lebanon and giant sequoia.

Heaven for a dinosaur-loving kid, **Dinosaur Place** is literally a dinosaur playground. Kids can climb up a Pachyrhinosaurus, a T-Rex Tower or a huge web, play miniature golf, navigate a maze, and cool off at the splash pad (they'll need a bathing suit and water shoes). Along 1.5 miles of wide, flat, wooded trails, 50 life-sized dinosaurs are ready to mug with you on Instagram. The 60-acre site also has indoor activities, a lunch spot and a volcano that erupts on cue. Attractions introduced in 2022 include a miniature train ride, a pedal-car track and a pedal-kart experience for kids aged two to five.

Historic Lunch

If you're in Rocky Hill on a summer day with good weather, a cool spot for lunch is **Ferry Park Grill**. For a seasonal casual restaurant where you eat at picnic tables, the menu is surprisingly extensive. Beyond the requisite burgers and lobster rolls, this restaurant on the Connecticut River – next to the landing of America's oldest continuously operating **ferry** – serves great barbecue and a salad with seared ahi tuna. If you're there from April to November, have $2 and want to be part of history, spend five minutes crossing the river to Glastonbury on a route that's been carrying passengers since 1655.

Listings

BEST OF THE REST

Antiques & Collectibles

Wayne Mattox Antiques

Woodbury has been called the antiques capital of Connecticut; its best-known purveyor is Wayne Mattox, as seen on *American Pickers*.

Antiques Marketplace

Putnam is another hotbed for antiques and collectibles. The largest shop here has four floors packed with seemingly every item imaginable from every period.

Scranton's Shops

In quiet South Woodstock, 85 dealers sell antiques, collectibles, art and crafts in a former blacksmith shop.

Stratford Antique Center

Look for the 16,500-sq-ft blue building and exit I-95 to browse everything from vintage clothing to lighting fixtures and country furniture from 200 dealers.

Hiking Trails

Bull's Bridge River Walk

Passing one of Connecticut's famous covered bridges and meeting with the Appalachian Trail, this Kent river walk includes waterfalls, a small gorge and an old power station.

Farmington River Trail

This 18-mile loop trail mostly follows the Farmington River and connects to the Farmington Canal Heritage Trail, a 56-mile rail trail and a canal towpath through 11 towns.

White Memorial Conservation Center

Encompassing 4000 acres in Litchfield, this is the largest wildlife refuge and nature center in Connecticut. Orient yourself at the museum and choose from 35 miles of trails.

Talcott Mountain State Park

Many a hiker has completed the ascent to the 165ft Heublein Tower in Bloomfield. This moderate 1.5-mile stretch is part of the 40-mile Metacomet Trail.

Feast on Seafood

Shell & Bones Oyster Bar & Grill $$$

This romantic spot on the New Haven waterfront has a raw bar and uses only sustainable ingredients. There's both an outdoor deck and indoor fireplace.

Lenny & Joe's Fish Tale $$

Crowds have been flocking to Lenny & Joe's since 1979 for generous portions of fried clams and lobster dinners. There are two locations of this casual eatery, in Westbrook and Madison.

Max Fish $$$

An ahi poke bowl and buffalo shrimp are two out-of-the-ordinary selections at this Glastonbury crowd pleaser. Diners can also

Farmington River Trail

order a 'best of both worlds' (both hot and cold) lobster roll.

Captain's Cove $$

Tucked away in a marina in Bridgeport, this casual seasonal indoor-outdoor restaurant and bar can get lively. Browsing the colorful little boardwalk boutiques is part of the fun.

Museums & Galleries

Mashantucket Pequot Museum & Research Center

Walking through a re-created Pequot village is a highlight of this enormous museum on the Foxwoods Resort Casino property.

Old State House

You can tour the beautifully re-created rooms of the 1796 former state capitol in Hartford, designed by Charles Bulfinch, and learn about the important events that took place not only in this building but in the whole state.

Yale University Art Gallery

Come here for van Goghs and Hoppers plus a stunning portrait of George Washington and a Paul Revere teapot. Don't miss the sculpture garden and rooftop terrace.

Yale Center for British Art

Major artists represented in the largest collection of British art outside Britain include Turner, Constable and Gainsborough. Both Yale museums are free and in remarkable buildings designed by Louis Kahn.

Only in Connecticut

Old New-Gate Prison

Descend into a cold, damp former copper mine in East Granby to learn the surprising story of America's first state prison.

Gillette Castle

On a visit to the East Haddam castle home of an eccentric actor, visitors learn about William Gillette's personal railroad, feline fixation and Sherlock Holmes connection.

MICHAEL KING/GETTY IMAGES ©

Gillette Castle

Witch's Dungeon Classic Movie Museum

Fans of classic monster movies won't want to miss the costumes, props and memorabilia from movies like *Dracula* at this small Plainville museum.

Essex Steam Train & Riverboat

Step back in time and take a scenic ride in the Connecticut River Valley aboard a steam train, which can be combined with a riverboat ride.

Casinos & Amusement Parks

Lake Compounce

At the oldest continuously operating amusement park in the US (opened in Bristol in 1846), the fun includes a wooden roller-coaster and a water park.

Foxwoods Resort Casino

Quite the complex, the 2000-acre Foxwoods in Mashantucket has four hotels, restaurants, an outlet mall, spa, golf course, museum, zipline and theaters that attract headline entertainment.

Scan to find more things to do in Connecticut online

VERMONT

SCENERY | MAPLE SYRUP | SLOPES

Experience Vermont online

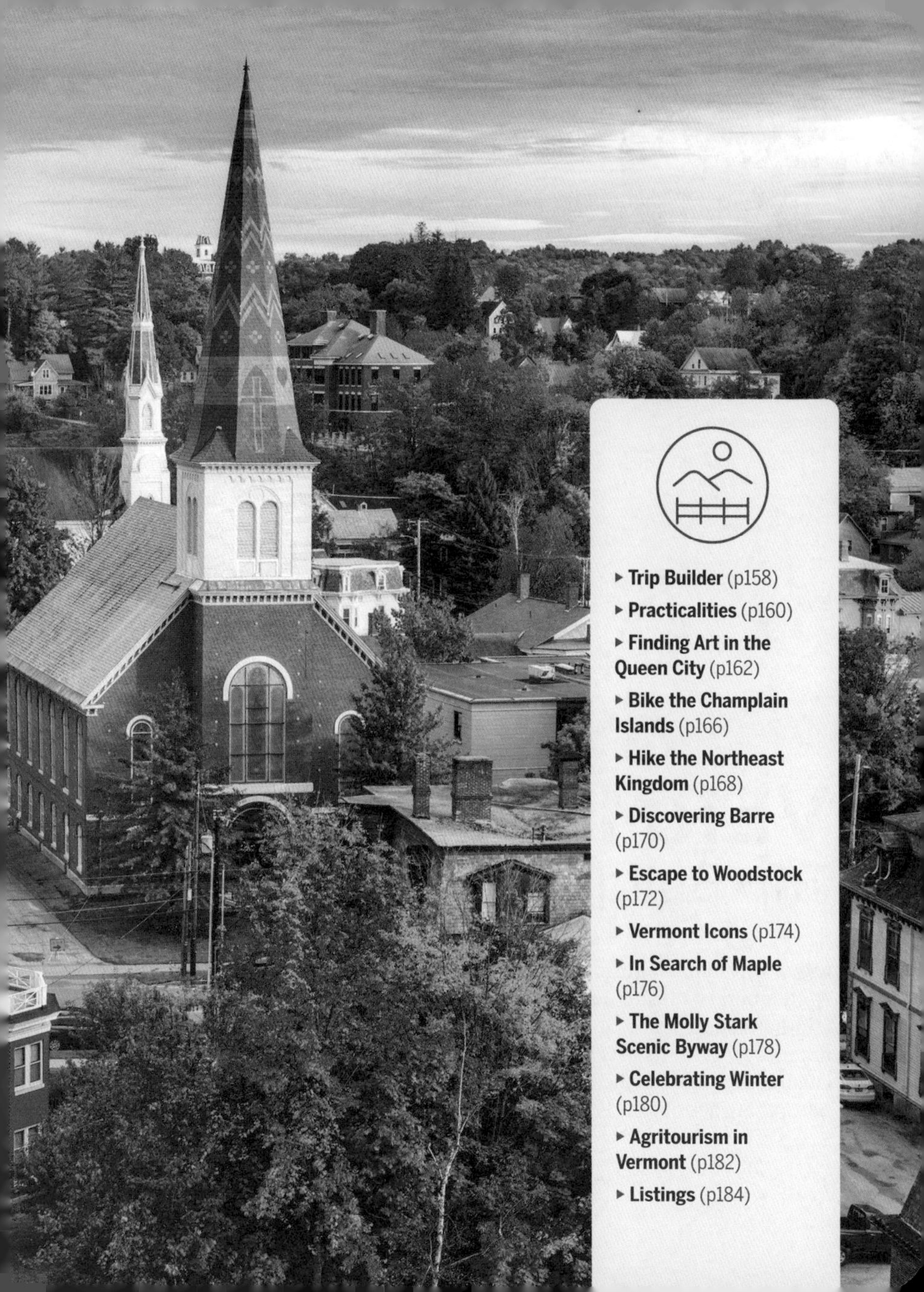

Travel back 480 million years at **Goodsell Ridge Fossil Preserve** (p167)
1hr from Burlington

Bike along **Burlington's waterfront** for lake views and public art (p162)
5mins from downtown Burlington

Explore local marine history at the **Lake Champlain Maritime Museum** (p184)
30mins from Middlebury

Say hello to the Jersey cows at **Billings Farm and Museum** (p173)
5mins from Woodstock

VERMONT
Trip Builder

Vermont is a fusion of classic New England and contemporary hipster culture with an independent, laid-back spirit and a disproportionate number of microbreweries. Its arts, history and farm-to-table cuisine compete for the visitor's attention with its natural attractions and outdoor activities.

Climb **Mount Olga** for jaw-dropping vistas of three states (p179)
30mins from Bennington

Savor a maple craft beer at a brewery on **Hogback Mountain** (p176)
25mins from Brattleboro
Take a dip in **Lake Willoughby** after an afternoon hike (p168)
30mins from Newport
Admire the artistry of the carved headstones at **Hope Cemetery** (p171)
25mins from downtown Barre
Hone your skating skills gliding on frozen **Lake Morey** (p180)
30mins from White River Junction
Meet the avian ambassadors of the **Vermont Institute of Natural Science** (p185)
15mins from White River Junction
0 50 km
0 25 miles
Lake Memphremagog
Newport
Colebrook
Island Pond
St Albans
Barton
Jeffersonville
Mt Mansfield
Morrisville
Groveton
Lyndonville
Lancaster
Berlin
MAINE
Stowe
St Johnsbury
Connecticut River
Green Mountains
VERMONT
Littleton
Waterbury
Montpelier
Barre
Waitsfield
Woodsville
Bridgton
Middlebury
Bradford
Randolph
Green Mountain National Forest
Brandon
White River Junction
Hanover
Killington
Lebanon
Rutland
Woodstock
Windsor
Franklin
Ludlow
Claremont
Newport
Merrimack River
Rochester
NEW HAMPSHIRE
Concord
Mt Equinox
Manchester
Bellows Falls
Hillsborough
Portsmouth
Arlington
Shaftsbury
Wilmington
Keene
Atlantic Ocean
Bennington
Brattleboro
North Adams
Greenfield
MASSACHUSETTS

Practicalities

EQROY/SHUTTERSTOCK ©

ARRIVING

Airport Buses and taxis go to and from Burlington International Airport (pictured), 3.5 miles from downtown. Manchester-Boston Regional Airport is more convenient for southern Vermont.

Train Amtrak's Vermonter, which offers carry-on bike service, runs from Washington, DC to St Albans with several Vermont stops. The *Ethan Allen Express* connects New York City with Rutland, where you can get a bus ($1 to $2) to Killington Ski Resort. All trains accept ski equipment as baggage.

HOW MUCH FOR A

half-gallon of maple syrup from $35

scenic lake cruise $32

half-day bike rental $25

WHEN TO GO

JAN–MAR
Perfect for outdoor winter sports; expect chilly temperatures and snow.

APR–JUN
Less crowded but often rainy. Spring wildflowers are in bloom.

JUL–SEP
Best weather for outdoor activities.

OCT–DEC
Great time to hike; weather can be changeable. Most seasonal attractions closed.

GETTING AROUND

Car Driving offers the most flexibility, allowing you to travel at your own pace. Rental cars are available in most major cities and towns as well as at the airport, which has the most agencies but not necessarily the cheapest rates.

Bus Greyhound, with hubs in Burlington and White River Junction, serves a limited number of communities, but several Vermont bus lines *(vpta.net)* connect towns within a region.

Bicycle Miles of rail trails, community bike paths and back roads make it easy to travel between towns or explore an area by bike. Mountain bikers have numerous options for off-road adventures.

EATING & DRINKING

Farm-to-table is more than a trend here. It's the standard at many restaurants where fresh, locally sourced foods such as grass-fed lamb or beef, aged cheeses and garden vegetables are served along with apple pie and maple desserts. Quebec's proximity influences offerings in the northern counties where *tourtière* (a French Canadian meat pie; pictured top right) and poutine (pictured bottom right) are menu staples. With more craft breweries per capita in Vermont than in any other state, the question may be less about where to stop but rather what to sample first.

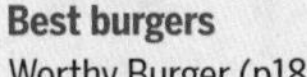

Best burgers
Worthy Burger (p184)

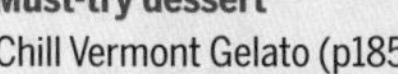

Must-try dessert
Chill Vermont Gelato (p185)

CONNECT & FIND YOUR WAY

Wi-fi Although widely available, don't expect internet connections to be fast in all locations, especially in rural areas with spotty cell service. Local libraries and coffee shops often have free public wi-fi, as do the state welcome centers on the interstates and other entry points.

Navigation While navigation by GPS works well in populated areas, for rural areas verify directions before heading out.

WHERE TO STAY

Accommodations are available to fit every budget, but lodging can be difficult to find during fall foliage season or near ski areas in winter, so advance reservations are a must.

Town	Pro/Con
Burlington	Abundance of options within walking distance of shops, restaurants and lake excursions; book early on college graduation and fall foliage weekends.
Montpelier	Centrally located, with a surprisingly diverse culinary scene; limited daytime downtown parking when the Vermont Legislature is in session.
St Johnsbury	Good base for hiking, but fewer attractions and harder to reach except by car.
Manchester	Ideal for a romantic getaway at a historic inn or pampered weekend at a luxury resort, but can be pricey. Nice mix of boutique shops, art galleries and fine dining.

MONEY

Although credit cards are accepted nearly everywhere, roadside stands, farmers markets and small businesses in some rural areas may be cash-only.

FALL FOLIAGE

From mid-September through October, the Vermont Department of Tourism and Marketing *(vermont vacation.com)* releases a weekly foliage report to direct visitors to areas with the best fall colors.

31 Finding Art in the QUEEN CITY

STREET ART | GALLERIES | MURALS

Burlington's art scene is as eclectic and surprising as the city itself. Its contemporary art galleries and university art museums not only educate but broaden perceptions. Abstract art shares street space with whimsical sculptures, and colorful murals pop up in unexpected places.

WANGKUN JIA/ALAMY STOCK PHOTO ©

How to

Getting here/around Burlington is 3½ hours from Boston or five hours by car from NYC. Burlington International Airport is 3.5 miles from downtown. Amtrak stops in Essex Junction, 7 miles north of the city. The compact downtown makes a car unnecessary; local buses and taxis are available.

When to go May to September, when streets come alive with festivals, outdoor concerts and alfresco cafes.

Don't miss In summer pushcart vendors sell handcrafted jewelry and one-of-a-kind crafts on the Church Street Marketplace.

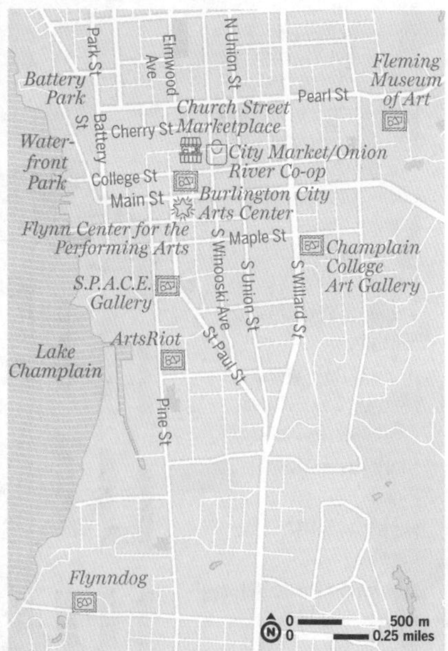

Artists & Makers

The heart and soul of the city's arts scene is the **South End Arts District**, a revitalized industrial neighborhood within walking distance of downtown and Lake Champlain. Abandoned warehouses have been transformed into exhibition sites and workspaces for artists of mixed disciplines. Meet them at the annual **South End Art Hop** in September, a three-day celebration of the arts organized by the South End Arts and Business Association.

Art Crawl

Visit the **Soda Plant**, once a Venetian gingerale bottling plant and now creative space for more than 30 artists and makers. Peruse the paintings at **Soapbox Arts**. Attend a talk or artist reception at the **S.P.A.C.E. Gallery** or

Top left Church St Marketplace. **Bottom left** Frog Hollow Craft Center (p164).

shop for jewelry, prints and other artwork. Grab a cappuccino at **Brio Coffeeworks** or smoothie at **Tomgirl Kitchen** before continuing along Pine St, the district's central artery. **Flynndog**, a community arts space with rotating exhibits, is here; so is **ArtsRiot**, a gallery, performance venue and cafe, the perfect spot for a night out. Or explore a different kind of art in the neighborhood – boutique chocolate making at **Lake Champlain Chocolates**, which offers free tours and samples.

Art Central

Downtown Burlington revolves around the **Church Street Marketplace**, a pedestrian thoroughfare with farm-to-fork restaurants, cozy coffeehouses, public art and shops like **Frog Hollow Craft Center**, a co-op selling products by Vermont artisans. Pop into the **Burlington City Arts Center** for thought-provoking contemporary art housed in an 1889 firehouse. The city's vibrant arts culture is also evident at Main St's **Flynn Center for the**

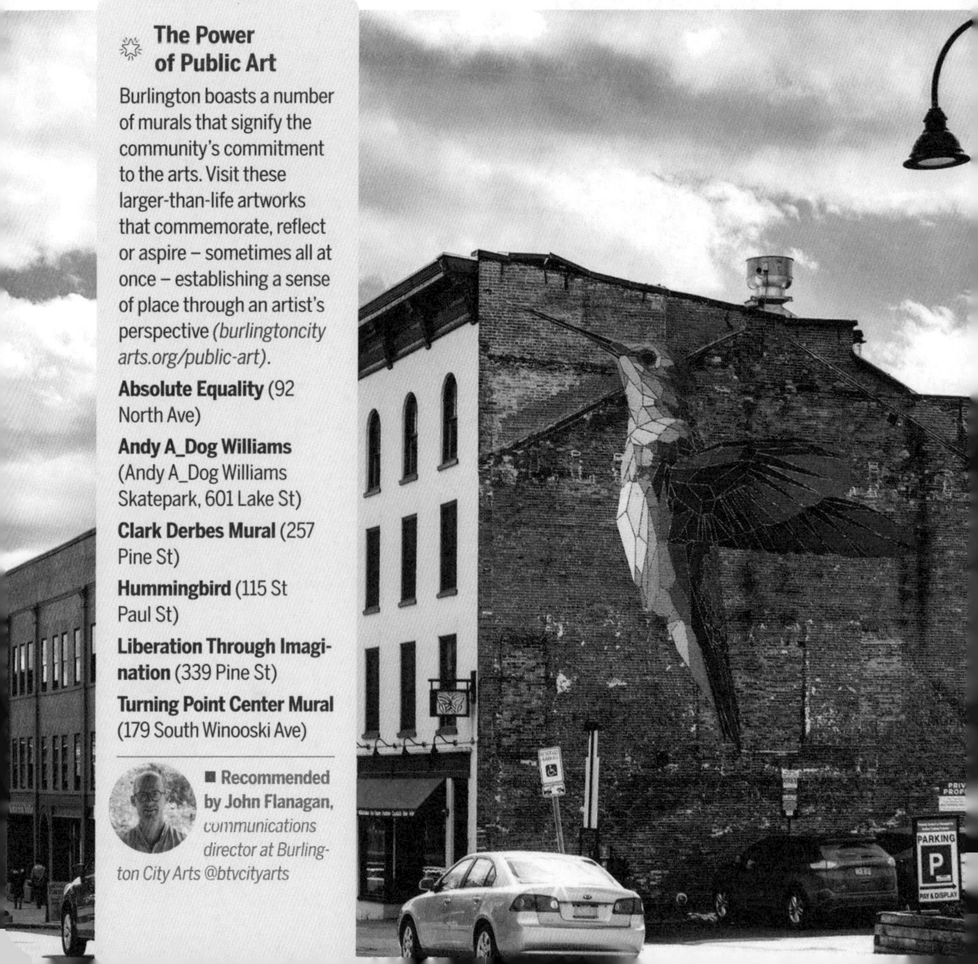

The Power of Public Art

Burlington boasts a number of murals that signify the community's commitment to the arts. Visit these larger-than-life artworks that commemorate, reflect or aspire – sometimes all at once – establishing a sense of place through an artist's perspective *(burlingtoncityarts.org/public-art)*.

Absolute Equality (92 North Ave)

Andy A_Dog Williams (Andy A_Dog Williams Skatepark, 601 Lake St)

Clark Derbes Mural (257 Pine St)

Hummingbird (115 St Paul St)

Liberation Through Imagination (339 Pine St)

Turning Point Center Mural (179 South Winooski Ave)

■ **Recommended by John Flanagan,** *communications director at Burlington City Arts @btvcityarts*

Unexpected Art

Enjoy more local art while you shop at **City Market Onion River Co-op** for Vermont cheese and wine for a lakeside picnic. Its two Burlington stores feature rotating exhibits of co-op members' art, while the newer South End location has farm-inspired abstract murals on two exterior walls.

DAN LEWIS/ SHUTTERSTOCK ©

Performing Arts, just off the marketplace. After dinner, catch a show at this art-deco theater that opened in 1930 as a vaudeville and movie venue.

On the Waterfront

Look up as you approach **Union Station** at the foot of Main St, where winged monkeys guard the clock tower. Hop on the Burlington Bike Path behind the station, heading south along the Lake Champlain waterfront to **Roundhouse Park** to view nine marble sculptures known as the **Water Treatment Plant Sculpture Collection**. Both **Waterfront Park** and **Battery Park**, north of the station, host public art that complements the lakefront setting, including *Equinox* and the aptly named *Amphibians*.

Campus Art

Head to the University of Vermont campus for a visit to the **Fleming Museum of Art**, where permanent galleries display Asian, Native American, American and European artifacts. The museum's collections number over 20,000 items, with several new exhibitions every year. Take a walk around campus to view more than a dozen larger pieces of public art, featuring contemporary, abstract and pop-art-inspired works. **Champlain College Art Gallery** in the city's hill section takes an edgier approach to art, featuring experimental art by faculty, students and outside artists.

FAR LEFT: DANIELLE MACINNES/PIQSELS © MURAL BY MARY LACY, WWW.MARYLACYART.COM
LEFT: RANDY DUCHAINE/ALAMY STOCK PHOTO ©

Left *Hummingbird* by Mary Lacy.
Top Lake Champlain from Waterfront Park. **Right** Union Station.

32 Bike the Champlain ISLANDS

CYCLING | NATURE | WINERIES

The Champlain Islands, a lake archipelago connected by bridges and causeways, is a cyclist's paradise. The terrain is mostly flat, and the absence of heavy traffic allows for a leisurely ride to soak up the seemingly nonstop water views and ambience of five laid-back communities. The natural attractions, including Vermont's only sand dunes and the world's oldest coral reef, are unparalleled.

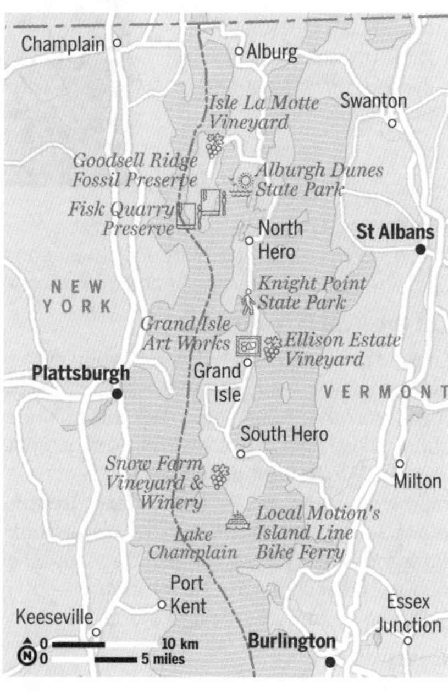

How to

Getting here The islands are a 25-minute drive from Burlington via I-89. In warmer months, cycle from Burlington to South Hero on the Island Rail Trail, crossing Lake Champlain on the Colchester Causeway and Local Motion's Island Line bike ferry.

When to go May through October, but pack rain gear in case of inclement weather.

Change of pace Rent a kayak at Hero's Welcome to explore the islands from the water.

Wind down Visit one of the wineries open to the public to sample wines from locally grown grapes. **Ellison Estate Vineyard** and **Isle La Motte Vineyard** are the islands' newest, while **Snow Farm Vineyard and Winery** has offered tastings and its popular Thursday-night summer concert series for decades.

One-stop shop On the shores of City Bay, **Hero's Welcome** is an island institution, stocking everything you didn't know you need from one-of-a-kind kitchen items and sundries to books and Vermont products. Order one of their signature sandwiches to eat at the dockside picnic area across the street.

Top right Biking trail, Lake Champlain. **Bottom right** Alburgh Dunes State Park.

JERRY HORBERT/SHUTTERSTOCK ©

Tiny Castles

You just might believe in fairies after biking South Hero's back roads. In the early 20th century, Harry Barber made several miniature castles with Vermont fieldstone, many with turrets, drawbridges, moats and even electricity. To view some, circle from US 2 down South St to West Shore Dr, heading north to Station Rd and back to US 2. This route also takes you past two pick-your-own apple orchards and a forest with hundreds of colorful birdhouses.

Made in Vermont A gallery-cafe in a 1790s farmhouse, **Grand Isle Art Works** features the works of over 70 local and regional artisans. Or check out **GreenTARA Space**, North Hero's newest gallery with a coffee bar in a refurbished 19th-century church.

Cool off Picnic or swim at one of the islands' five state parks. The walking trail in **Knight Point State Park** offers stunning lake vistas, while **Alburgh Dunes State Park** is worth a stop for its natural sand dunes, black-spruce bog and one of the longest sand beaches on Lake Champlain.

Geologic treasure Search for cephalopods, gastropods and other marine fossils in Isle La Motte at **Fisk Quarry Preserve** or **Goodsell Ridge Fossil Preserve**, the world's oldest fossilized coral reef.

JOE FERRER/SHUTTERSTOCK ©

33 Hike the Northeast KINGDOM

HIKING | BIRD-WATCHING | WILDLIFE

You're spoiled for choice for hikes in the Northeast Kingdom, Vermont's remotest region. Follow moose-maintained trails through boreal forests, or stroll along the shore of a glacial lake. Revel in the panoramic vistas from a rocky mountaintop, or bask in the quiet solitude of the North Woods as you go in search of wildlife. Can't decide? Sample them all.

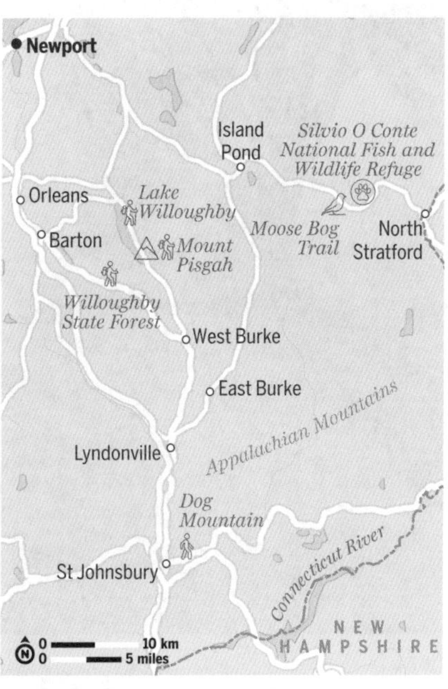

How to

Getting here/around Two interstates, I-91 and I-93, connect Boston and other major cities to the region. No trains and limited buses means you'll need a car to get around.

When to go Avoid spring when trails may be muddy or closed. Summer is ideal hiking weather, but the fall colors can be amazing. If hiking in winter, bring snowshoes and poles.

Plan ahead Cell service is spotty, and in many areas unavailable, so be prepared for emergencies when hiking the more remote trails *(trailfinder.info)*.

Panoramic vistas Multiple routes to the summit of **Mount Pisgah** reward hikers with unsurpassed views of the 6-mile long Lake Willoughby. The shortest, and most gradual route, is the 1.7-mile **South Trail**, which also offers great water views from **Pulpit Rock**, about a mile up the trail.

Lakeside stroll Appreciate the beauty of **Lake Willoughby**, a deep crystalline glacial lake, with an easy trek in **Willoughby State Forest** along the **South Beach Trail** that follows the shoreline before connecting with the **South Shore Trail** for a 2.1-mile loop.

Top right Spruce grouse.
Bottom right Hiking, Mt Pisgah.

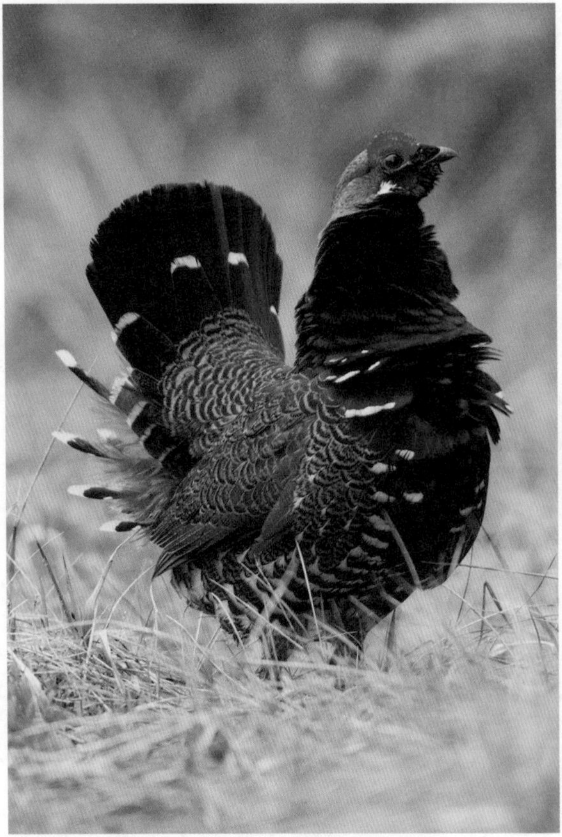

DOUBLE BROW IMAGERY/SHUTTERSTOCK ©

EDITH ROSS/SHUTTERSTOCK ©

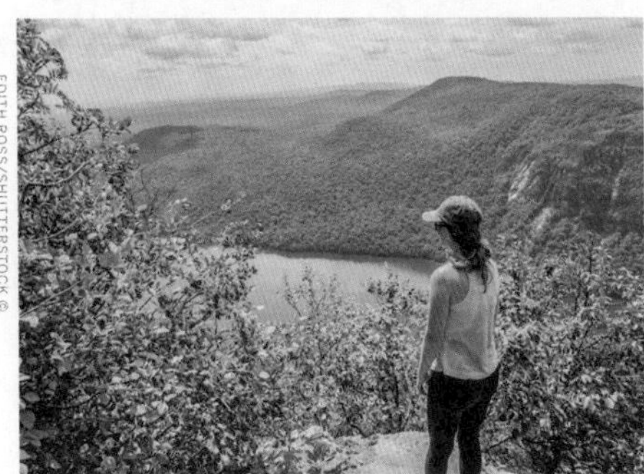

Unleashed

Walkers and dogs (no leashes required) are welcome at **Dog Mountain**, a 150-acre property in St Johnsbury with trails, ponds, a gallery of dog-related art and a chapel where visitors pay tribute to their departed pets.

Birders' paradise For an easy nature ramble, the **Moose Bog Trail** – with its wheelchair-accessible boardwalk – delivers. The 1-mile trail through boreal spruce-fir forest is popular with birders for sightings of the endangered spruce grouse and boreal chickadees. Curious Canada jays (or gray jays) often greet visitors who bring peanuts. The trail leads to a black-spruce woodland bog where you can find pitcher plants, Labrador tea, sundew and other classic bog plants.

Moose country Your best chance of spotting a moose may be in the Nulhegan Basin Division of the **Silvio O Conte National Fish and Wildlife Refuge**. A number of gravel roads crisscross the preserve, providing access to trails, wetland bogs and overlooks. Hike the **North Branch Trail**, a 4-mile loop along a river. If short on time, the **Nulhegan River Trail**, a 1-mile interpretive loop, can be accessed from the visitor contact station on VT 105.

34 Discovering BARRE

ARCHITECTURE | SCULPTURE | MEMORIAL ART

Barre (pronounced 'berry') lives up to its moniker, the 'Granite Center of the World'. Its Italianate-to-neoclassical stone architecture, impressive granite statues and creatively sculpted headstones in a bucolic hilltop cemetery are a testament to the artistry and craftsmanship of the legions of immigrant stonecutters who called this central Vermont city home in the 19th and early 20th centuries.

CHRISTIAN OUELLET/SHUTTERSTOCK ©

How to

Getting here/around Local buses connect the Amtrak station in Montpelier with Barre, a 20-minute ride. Downtown Barre is walkable, but you'll need a car to visit areas on the outskirts.

When to go Any season but dress for the weather, including layering in winter when snow is common and temperatures often dip below zero.

Public art If visiting in fall, stop by Studio Place Arts for the visual arts center's Rock Solid, an annual two-month showcase of stone sculptures by local artists.

DAVID LYONS/ALAMY STOCK PHOTO ©

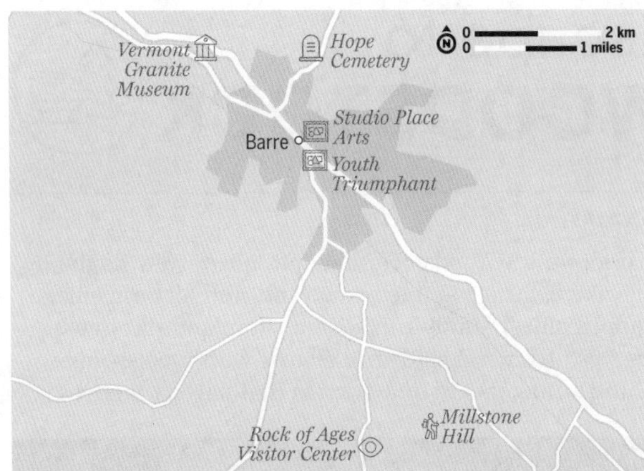

Carved in stone Wandering Barre's downtown historic district in search of streetscape sculptures is akin to a treasure hunt. The rewards are rich as you gaze upon **Youth Triumphant** with its curved whispering wall, or the more modern and whimsical 74ft-long **zipper**, centerpiece of a pocket green space, or the ghoulish **gargoyles** bookending a serpentine bike rack on Main St.

Art of stonecutting A 23ft-high statue of a sculptor holding a chisel and hammer pays homage to master stonecutter Carlo Abate, who founded a school in 1900 to teach design and sculpting to granite industry workers. The **Stone Arts School** continues that tradition, sharing space in a massive abandoned granite shed with the **Vermont Granite Museum**.

Outdoor museum of art Among the 10,500 elaborately carved headstones and crypts at **Hope Cemetery** are an overstuffed armchair, a race car etched with the number 61, and a loving older couple holding hands in bed for all eternity. The cemetery's 65 acres are the final resting place for many stoneworkers, most of whom carved their own memorials – a lasting tribute to these talented artisans.

Rock on Watch as steel derricks slowly hoist up gargantuan blocks of gray granite on a guided tour of the world's largest operating deep-hole granite quarry. The 40-minute tour leaves from the **Rock of Ages Visitor Center**, where you can learn about Vermont's granite industry before testing your prowess on an outdoor granite bowling lane.

Top left Rock of Ages. **Bottom left** Headstone, Hope Cemetery.

Exploring Forgotten Quarries

A vast network of multiuse trails wind through hardwood and coniferous forests, past quarry ponds, grout piles and rusting mining equipment on abandoned quarry lands at **Millstone Hill** (*millstonetrails.com*). Adventurous mountain bikers should seek out **Gnome Man's Land**, while the **Barre Town Forest** and **Canyonlands** trails are best suited for less experienced bikers, hikers, birders and snowshoers. The **Grand Lookout Trail**, a favorite for its expansive vistas stretching from Lincoln Gap to Jay Peak, features sculptures carved by local artists and interpretive signage about historic quarry processes and machinery. Mountain bikers pay $10 for a day-use pass. All other recreational use is free.

35 Escape to WOODSTOCK

VILLAGE | RIVER VIEWS | HISTORY

Of all the towns in Vermont, it's Woodstock that epitomizes New England with its rich architectural heritage, farm-to-table restaurants and historic village green. It lays claim to Vermont's oldest family-run general store and the state's only national park. Farmers fresh from the fields rub elbows with townspeople and visitors at cozy diners, and strangers are only friends that haven't met yet.

REIMAR/SHUTTERSTOCK ©

How to

Getting here/around Woodstock is 2½ hours from Boston or 1½ hours from Burlington by car. Once you arrive, just park and explore on foot.

When to go Woodstock is a four-season destination. Fall foliage season is spectacular but busy. Visit midweek to avoid the crowds.

Local happenings Check the Woodstock Town Crier (the public chalkboard in the heart of the village) for news of chicken-pie suppers, country dances and other local events.

JENLO8/SHUTTERSTOCK ©

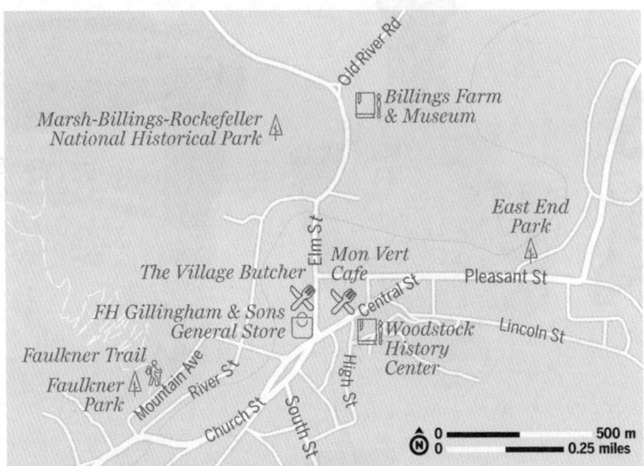

Steeped in history Stroll through the village admiring the historic 18th- and 19th-century architecture. Browse its one-of-a-kind shops and galleries before continuing to the town green ringed with Federal, Georgian and Greek Revival buildings.

Lunch with a view From the green, cross the Middle Covered Bridge spanning the Ottauquechee River. At Faulkner Park, a short walk away, access the **Faulkner Trail** to Mount Tom's South Peak, a 2.75-mile round-trip hike. Pack a picnic to eat at the overlook with amazing mountain views.

From soup to nuts Splurge on Vermont products at **FH Gillingham & Sons General Store**, Vermont's oldest single-family-owned general store (established in 1886).

Life on the farm Learn about agrarian life past and present at **Billings Farm and Museum**. Tour an 1890 farmhouse, kitchen garden and historical displays in 19th-century barns, and visit a working dairy and sheep farm on the same grounds.

History preserved Continue your visit at the **Marsh-Billings-Rockefeller National Historical Park**, Vermont's only national park. Ranger-led tours of the art-filled Queen Anne mansion provide a glimpse into the lives of its former owners. The mansion and Carriage Barn Visitor Center are open late May to late October, but the 20 miles of trails and carriage roads on the 550-acre property are free for hiking, horseback riding and snowshoeing year-round.

Top left Billings Farm and Museum. **Bottom left** FH Gillingham & Sons General Store.

Have a Picnic

Pick up a sandwich at **Mon Vert Cafe** or **The Village Butcher** for a picnic at East End Park or the Woodstock History Center lawn, both overlooking the Ottauquechee River.

■ **Tip from Elizabeth Daniels,** *owner of Vermont Crafted Goods Co @alifeinvermont*

Vermont ICONS

01 Maple syrup

Tapping maple trees to make syrup is a springtime tradition, often continued by generations of the same family.

02 Morgan horse

One of the country's earliest horse breeds, this gentle-natured saddle horse was named after its first breeder, Justin Morgan of Randolph.

03 Ben & Jerry's

From its humble beginnings at a renovated gas station in Burlington, the legendary ice cream has gained a worldwide following.

04 McIntosh apple

This versatile variety, as popular for eating fresh as for making cider, accounts for about 50% of Vermont's annual apple crop.

05 Village church

The white-steepled church, a landmark seen in many towns and villages around the state, is reminiscent of the traditional New England house of worship.

06 Leaf-peeping

The abundance of native sugar maples in a state that's 75% forested means a vibrant display of color every autumn.

07 Cheddar cheese

Its creamy texture and sharp, distinctive flavor set the classic white Vermont cheddar cheese apart from those produced in other regions.

08 Covered bridge

Vermont has more than 100 covered bridges, which is more per square mile than any other state.

09 Holstein cow

This black-and-white cow, the most common dairy breed, is a popular sight on farm pastures throughout Vermont.

10 Alpine skiing

A cold, snowy climate and mountainous terrain add up to some of the best skiing on the East Coast.

37 In Search of MAPLE

SUGARHOUSES | MUSEUMS | CRAFT BEER

If there's one product that's associated with Vermont, it's maple. Visit a sugarhouse to learn about the age-old tradition of sugaring; delve into its history at a maple museum; sample sugar on snow, served with a sour pickle and doughnut; then stock up on syrup and Vermont maple products before you hop on the road to head home.

RANDY DUCHAINE/ALAMY STOCK PHOTO ©

How to

Getting around Spring is mud season, so a 4WD vehicle is essential as unpaved back roads can be muddy.

When to go Sugaring is in full swing from February, when trees are tapped, through late March for boiling. Go in summer to taste maple products and tour maple museums and sugarhouses.

Sugarhouse tour Many sugarhouses *(vermont maple.org)* welcome visitors in season, but call ahead to ask if they're boiling that day, and dress for the cold.

JESSAMYN WEST/FLICKR/CC BY-NC-SA 2.0 ©

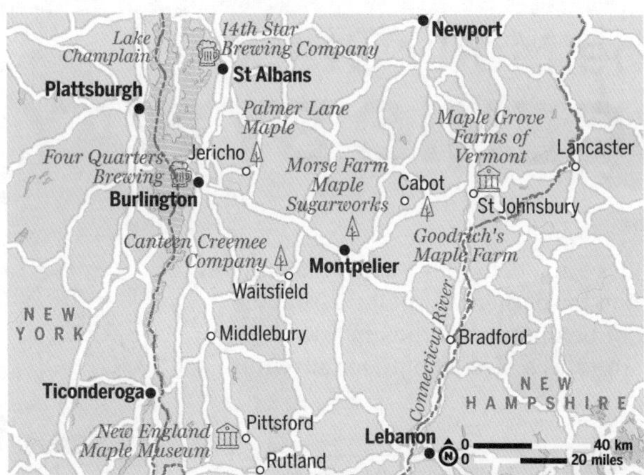

Tap to table Tour the 40-acre sugar bush and sugarhouse at **Merck Forest and Farmland Center** in Rupert to learn how sap becomes syrup. **Goodrich's Maple Farm** in Cabot offers tours and sugar on snow, a Vermont tradition, as does **Morse Farm Maple Sugarworks** in Montpelier, among other sugarhouses.

Museum tours Take a selfie with the world's largest jug of maple syrup at the **New England Maple Museum** in Pittsford before viewing the dioramas, murals and maple-sugaring artifacts. The museum at **Maple Grove Farms of Vermont** in St Johnsbury tells the story of maple sugaring through a video and vintage equipment. The gift shop has free samples and maple products.

Seasonal sips Vermont is known for its craft beers, and maple makes an appearance in many brews. Visit the taproom at **Four Quarters Brewing** in Winooski for a glass of Eleven Below or Bernie's Smitten Mittens; or **14th Star Brewing Company**, a veteran-owned brewery in St Albans, for its Maple Breakfast Stout. At **Beer Naked Brewery** on Hogback Mountain in Marlboro, enjoy the views with your brews including its popular Maple Brown Ale.

Sweet treat Indulge in a maple creemee, a uniquely Vermont summertime treat. **Palmer Lane Maple** in Jericho will top your cone with homemade crunchy maple candy sprinkles. Or try a maple and chocolate swirl with a dollop of cotton candy at Waitsfield's **Canteen Creemee Company**, also renowned for its inventive sundaes.

Top left New England Maple Museum. **Bottom left** Maple Creemee.

Worth the Trip

Mark your calendar for the annual **Vermont Maple Open House Weekend** (late March) and the three-day **Vermont Maple Festival** in St Albans (late April).

38 The Molly Stark SCENIC BYWAY

HIKING | NATURE | HERITAGE

Although only 48 miles long, the Molly Stark Scenic Byway provides a sweet introduction to southern Vermont – from the Revolutionary War history of Bennington to the hip arts and culinary scene of Brattleboro, with a dash of outdoor adventure and stunning scenery.

Trip Notes

Getting here VT 7 will bring you to Bennington, the western terminus. To start from the other end, take I-91, Exit 2, to Brattleboro to access the byway (VT 9).

When to go Travel in summer or fall when road conditions are good and the state parks are open. Expect heavy traffic in foliage season.

Lunch stop Mingle with the locals at Dot's in Wilmington while enjoying hearty, locally sourced food.

Brattleboro Tips

Sip Belgian-style sours brewed with Brattleboro wild yeast at **Hermit Thrush Brewery** or Snowdrop Gin at **Saxtons River Distillery**.

View contemporary art at the **Brattleboro Museum and Art Center**.

Visit **Retreat Farm** for the Thursday Food Truck Roundup with live music in summer, or to explore its 10 miles of woodland trails year-round.

Recommended by Gregory Lesch, *executive director of Brattleboro Area Chamber of Commerce @brattchamber*

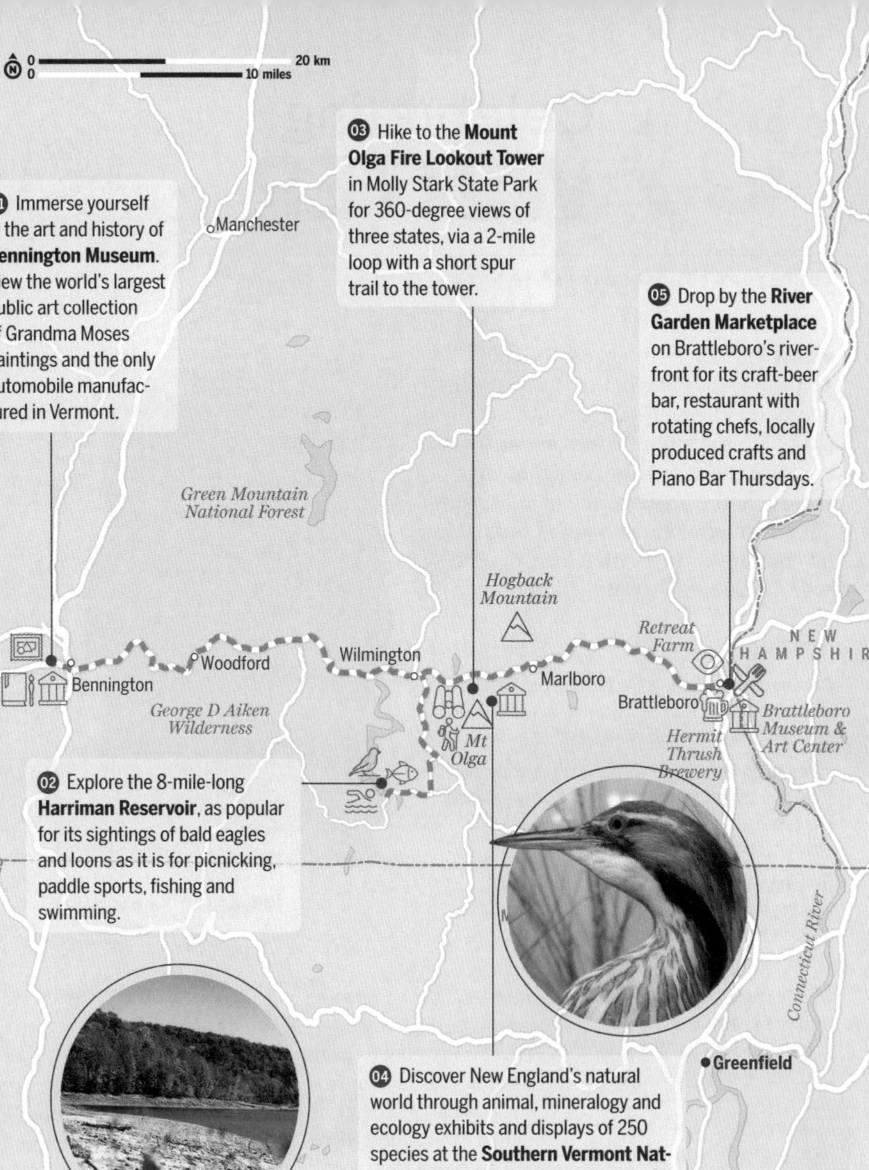

01 Immerse yourself in the art and history of **Bennington Museum**. View the world's largest public art collection of Grandma Moses paintings and the only automobile manufactured in Vermont.

02 Explore the 8-mile-long **Harriman Reservoir**, as popular for its sightings of bald eagles and loons as it is for picnicking, paddle sports, fishing and swimming.

03 Hike to the **Mount Olga Fire Lookout Tower** in Molly Stark State Park for 360-degree views of three states, via a 2-mile loop with a short spur trail to the tower.

04 Discover New England's natural world through animal, mineralogy and ecology exhibits and displays of 250 species at the **Southern Vermont Natural History Museum** at the Hogback Mountain Scenic Overlook.

05 Drop by the **River Garden Marketplace** on Brattleboro's riverfront for its craft-beer bar, restaurant with rotating chefs, locally produced crafts and Piano Bar Thursdays.

39 Celebrating WINTER

ADVENTURE | SNOW | WINTER SPORTS

Vermont winters can be cold and snowfalls epic. But that also means plenty of opportunities for outdoor play. Skip the alpine slopes and instead embrace the season by lacing up your skates, taking a sleigh ride or venturing out on a moonlight snowshoe walk. Cap off your adventure with a local craft beer or a slopeside candlelight dinner.

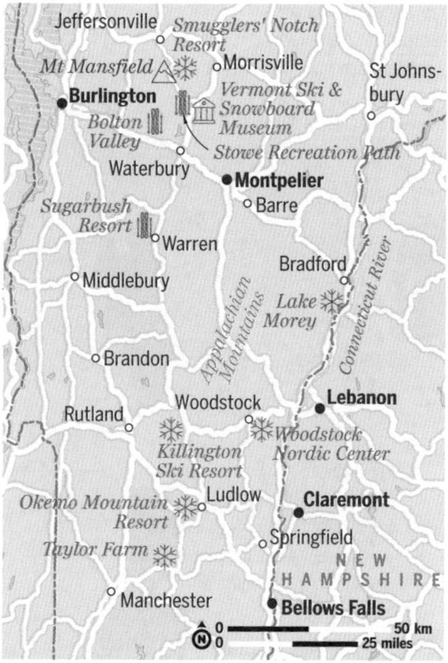

How to

Getting around A car is the best way to travel around the state, although good winter tires and 4WD are a must for safe winter driving.

When to go Many activities are weather-dependent, so always call before you go. Weekdays are generally less crowded and may be less expensive, both for activities and lodging.

Staying warm Choose function over fashion, wearing layers including polyester or wool close to the skin to absorb sweat and prevent chill.

Old-fashioned fun Grab your ice skates and head to **Lake Morey** in Fairlee to skate on the longest track in the country. The 4.3-mile groomed oval track is monitored daily for safe ice conditions. Access is free from the Fairlee Town Beach or **Lake Morey Resort**, which also offers skate rentals.

Mush Meet the huskies and learn about dogsledding before heading out on a brisk ride through snowy forests with an experienced musher at **Eden Ethical Dog Sledding** in northern Vermont.

Dashing through the snow Experience winter's beauty on a horse-drawn sleigh ride at **Taylor Farm** in Londonderry, with a bonfire stop for marshmallow toasting and hot cider.

Reaching new heights Hang onto your hat as you travel up to 25mph on the Timber Ripper Mountain Coaster at **Okemo Mountain Resort**. Riders control the speed of their sled-like cars as they navigate the twists and turns through the woods on the 3100ft track with a vertical drop of over 375ft. The Beast Mountain Coaster at **Killington Ski Resort** also thrills with its 360-degree corkscrews on a 4800ft-long track.

Preserving history Visit the **Vermont Ski and Snowboard Museum** in Stowe to explore the history of this mountain town and winter sports in New England, then hop on the **Stowe Recreation Path** for an easy 5.3-mile ski trek from the village center to a covered bridge.

Beyond the Slopes

Go fat biking at **Woodstock Nordic Center** or on 30 miles of groomed single track maintained by the Kingdom Trail Association near **Burke Mountain**.

Take a guided hike or ride in a heated snowcat up the mountain to **Allyn's Lodge** for a candlelight fireside dinner. Bundle up to ski down the freshly groomed track or catch a ride back to base at **Sugarbush Resort**.

Bolton Valley offers a point-to-point skinning backcountry experience with descent options into Waterbury and parts of Stowe, including to the **von Trapp Brewing Bierhall f**or an après-ski Austrian lager.

Enjoy a family-friendly evening at **Smugglers' Notch Resort**, with a short snowshoe hike to a cozy campfire to toast s'mores and toes.

■ **Recommended by Bryan Rivard,** *director of communications at SKI Vermont @ski_vt*

Above Sugarbush Resort.

YIWENZ/SHUTTERSTOCK ©

Agritourism in Vermont

VERMONT'S HERITAGE IS WELL ROOTED IN AGRICULTURE

Farmers make up less than 2% of the US population and most people have no connection to agriculture. Agritourism in Vermont and elsewhere has helped remedy that disconnect. Farms open their doors to the public by hosting tours and farm stays or selling products at stands and farmers markets.

Left Randall Lineback cows. **Middle** Maple sugarhouse. **Right** McIntosh apples.

CGLADE/GETTY IMAGES ©

From Dairy to Maple

Traveling on the back roads of rural Vermont, you may conclude that the state has more cows than people. While that's not quite true, Vermont is the largest dairy-producing state in New England. It has more than 650 farms with 125,000 cows producing over 2.5 billion gallons of milk a year – milk that's sold fresh or turned into cheese, butter and other dairy products.

It's not just dairying that's important to the economy and the working landscape of Vermont. The state supports a diversified agricultural spectrum with farms raising sheep, beef, goats, poultry and even emus.

In addition to poultry and livestock, there's maple. Vermont holds its own as the biggest maple-producing state in the country. Apples are also a major industry. McIntosh accounts for more than 50% of the apple crop statewide, and more than 150 varieties are grown here, including several heritage varieties.

Merino Mania

Farms in the early 1800s were small and self-sufficient. Families planted vegetable gardens and kept a few milking cows and chickens. A small flock of sheep provided fleece to be carded, spun and woven to make clothing. Wheat was the main commercial crop, though beef and turkeys were also raised for export.

In 1811, William Jarvis, US consul to Portugal, brought 4000 Merino sheep to Vermont from Spain. With the introduction of these sheep, prized for their fine wool,

IMAGE A NATION/SHUTTERSTOCK ©

RICHARD PRATT/SHUTTERSTOCK ©

everything changed. Sheep soon became ubiquitous with textile mills springing up in Winooski and other river towns, an economic boost to those communities. By 1840 Vermont had over a million sheep, about six times the human population.

The sheep boom was fairly short-lived, however. Westward expansion of the railroads meant increased competition for markets from farms in the Midwest, where grazing land was more plentiful and it was cheaper to raise sheep.

By 1840 Vermont had over a million sheep, about six times the human population.

Cows Are King

Dairy farms soon replaced sheep operations, and today dairying continues to be the primary farm industry in the state. Although most people associate Holsteins – the black-and-white cows you see grazing on green hillsides – with Vermont, until the mid-1900s, Jerseys were the predominant breed although some farmers preferred to milk Ayrshires, Brown Swiss or Guernseys. In recent years, the Randall Lineback, a rare heritage breed originally bred for milk, meat and as a draft animal, has been reintroduced to the state.

Today, agritourism is a growing industry in Vermont, with many farmers supplementing their income through direct sales of local products. They are also inviting the public to visit, charging for experiences such as farm tours, corn mazes, hayrides and other recreational activities. Picking apples in the fall, visiting a sugarhouse to learn about maple sugaring or helping collect eggs at a farm – all of these activities are part of agritourism in Vermont.

Fun on the Farm

Only a few generations ago, most families – if they weren't farmers themselves – had relatives, friends or neighbors living on farms. So where their food came from was no mystery. Today, agritourism plays an important role as pick-your-own apple and berry operations, farm stands, and harvest events provide an opportunity to experience firsthand the sights, smells, sounds and tastes of a working farm. Many wineries, cideries and breweries offer tours and tastings. Vermont also has several designated food trails including a **Cheese Trail** and **Maple Creemee Trail**. Visit **Dig In Vermont** *(diginvt.com)*, which lists farm and food experiences and events, to build your own itinerary.

Listings

BEST OF THE REST

Just Add Water

ECHO Lake Aquarium and Science Center

Interactive exhibits provide an informative look at the ecology, culture and history of the Lake Champlain Basin, but it's the indigenous aquatic species in its touch tanks and aquariums that steal the show.

Spirit of Ethan Allen

Relax on a sunset cruise or join in the fun of the Comedy Quest Dinner Show. Ask about the Bike and Boat package, a 4-hour bike rental and 1.5-hour scenic narrated cruise on Lake Champlain.

Lake Champlain Maritime Museum

Watch conservators restoring artifacts and board a replica of a 1776 gunboat to explore Lake Champlain's history. Vintage boats and exhibits in 14 buildings tell the rest of the story.

Northern Star Cruises

A 1920s-style steamer offers scenic dinner and brunch cruises on Lake Memphremagog, which straddles the US–Quebec border, with narration on local history (including Prohibition-era smuggling) and wildlife.

Brews & Chews

Alchemist Brewery $

Heady Topper, among the most sought-after IPAs, is the draw here, but the tour is informative and the beer garden (open in summer) is a convivial social scene not to be missed. Located in Stowe.

Hill Farmstead Brewery $

This world-class brewery offers stunning views of the Green Mountains and expertly crafted farmhouse ales with names such as Peleg, Ephraim and Anna, named after founder and brewer Shaun Hill's ancestors.

Red Clover Ale Company $

A relative newcomer to the craft-beer scene, this brewery in Brandon is already winning accolades for its rotating selection of artisan beers. Many are named after birds including Sapsucker, a maple stout.

Worthy Burger $$

Angus-Wagyu beef, turkey and black-bean burgers are served with crisp Belgian-style fries. A build-your-own option offers kimchi, bacon jam and other toppings. Pair with a Vermont brew from its extensive beer list. Located in South Royalton.

Prohibition Pig $

A casual atmosphere with a creative menu specializing in smoked meat. Try the slow-smoked beef brisket with a side of duck-fat fries and a house-made beer from the on-site brewery. Located in Waterbury.

Lake Champlain Maritime Museum

One-of-a-Kind Museums

Shelburne Museum

Set on 45 acres, this museum of early Americana has more than 30 historic buildings, a circa-1903 Dentzel carousel and fully restored 220ft steamboat that once plied the Lake Champlain waters.

Vermont Institute of Natural Science

Live bird shows introduce resident owls and other avian ambassadors, while the Forest Canopy Walk provides a bird's-eye view of the treetops at this avian rehabilitation and nature center in Quechee. Open year-round.

Fairbanks Museum and Planetarium

Home to Vermont's only public planetarium, this St Johnsbury museum founded in 1889 reflects the Victorian-era passion for travel with its eclectic collections of natural science specimens and ethnological treasures. Don't miss the bug art mosaics.

Birds of Vermont Museum

This unique collection contains more than 500 realistic wood carvings of birds arranged in dioramas of their habitats, the lifetime work of just one man. Located in Huntington.

Presidential Places & Estates

Calvin Coolidge State Historic Site

Explore the rural village that shaped the president's early life. Stop by the homestead, square-steepled church and general store. Artisan cheese sells at the cheese factory, founded by his father in 1890. Located in Plymouth.

Hildene

Marvel at presidential son Robert Todd Lincoln's summer estate in Manchester with a tour of his Georgian Revival mansion, perennial gardens, goat dairy, cheese-making operation and restored Pullman train car.

Calvin Coolidge Homestead

Shelburne Farms

Observe how farmhouse cheddar is made at the Farm Barn and visit the animals before taking in the vistas on 10 miles of walking trails on this 1400-acre agricultural estate.

Sweet Spots

Ben & Jerry's Ice Cream $

A fun factory tour of this famous ice-cream maker offers a peek at the production process, while the outdoor Flavor Graveyard memorializes Wavy Gravy, Bovinity Divinity and other 'dearly de-pinted' flavors. Located in Waterbury.

lu•lu $

This shop in Vergennes churns out small-batch artisan ice cream in unexpected flavors such as orange cardamom and curried peanut butter. The menu changes daily but always includes one or two vegan options.

Chill Vermont Gelato $

Vermont milk and other natural ingredients go into making Sicilian-style gelato in rose and mango cream, coconut and ginger and other inventive flavors. Well-worth the wait if the line is long. Located in Montpelier.

Scan to find more things to do in Vermont online

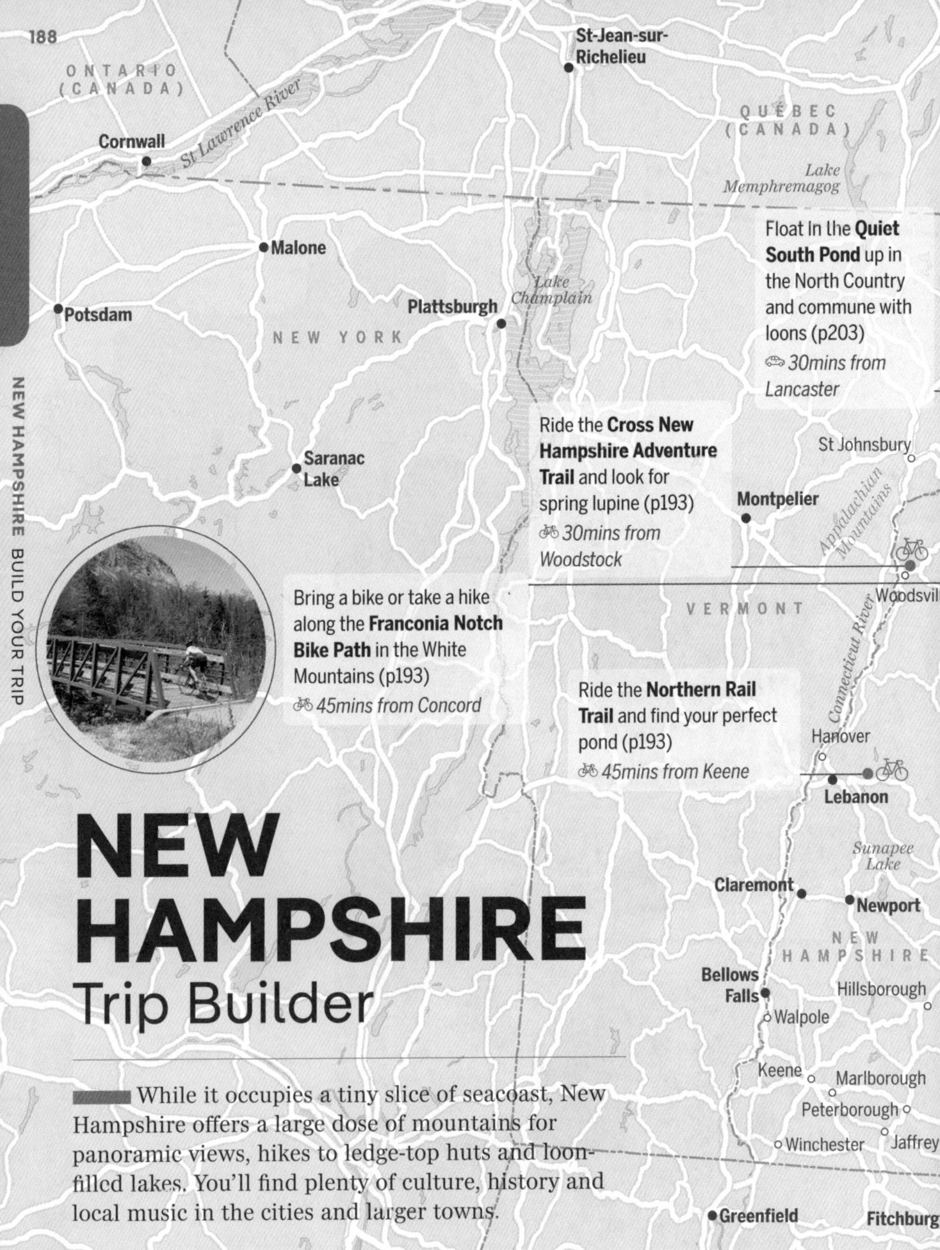

Float in the **Quiet South Pond** up in the North Country and commune with loons (p203)

30mins from Lancaster

Ride the **Cross New Hampshire Adventure Trail** and look for spring lupine (p193)

30mins from Woodstock

Bring a bike or take a hike along the **Franconia Notch Bike Path** in the White Mountains (p193)

45mins from Concord

Ride the **Northern Rail Trail** and find your perfect pond (p193)

45mins from Keene

NEW HAMPSHIRE
Trip Builder

While it occupies a tiny slice of seacoast, New Hampshire offers a large dose of mountains for panoramic views, hikes to ledge-top huts and loon-filled lakes. You'll find plenty of culture, history and local music in the cities and larger towns.

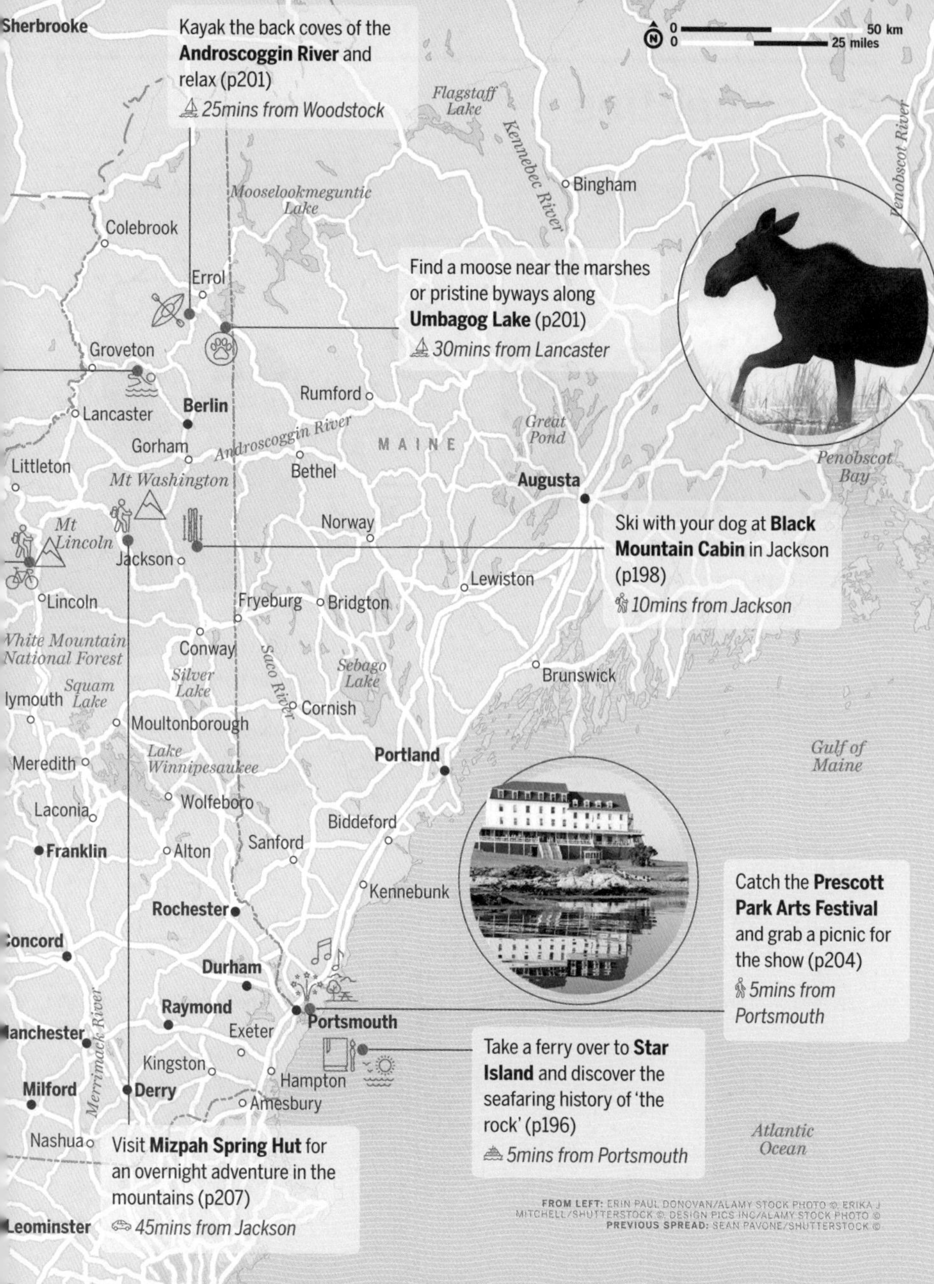
Kayak the back coves of the **Androscoggin River** and relax (p201)
25mins from Woodstock
Find a moose near the marshes or pristine byways along **Umbagog Lake** (p201)
30mins from Lancaster
Ski with your dog at **Black Mountain Cabin** in Jackson (p198)
10mins from Jackson
Catch the **Prescott Park Arts Festival** and grab a picnic for the show (p204)
5mins from Portsmouth
Take a ferry over to **Star Island** and discover the seafaring history of 'the rock' (p196)
5mins from Portsmouth
Visit **Mizpah Spring Hut** for an overnight adventure in the mountains (p207)
45mins from Jackson
0 50 km
0 25 miles
Sherbrooke
Flagstaff Lake
Kennebec River
Penobscot River
Bingham
Mooselookmeguntic Lake
Colebrook
Errol
Groveton
Lancaster
Berlin
Rumford
Gorham
Androscoggin River
MAINE
Great Pond
Penobscot Bay
Littleton
Mt Washington
Bethel
Augusta
Mt Lincoln
Jackson
Norway
Lewiston
Lincoln
Fryeburg
Bridgton
White Mountain National Forest
Conway
Silver Lake
Saco River
Sebago Lake
Brunswick
Squam Lake
Plymouth
Cornish
Moultonborough
Meredith
Lake Winnipesaukee
Portland
Gulf of Maine
Wolfeboro
Laconia
Biddeford
Franklin
Alton
Sanford
Kennebunk
Rochester
Concord
Durham
Raymond
Portsmouth
Manchester
Merrimack River
Exeter
Kingston
Hampton
Milford
Derry
Amesbury
Nashua
Atlantic Ocean
Leominster

Practicalities

ANDY SHIH/SHUTTERSTOCK ©

ARRIVING

Air Boston Logan International Airport, 50 miles from the New Hampshire border, has the best international deals. Manchester-Boston Regional Airport is about an hour from most destinations.

Bus, train and car Buses from Boston can get you to Portsmouth. Trains go to Durham and Dover but service beyond that is limited. The best option to cover the most ground and provide the most flexibility is to rent a car.

HOW MUCH FOR A

Lobster
$15

Microbrew
$7–10

Maple syrup
$8–15

GETTING AROUND

Car Renting a car is your best bet for state-wide exploring. Better yet, rent a camper or van for a camp-as-you-go experience.

Public transportation From Boston, take C&J Bus Lines to Seabrook, Portsmouth and Dover, or the daily Amtrak Downeaster train to Exeter, Durham and Dover.

Shuttle buses These convenient services in the White Mountains include Trail Angels Hiker Services, Mountain Courier Shuttle, and the best bet, Appalachian Mountain Club (AMC) Hiker Shuttle (*outdoors.org/shuttle*). Reservations are strongly suggested in the summer.

WHEN TO GO

JUN–AUG
Most crowds; warmest weather; best swimming and hiking; bugs.

SEP–OCT
Leaf-peeper crowds; still swimming weather; stunning hiking; no bugs.

NOV–MAR
Early season skiing deals; prime winter hiking; cozy inns with fireplaces.

APR–MAY
Best lodging deals; no crowds; limited bugs.

EATING & DRINKING

Walkable Portsmouth (pictured top right) has upscale to down-on-the-decks dining options and morning wake-ups at local bakeries. Cruise into Manchester, Keene and Concord for ethnic specialties and mom-and-pop cafes and grills. Mountain towns have après-ski/hike vibes, fireplaced pubs and quaint bistros, while the North Country offers comfort dining and funky brewpubs.

Best beers with a view
Woodstock Inn Brewery (p211; pictured bottom right)

Best clam chowder on the beach
Petey's Summertime Seafood (p210)

CONNECT & FIND YOUR WAY

Wi-fi Limited to larger metro areas. Cell coverage is good throughout most of the state but spotty in the mountains and the far north. The 5G service is currently limited to the metro areas.

Navigation GPS navigation is good throughout the state.

WEATHER ALERT

Always check the mountain weather before you go – the higher the elevation, the wilder the weather. Useful resources for snow conditions are granitebackcountryalliance.org, mountwashington.org and skinh.com.

WHERE TO STAY

There's an array of stays to fit any budget or activity level. These towns up the cozy quotient, with lakeside lounging, mountain views, seaside culture and history, and small-town charm.

Town	Pro/Con
Jackson	Historic inns for skiing, hiking and biking in the White Mountains. Some budget, mostly pricey.
Concord	Centrally located mid-state with museums, art galleries and quirky dining options.
Portsmouth	Elegant seaside town with excellent dining and artisan shopping. Congested and pricey in the summer and fall.
Keene	College town vibe. Nearby are the quiet western lakes and rolling hills.
Woodstock	Rustic mountain town with local brewpub and nearby swimming holes and waterfalls.
Lancaster	North Woods location featuring local inns, campgrounds and family-run budget hotels.

MONEY

Get a Recreation Pass (from USDA Forest Service) for discounted fees. For hiking emergencies, buy a New Hampshire Hike Safe Card (from NH Fish and Game).

39 Ride the RAILS

CYCLING | MOUNTAINS | NATURE

Does crushed gravel, dirt lanes, fields of lupine and empty country roads sound like a perfect solution to stressful cycling? Then try hitting two of the state's rail trails: Northern and Cross New Hampshire Adventure. Add in views of the Presidential Range and quiet lakeside picnic spots, and you get to enjoy two weekends of solitude.

PEGGY NEWLAND/LONELY PLANET ©

How to

Getting here Cross New Hampshire Adventure Trail *(xnhat.org)* has various day parking locations. For Presidential Rail Trail access, park at Dolly Copp (Pinkham B Road) in Randolph. Northern Rail Trail's *(northernrailtrail.org)* official Welcome Center is located in Andover's Highland Lake Inn.

When to go Late spring through foliage fall; make sure to add the Lupine Loop to your Presidential Rail Trail ride in mid-June for flower fireworks.

Mind the mud Mud season can last through late spring.

JERRY AND MARCY MONKMAN/ ECOPHOTOGRAPHY.COM/ALAMY STOCK PHOTO ©

Northern Rail Trail The 48-mile Northern Rail Trail is the longest managed trail in New Hampshire, with cushy cinder-ballast surface and loops through farmland, around postcard-perfect ponds and past decommissioned depots. Pecco Beaufays, at the **Highland Lake Inn's** Welcome Center, knows about the trail's history and excellent turnoffs for picnics, lake swimming and historical tours. Start here and make a 60-mile trip to and from Enfield or Mascoma Lake, taking additional dips in Eagle Pond in Wilmot and Mirror Lake in Canaan, and a lunch stop at **Danbury General Store**. Take in Mt Cardigan views in Grafton, then roll back through Keniston Covered Bridge in Andover for a final float in Highland Lake.

Cross New Hampshire Adventure Trail Pick mountains on all sides and you've got the Presidential segment – a crushed 'velour' ride on smoothed gravel with some paved roads. Best of all: there's limited or no traffic for 20 miles, and it's gradually uphill. Start off through tunnels of fir with the Moose River to entertain you and swimming-hole potential. Eventually, you'll be riding through meadows of lupine, crossing bridges over marshes and following the Israel River's wild meander. You can pop off the dirt and ride the pavement of rolling, lupine-filled, Valley Rd and Rte 115B to Marsh Rd. Don't miss Cherry Pond and the **Pondicherry Wildlife Refuge**, with views over heron-filled marshes and the Pliny and Presidential Ranges as your mountainous amphitheater. If you can't leave this area, stay at **Israel River Campground** and explore further through Littleton and onto Woodsville and the Vermont border. Or return to Randolph – a downhill joy.

Top left Cycling, Northern Rail Trail. **Bottom left** Pondicherry Wildlife Refuge.

Other Dirt Buddies

Franconia Notch Bike Path Ride downhill 10 miles from Franconia to Lincoln, past the Flume Gorge's waterfalls and plenty of mountain views. Then ride back up 10 miles for dips in Echo and Profile Lakes.

Rockingham Rail Trail From Manchester through to Newfields, share the road with dogs, runners and occasional 'four-wheelers' (ATV bikes).

Odiorne Point State Park trails Cruise past sunken forest, marshes, empty harbor beaches and abandoned military forts.

Cheshire Rail Trail Enjoy 42 miles of woodland, arched bridges and deep ravines for lunch spots near Keene. Some paved sections, most dirt.

40 Adventures with FIDO

SKIING | HIKING | SWIMMING

There's nothing better than taking a furry friend along with you to get wild on adventures. The White Mountains are a free-for-all with many dog-welcoming hikes, while the Atlantic, full of waves and with occasional surfers, invites for a 'refreshing' swim. Bring a leash for cliff scrambles and for the dog chasing ever-beguiling seagulls.

How to

Getting here All locations mentioned here have free, small parking lots and most are off main roads.

When to go Go early to park. Check the weather forecast as storms pop up often in the humid summer and mid-winter.

What to bring Water is a must; plus a snack kibble for the dog and a shareable sandwich for you. Pick up the poop – there are fines for leaving Fido's contributions. You'll need a wetsuit for winter swimming.

Jenness Beach For off-leash wave leaps with the dog, go from dawn to 9am and again after 7pm. There's plenty of space for racing around on the beach, chasing seagulls and fetching sticks. Romp in the chilled Atlantic waters or ramble along the rocky cliffs, with views to the Isles of Shoals. Grab a picnic for sunset.

Bear Notch Ski Area Skate or ski all day with the dog. Explore trails through frosted pine and aspen, or enjoy races through meadows over bridges and wide fields of snow. Ask if they are offering the 'fresh bread' bell and zip down to the barn for an 'all dogs welcome' lunchtime feast of homemade soups and right-out-of-the-oven breads.

Jackson Ski Touring This is panoramic Nordic perfection, with some dog-friendly trails and over 60 miles of skate and classic groomers.

Waterfall Wonder

Jackson Falls offer layered swimming pools for dips with the dog, with ledge views down to **Jackson Village**. Hike the river to find the best cascades and calm spots, sit in a waterfall or find a sandy perch. There's some slippery climbing, so wear water shoes or old sneakers for rocky rambling. Go early, due to limited parking and afternoon crowds, or nab a parking spot in pretty Jackson and have a short amble up. Fall asleep to the babbling brooks, and be sure to grab a sandwich and homemade dog biscuits at **J Town Deli**.

Imp Face Trail Fall foliage is fantastic, but summer allows for dips in the various cascading waterfalls. Hike this trail counterclockwise for around-the-rim viewing of unique canyon bell curves. Granite profile shows a 'mis-shapen face of a wood sprite' – it's an obstacle course of moss forests and easy rock scrambles. On Imp Cliffs (be sure to leash a rambunctious pup here), there are views over the Northern Presidential Range. After a nap on the sun-warmed ledge, head down to a waterfall for a dip with the dog.

Above Jackson Ski Touring.

ALLAN WOOD PHOTOGRAPHY/SHUTTERSTOCK ©

Shipwrecks & Sunsets on 'the Rock'

A MURDEROUS HISTORY AND A MAGNIFICENT VIEW

Isles of Shoals can be reached by ferry from Portsmouth, but it's a world away. Come for the day or stay for a weekend at this rocky outpost off the coast, to learn about its flamboyant past, explore the historic garden and enjoy the gorgeous sunrise and sunset views.

Left Lighthouse, White Island. **Middle** Black-backed seagull, Appledore Island. **Right** Celia Thaxter's Garden, Appledore Island

History of the Islands

John Smith of Jamestown, Virginia, wanted to name these islands Smyth's Isles in the early 1600s, but local fishing families had already called them Shoals due to the jagged coastline with plentiful fish. Even so, John Smith shares a memorial plaque with the larger obelisk dedicated to Shoals' beloved minister, Reverend John Tucke, on **Star Island**. These tiny islands in Maine and New Hampshire waters all have exposed craggy shelves. Unfortunately, they were often landing bases for many shipwrecks, supposed sunken treasures and the many legends of Blackbeard and Phillip Babb burying their golden loot. Described by Captain Levett, another early explorer in the 1600s, as without 'good timber-tree or good ground for a garden,' it's a place to bring your imagination. The largest, **Appledore Island**, is thought to be haunted by spirits of a fire-ravaged hotel, but it's now home to **Shoals Marine Laboratory** and the famous, nesting and dive-bombing, great black-backed gulls. **White Island** holds the lighthouse and keeper's house, but **Smuttynose Island** has the stories of pirates, shipwrecks, hidden treasure and murder. Just across Gosport Harbor from Star Island, it's worth swimming or kayaking to for more exploration. Visit the caretaker at **Haley House** and find out where the caves and graves are hidden.

Clapboard Inn

You can see the **Oceanic Hotel** from the beaches of New Hampshire – it resembles a ghostly ship on a craggy ledge of Star Island. Don't let that scare you, because this hotel has the best wraparound porch anywhere in New England, with sunrise and sunset views. The only island accessible to

REMO NONAZ/SHUTTERSTOCK ©

MARCUS BAKER/ALAMY STOCK PHOTO ©

day-trippers and weekend getaways, this is like summer camp on a massive rock with a revamped boarding-house history and 'pass the dish' family-style dining. Windows are flung open for ocean breeze in the bedrooms, and Victorian charm is still apparent in the pink-tinged parlors filled with maps, books and reading nooks. A grand piano sits in the sunroom awaiting singers. Like any good summer camp, Star Island has yoga retreats, astronomy and painting classes, but most folks come for the peacefulness – a chair by the craggy beach, a kayak float around the harbor or a bird-watching forage. No television, limited wi-fi, but an open-air **Art Barn** with paints available connects you to creativity on the coast. Fall asleep to crashing waves.

Windows are flung open for ocean breeze in the bedrooms, and Victorian charm is still apparent in the pink-tinged parlors filled with maps, books and reading nooks.

Celebrated Island Garden

Think cornflower, cosmos, phlox and poppy, add some wild daisies, and you've got this Appledore Island garden created in the late 19th century by poet and lighthouse keeper's daughter Celia Thaxter. She described herself as a lonely child, with flowers as friends. You'll want to plop down in this wild, windswept and fragrant garden and dream of island living, but don't forget to explore the **Devil's Dance Floor** rocks or splash in the sea at **Broad Cove**. Only open June to August and reached via research vessel, it's an adventure with blooming sunflowers and dahlias on rugged trails with careening seagulls.

Island Sunrise & Sunset

Wrap yourself up in a blanket from the Oceanic Hotel, grab an early cup of coffee from the porch, and find a perch just past the Art Barn rocks. The sun will come slow, red at the horizon, and suddenly fill the sky, your world brightening pink. Some folks add yoga on the rocks, but it's also lovely to take a kayak out into the harbor and float around at sunrise. Sunsets are stunning on the porch, sky shading to purple, with twinkling lights glowing from the mainland. Lanterns flicker for night walks up to the chapel.

41 Backcountry STASHES

PARTY | SKIING | OUTDOORS

You don't have to be a top athlete to go backcountry in New Hampshire, you just need to know the trails and the events. There are plenty of quiet paths for snowy hiking or snowshoeing in the mountains. Bring a winter picnic and relax, or get your pulse racing on the elevated pitches of powder on backcountry runs and organized group tours.

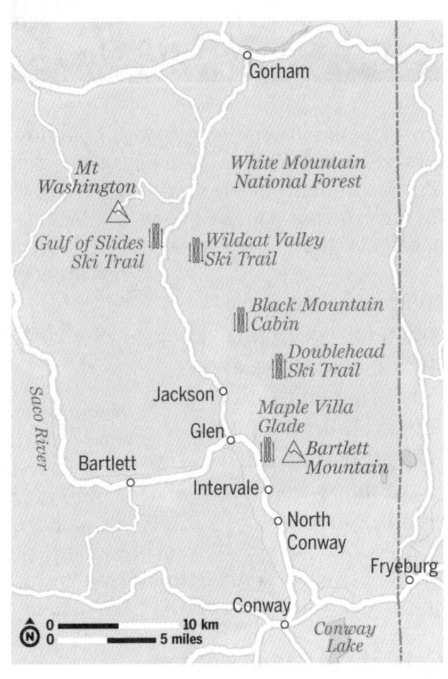

How to

Getting here Plan ahead with Granite Backcountry Alliance and Ski the Whites websites.

When to go Throughout winter for Friday Night Lights on various mountains. Check the weather and ski reports beforehand.

Best views Hike up Doublehead Trail's Middle Path and take a right at the top to follow the ridgeline to three viewpoints: Carter Notch, Tin Mountain and Bald Face. Continue onto North Doublehead and Mt Washington views from the cabin. Ski down.

Black Mountain Cabin You'll find moderate grades on the hike up, but recently cleared, wide expanses along the ridgeline for the smooth line downward. There's a mountain cabin at the top, with a luxe composting toilet, and views of Mt Washington and the Wildcat Range as your reward. Watch out for a waterfall crossing toward the bottom of the trail. Bonus: ski the backside and join the **Jackson Cross-Country** trails.

Doublehead Ski Trail Ski-tour it up the gradual, double-tracked trail with skis (or snowshoes) on, and you'll be rewarded with alpine views of Jackson Village, Carter Dome and over to Maine's lake district. A mountain cabin allows overnight camping (with booking). It's a perfect day trip for gliding downhill through aspen grove, spruce spurs and rolling, wide turnoffs. With a 1500ft elevation, you'll deserve that après-ski

Backcountry Pro Tips

For more backcountry fun, try these additional trails: **Maple Villa Glade** on Bartlett Mountain, **Wildcat Valley Ski Trail** and **Gulf of Slides Ski Trail** near Mt Washington.

The following items make backcountry skiing more enjoyable: down knickers, hand warmers and extra layers; lightweight helmet; and a backcountry pack filled with power bars.

■ **Recommended by Andrew Drummond,** *owner of Ski the Whites store in Jackson @ski_the_whites*

beer at **Wildcat Lounge** (p210) down in Jackson.

Granite Backcountry Alliance DIY routes for novice and expert skiers and snowshoeing enthusiasts. Come in early spring for **Wild Corn Shindig**: two days of demos, races, tours, music, themed costumes and craft beer.

Friday Night Lights Join the **Ski the Whites** crew for group-safe routes with lanterns lighting the way. Friday Nights are hosted at various White Mountains ski areas. Loosen your boots, throw on some 'skins' and zip-walk yourself up to various snow parties downhill.

Above Mt Washington from Wildcat Valley Ski Trail.

42 Canoe Trails & RIVER FLOATS

CANOEING | RAPIDS | NATURE

There's plenty of moving water in New Hampshire and if you have a canoe, rivers, rapids and loon-filled ponds await your paddling. Simplify your gear and go with outfitters for an organized trip downriver. For wild water and do-it-yourself paddling routes, check out the Northern Forest Canoe Trail, with over 700 miles of routes in New England.

How to

Getting here Take Hwy 93 north from Keene or Concord to Rte 3 and Rte 110, or Rte 16 north from the seacoast.

When to go Avoid summer weekends or long-holiday weeks (July 4), or you'll be sharing the water with day-trippers and large groups. Go mid-week at an out-of-the-way lake or river.

Find your personal put-in Most state parks offer boat launches or suggest launches for canoes. Go with friends and two cars for put-in and take-out ease.

Stark Base yourself at **Percy Campground** for river-bound camping and canoe rentals on the Ammonoosuc. Ramp up with Class II rapids under the **1862 Stark Covered Bridge**, float the flat flow past the village, or go for it with a do-it-yourself paddle on the Upper Ammonoosuc. Tip: strap a rental canoe to your car (haul a bike for the ride back to the car afterward) and find a put-in 10 miles upriver. Explore islands for picnics and naps. Float in the shallows; tie-up at a sandbar. If you get stuck in the narrows, all the better. **Christine Lake** is great for

Top right Campfire, Umbagog Lake. **Bottom right** 1862 Stark Covered Bridge.

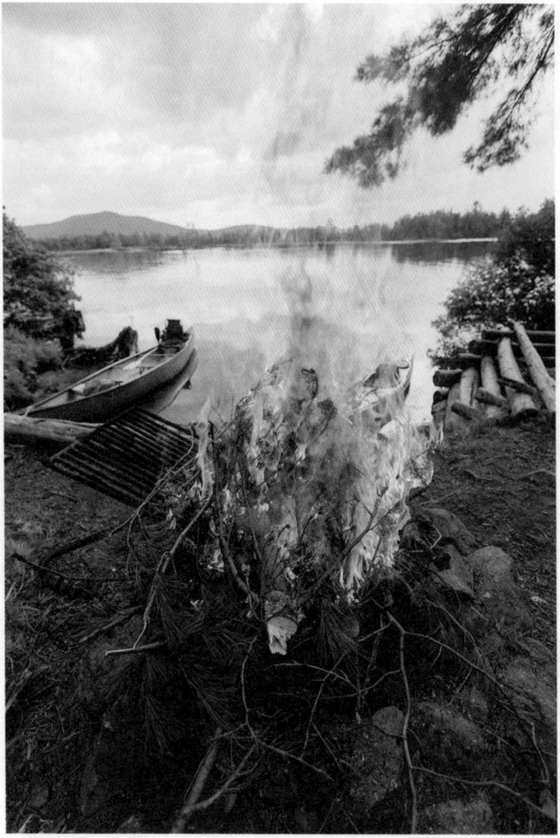

Sea Kayaking with Seals

Head over to the **Seacoast Science Center** in Rye for an organized tour, or rent a sea kayak and explore Sagamore Creek, Leachs Island and Piscataqua Back Bay at leisure.

a paddle, with plenty of loon watching and clear lake swimming.

Umbagog Lake State Park Errol is the pulse of river rafting or quiet glides through the Umbagog National Wildlife Refuge. Canoe to your campsite on a remote island and fish for dinner on the lake. Try **Big Island** off Thurston Cove and you'll be in loon symphony land, with dozens of paddling routes. Transport your canoe and self to the **Steamer Diamond Boat Launch** for a day trip through Bear Brook's nooks and crannies. Egrets, eagles, loon and osprey will greet you everywhere, especially midweek and in early mornings.

Errol For Class II and III rapids, **Northern Waters Outfitters** does a half- or full-day throttle through the rumblers of the Androscoggin River.

43 WATERFALL Wonderlands

WILDLIFE | WATERFALLS | RAVINES

The Northern Presidential Range is ruggedly accessible for all things North Woods. Take a waterfall walk past mossy glens and cascading ravines, and along rough-hewn bridges over brooks. Find a camping spot smack-dab in the middle of moose country, and swim in nearby mountain ponds. Wake up early to spot moose along the Ammonoosuc River.

How to

Getting around Rent a car, add a bicycle and bring your mud boots.

When to go Mid-May through late October. Get a morning move-on. Get up at dawn to be rewarded by munching moose in the marshes.

Safe hiking Note all the hiking references to Devils! Nothing to fear: just steep jaunts, hidden caves, jagged cliffs and rocky ravines.

Muddy meanderings Backroads and dirt lanes can be your moose-finding secrets. Heading out on Rte 110 toward the historic town of Stark, turn where the mood strikes you along the Dead River, Bell River or Phillips Brook, but bring your mud-kickers for the marshes. Take a hike up **Devil's Ledge** for views over the village.

Camping There are hiking trails and stream-fed swimming pools in the **Moose Brook State Park**. Camp overnight and have quick access to 'Moose Alley' on Rte 110.

Top right Gordon Falls, Randolph Paths. **Bottom right** Devil's Hopyard.

ERIN PAUL DONOVAN/ALAMY STOCK PHOTO ©

ERIN PAUL DONOVAN/ALAMY STOCK PHOTO ©

Where's the Moose?

NH Fish and Game suggestions for moose-spotting:

Rte 3 north of Pittsburg to the Canadian border

Rte 16 north of Milan to the Maine border

Rte 26 east of Dixville Notch to the Maine border

Rte 112 east of Lincoln to Bear Notch Rd

Rte 110 north of Berlin to Route 110A

Bike to find moose
Grab your mountain bike for mud-stomping and moose-watching through beautiful, smoothed and groomed, **Coos Cycling Club's** trails. Howie Roll is a favorite, with limited mucky traps and plenty of rolling fun.

Hike to the falls It's waterfall world at **Randolph Paths** for a number of beauties: Cold Brook, Salrock, Tama, Gordon, Coosauk, Hitchcock and Stairs Falls. Look for the Devil's Kitchen gorge, Bumpus Brook and the caves and lairs of Bear Pit.

Clean yourself up There are plenty of waterfalls, brooks and lakes to wash off all the mud in moose country. The **Quiet South Pond** in Stark offers mountain views and a quick hike up to the **Devil's Hopyard** ravine.

44 MUSICAL Portsmouth

FESTIVALS | JAZZ | HISTORY

Portsmouth is a mecca of jazz clubs and on-the-law festivals. Known as the 'Colonial city by the sea,' it has blossomed into a home for local musicians who make it big. From duos playing banjos and harps on sloops along the Piscataqua River to speakeasy vibes of fresh bebop, there are walkable club tours or find-it-yourself discoveries.

PERNELLE VOYAGE/SHUTTERSTOCK ©

Trip Notes

Getting around There's free parking at the City Hall lot; it's a pleasant walk to town. Rent a bicycle for a town-and-country tour along Rte 1B.

When to go Summer for outdoor concerts, winter for front-row seats.

Get a seat Spread your blanket early at the Prescott Park Arts Festival. Reserve tickets for jazz clubs.

By the sea Visit the Seacoast Science Center for ocean sounds, or if you want a beach day, head to the Great Island Common.

Banjo on the Boat

Head to the Gundalow's cargo-barge concerts on the **Piscataqua River.** Sidewalk Tom, with his banjo, is one of the varied musicians who entertain small-boat tours sailing past lighthouses, historic districts, the harbor and shipyards. Afterward, stroll the Colonial neighborhoods in Strawbery Banke.

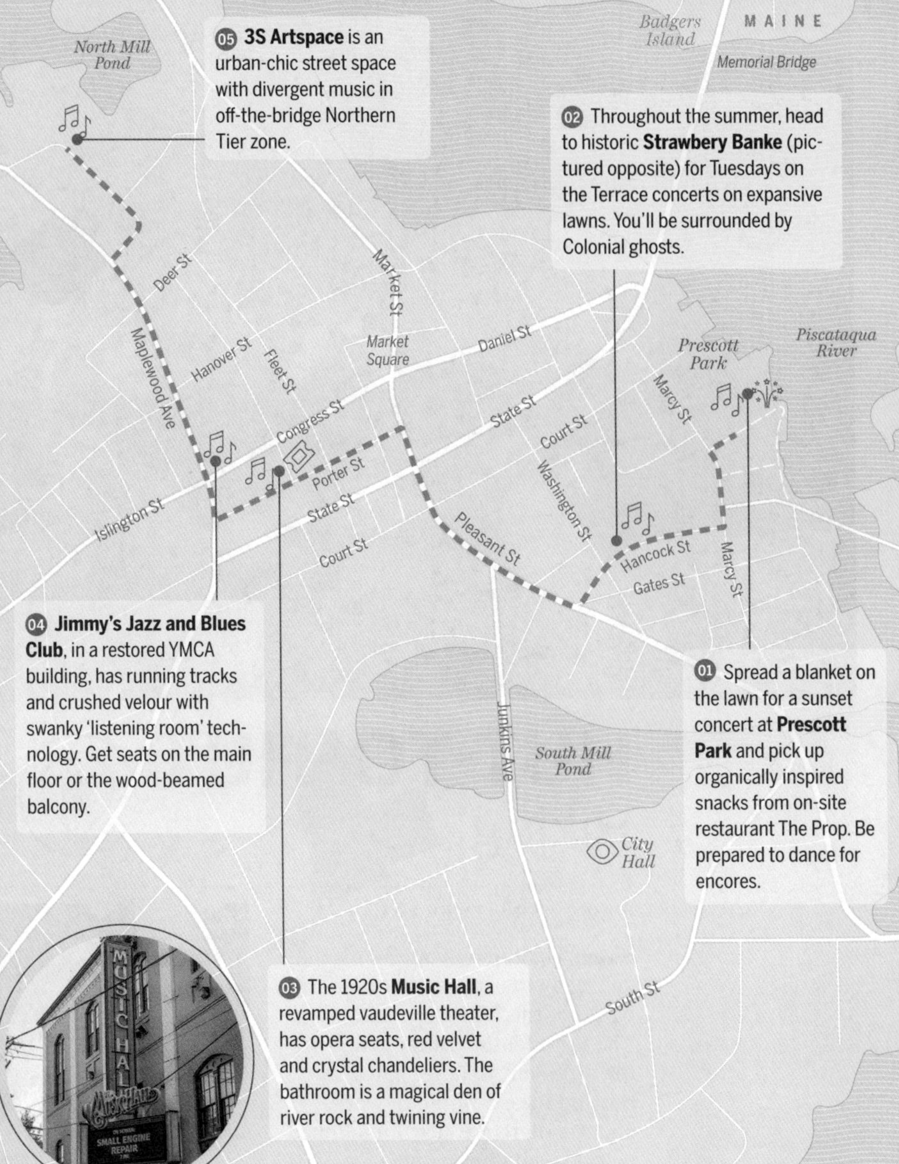

WAREWARDSON/SHUTTERSTOCK ©

45 HUT-TO-HUT Hiking

HIKING | MOUNTAINS | WILDLIFE

Tighten up your boots and get ready to explore the wonderful world of the White Mountains. The Presidential Range is known for turbulent weather patterns, but you have nothing to worry about – there are cozy huts linked by trails, all offering wood-stove warmth and wilderness views.

PEGGY NEWLAND/LONELY PLANET ©

How to

Getting here/around It's a three-hour drive from Boston to the trails. Use the Hiker Shuttle service (through AMC) for drop-off/pick-up between the hikes or huts; it's available during summer months. Reserve ahead.

When to go Reserve huts through the AMC website from May to October; avoid holiday weekends. For tent platforms or rustic shelters in the deep woods (contact USDA Forest Service for information), it's first come, first stay – go midweek.

Top tip Earplugs are a must when bunking in the huts if you are a light sleeper.

NORTHWOODS/SHUTTERSTOCK ©

Mizpah Mayhem

On the **Crawford Path** – the oldest continuously maintained hiking path in America – it's 8.5 miles over moss ledges, silver cascades and view-worthy branch-offs to Elephant Head and Mt Webster before a 360-degree whirl on Mt Jackson. Look for gray jays, the snack-stealing birds of the White Mountains, as you tromp over boggy logs. Take a refreshing soak in Mizpah Spring as you listen for the distinctive call of Bicknell's thrush.

From the front porch of **Mizpah Spring Hut**, there are forever vistas across Oakes Gulch and over the Southern Presidential Range, but listen for the dinner 'hut gong.' Become part of friendly jostling for bench space, as 'croo' members (caretakers) place bowls of fresh salads and steaming lasagne on tables. Hiking

DANITA DELIMONT/ALAMY STOCK PHOTO ©

Mountain Pools & a Brew

Have a dip in the **Centennial Cascades** before returning to the Highland Center in Crawford Notch. Grab an Adirondack chair and a local brew for a summer concert series. With the moon rising over shadowed peaks, and stars overhead, what better way to celebrate a 'hutter'?

Top left Hiking Mt Eisenhower (p209).
Bottom left Zealand Falls Hut (p208).
Top right Gray jay.

pals are quickly made, and soon guitars come out and there's singing. Mizpah Spring Hut is log-cabin-comfy with shelves full of books, games and cards, and there's always a whiff of fresh cookies; but don't forget to nab a bed in the 'vertical' sleeping rooms (bunks with ladders connecting bed to bed). Grab a book from your backpack for some headlamp reading before you fall sleep. Lights are out at 9:30pm, because early coffee is number-one priority before the next day's jaunts.

Zealand Chill & Slide

Take the Hiker Shuttle to the **Zealand Falls Trailhead** and tackle the short and sweet incline on old logging and railway routes for a pleasant afternoon, stopping for cooling dips in Whitewall Brook and Zealand Pond. You can rest up at **Zealand Falls Hut**, not far from the namesake waterfall. Awaiting you the next day is a 5.5-mile scramble back to the Highland Center in Crawford Notch along the A-Z and Avalon trails.

Spotting Wildlife on the Trails

Bald eagle Watch them cruise the thermals along the ravines of a 4000-footer mountain.

Beaver Downed trees? Dammed ponds? Beavers are near. In the morning, hear them slap tails on marshes.

Black bear Elusive along well-traveled trails but active near blueberry bushes. Caution: be prepared for protective mothers with cubs on less-traveled trails in the spring.

Coyote You'll hear them yipping at dusk along the trails, but they are a rare sighting. If you have a dog, add a bell to the collar.

Red fox Spy them in meadows at twilight or along backroads between trails.

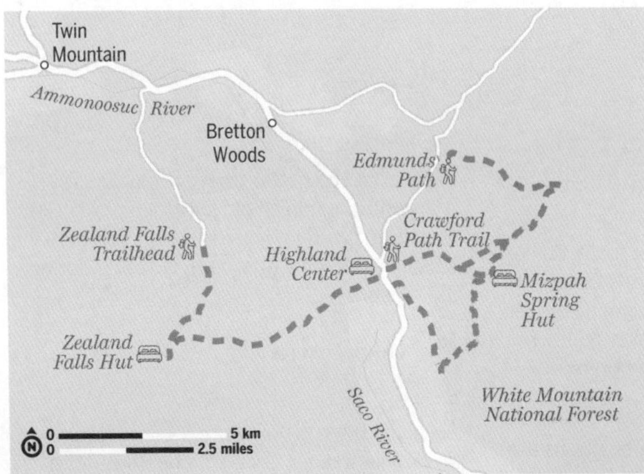

Left Beaver, New Hampshire.
Below Zealand Falls.

Highland Swank

After a fully loaded breakfast, you'll find alpine bliss. The Crawford Path takes you on a peak-bagging tour, with Mt Pierce as the first cairn-strewn highlight, but stay focused for Mt Eisenhower, a 4760ft charmer. An old-man mountain, with its bare dome and hardy wildflower fringe, this is the place to sit and stare at the Presidentials in all directions: Franklin, Monroe, Washington, to name just a few. **Edmund's Path** is the decline back down and it's rocky, rooty and full of stream crossings.

Mt Clinton Rd, a well-tended fire road, takes you back for a celebratory stay at the **Highland Center**. That night, treat yourself to a luxe single room, decked out in L.L.Bean decor, with views through Crawford Notch. After another filling 'croo' dinner, it might be easy to just pass out, especially after downing a happy-hour beer – but you really shouldn't. The stars are about to have a light show.

Listings

BEST OF THE REST

Nibbles & Nosh

Wildcat Lounge $$

Head to the garden out back for local music or enjoy après-ski in the bar that's filled with chairlift seating and vintage ski gear. Located in Jackson, a classic New England ski town with plenty of shops. Craft beers on tap.

May Kelly's Cottage $$

Irish pub sessions on Sunday afternoons are the place to find local musicians. The back deck has lovely views of Moat Mountain and the Saco River, so be sure to grab a bench early and enjoy Guinness on tap.

The Inn at Thorn Hill $$$

This Jackson venue offers farm-to-table elegance in the dining room, but the best place is on the wraparound porch during happy hour with daily specials from the pub.

Petey's Summertime Seafood $$

Come with sandy feet and sundresses over swimsuits, order a lobster roll and ice cream at the side window, and head back to the beach in Rye. Or, if the porch deck is open, eat lobster on skewers.

Ceres Bakery $

Get a Penhallow cookie and a bowl of lentil soup and watch the action in Portsmouth. Lines go out the door, so go after the coffee rush or before the lunch hordes of summer.

Moxy $$$

Funky vibe and small plates, with outdoor views of the Portsmouth harbor from street-side tables. Sitting at the bar in front of huge windows is sublime in snowy winter. Rotating wine menu and wine tastings.

Margaritas Concord $$

What could be better than nachos and margaritas inside an old jail in Concord? Get bean burritos and never-ending chips and salsa in your individual cells. Go early during ski season.

Cool Towns

Eaton

Lakeside town in the White Mountains with an excellent diner. Grab a picnic table for a sunset dinner along Crystal Lake. Look for the rope swing on the south end and leap in the mountain-spring-fed waters.

Bethlehem

Funky brewpub, great cafes and an independent theater in an unknown nook of the White Mountains. Downtown is small but loaded with charm, and there's a tree farm for viewing perfectly coiffed spruce and fir.

Littleton

Head to Chutters, the 'world's longest' candy counter with penny candies, atomic fireballs, sour pumpkins, sweet tarts and chocolate drops near Woodstock. Eat to your heart's

Chutters, Littleton

content after a day spent hiking the local-built trails in the White Mountains.

Rye

Take some surfing lessons on Jenness Beach at Summer Sessions Surf Shop near Portsmouth. Grab a hot drink and bagel sandwich after surfing at Sandpiper Cafe next door and find a sandy spot for lunch.

New Castle

A historic New England coastal community close to Portsmouth, located along Rte 1B. Stop at the 32-acre Great Island Common for a day on the cove-side beach. Bathhouses, picnic tables and a playground keep everyone happy.

Peterborough

Explore art galleries and excellent cafes on scenic Contoocook River. Close to Keene, the western lakes region and majestic Mt Monadnock, it's worth the side trip. Famous writing enclave nearby at MacDowell.

Holderness

Quaint New England town near Squam Lake and Concord. The filming location of the 1981 Academy Award–wining movie *On Golden Pond* adds even more charm. Kayak past Church Island and watch a wedding take place.

Brews with a View

Woodstock Inn Brewery $$

A rollicking and happy crowd to join for garden noshing and craft brews. Make sure to take advantage of the swimming hole across the street in Woodstock.

Elm City Brewing $

With a college-town vibe but an excellent menu, this brewery offers specials and rotations of various seasonally inspired brews near Keene.

Henniker Brewing Company $

Go to the Wurst Festbier festival and it's like you're at a German Oktoberfest. In the rolling

MIRA/ALAMY STOCK PHOTO ©

Peterborough

western hills near Concord, head for the patios and call it a day. Perfect porters and ales.

Tuckerman Brewing Company $$

Classic New England beer garden and local music in the White Mountains near Conway. The craft brews have beautiful labels made by a local artist. Cornhole tournaments and Acoustic Sundays in the tasting room.

Ledge Brewing $

Surrounded by the White Mountains, this is the hip zone for craft brews after hiking, skiing or cycling. Flop on couches, play a game of cornhole, or take turns sitting in the Giant Chair.

Throwback Brewery $$

Reserve a firepit or find an Adirondack chair in the fields of this women-owned farm near Portsmouth. Beautiful barn, organic snacks and excellent beer, plus yoga on Sunday mornings.

Woodman's and Shackett's $

Bristol (near Concord) is the best tiny town, with two breweries plus vintage music store. Check out the walking trails along the Pemigewasset River or take a dip in Newfound Lake, which is mountain-fed and refreshing.

Scan to find more things to do in New Hampshire online

MAINE
COASTLINE | FORESTS | CULTURE
Experience Maine online

MAINE

Trip Builder

Maine is not one place but many – featuring coastal towns, lakes, mountains, remote North Woods, misty islands and beautiful Acadia National Park. The vibe is flannel-shirt-wearing comfort while eating seafood at picnic tables and local pubs, but culture can be found at festivals and seaside galleries. Pick your part of Maine and explore.

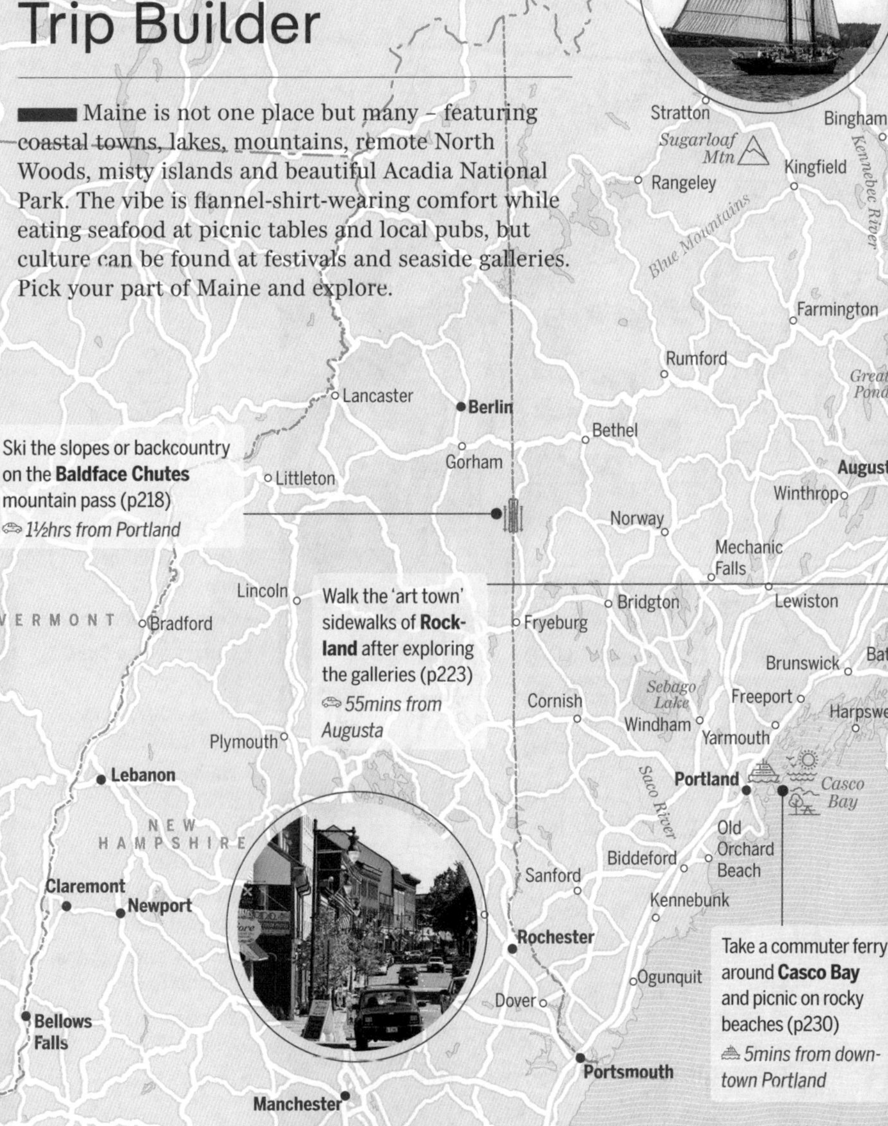

Ski the slopes or backcountry on the **Baldface Chutes** mountain pass (p218)
1½hrs from Portland

Walk the 'art town' sidewalks of **Rockland** after exploring the galleries (p223)
55mins from Augusta

Take a commuter ferry around **Casco Bay** and picnic on rocky beaches (p230)
5mins from downtown Portland

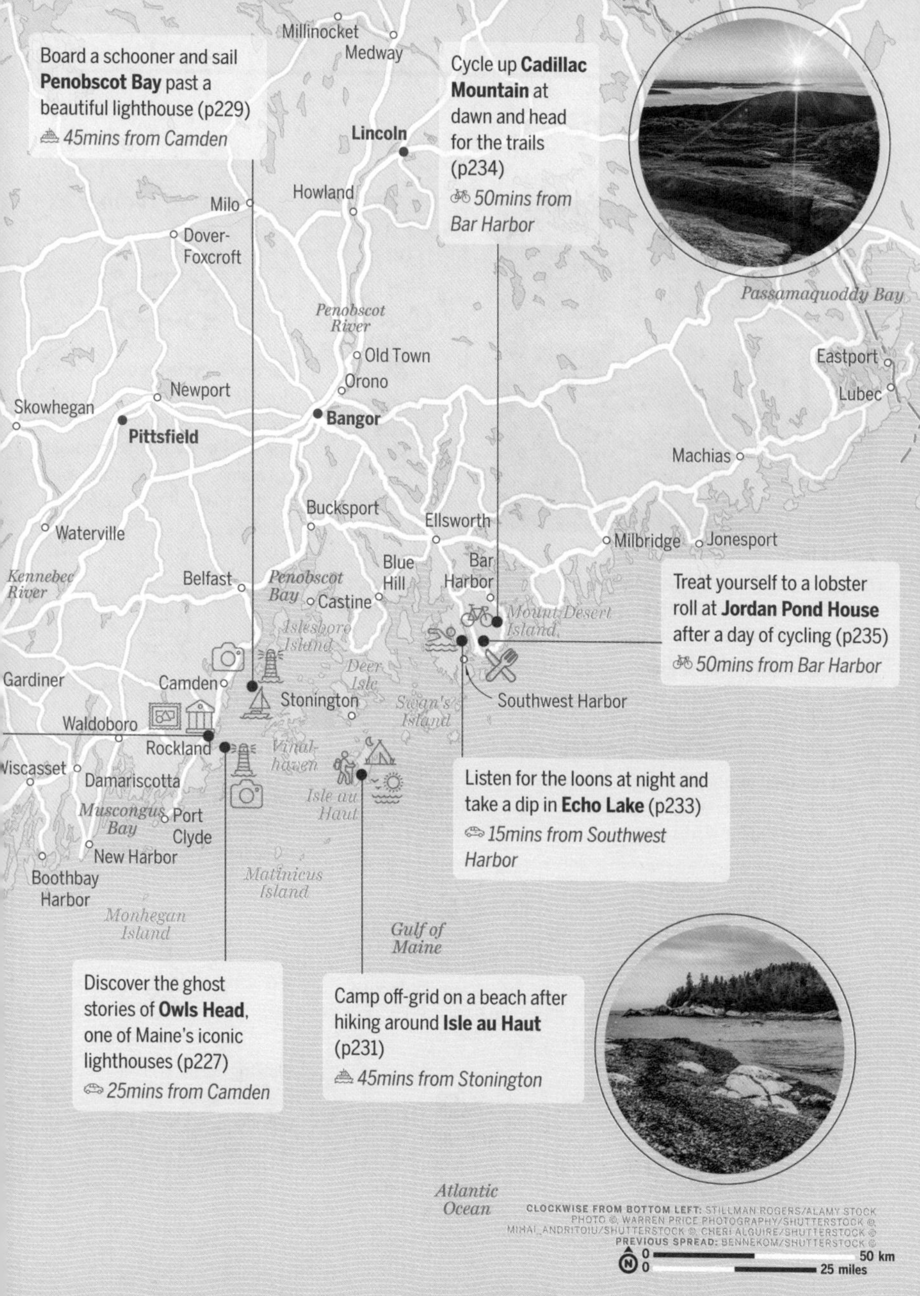

CLOCKWISE FROM BOTTOM LEFT: STILLMAN ROGERS/ALAMY STOCK PHOTO ©, WARREN PRICE PHOTOGRAPHY/SHUTTERSTOCK ©, MIHAI_ANDRITOIU/SHUTTERSTOCK ©, CHERI ALGUIRE/SHUTTERSTOCK © PREVIOUS SPREAD: BENNEKOM/SHUTTERSTOCK ©

Practicalities

ARRIVING

Bangor International Airport A smaller airport, this is the closest to stunning Acadia National Park and Down East Maine. Renting a car is essential.

Portland International Jetport (pictured) Maine's primary airport, serviced by budget airlines. Closest to beaches, Portland and the midcoast's art galleries. Best to rent a car for exploring.

Local regional airports Throughout Maine for private-jet access to remote locations across the lakes region and the North Woods.

HOW MUCH FOR A

Lobster off the boats $15

Moxie at general stores $1

Blueberry pie at town festivals $3

WHEN TO GO

JUN–AUG
Most crowded; perfect weather for beach and lake dips; insects.

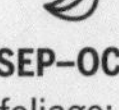

SEP–OCT
Stunning foliage; lighthouse tours and bicycle rides; no insects.

NOV–MAR
Cold but cozy; ice skating and downhill snow adventures.

APR–JUN
Mud season; lodging deals; empty beaches, art walks and rail-trail rides.

GETTING AROUND

Car and bicycle It's best to rent a car in Maine for access to remote towns, coves and hiking locations. There are cycling routes throughout Maine – some rail trails, some country roads. It's busy along the coast.

Public transportation The Amtrak Downeaster train links places from Boston to Portland. Bus services are limited, and available within the city centers of Bangor, Portland and along the coast during the summer.

Walking Portland is the most walkable. Most Maine towns have walking routes but you'll need a car to get there.

EATING & DRINKING

Portland is known as the foodie zone of Maine, with multiple outdoor eateries on the harbor as well as Michelin-starred bistros and specialty dining. Camden and Rockland are close seconds. Lobsters are abundant everywhere along the coast and inland. Out-of-the-way barn dinners, wine tastings, unique pizza cafes and brewpubs are highlights for 'where the locals eat' experience, with fewer crowds and local musicians playing blues, folk and country.

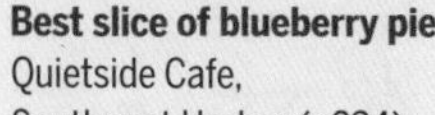

Best slice of blueberry pie
Quietside Cafe, Southwest Harbor (p234)

Must-try lobster roll
Off-the-boat-fresh at Seagull Seafood (p229)

CONNECT & FIND YOUR WAY

Wi-fi Generally available in cafes, restaurants and public facilities in the larger urban areas. Cell networks have good coverage in the southern and central portions of the state; it can be spotty along the coast and in the mountains.

Navigation Since connection can be spotty, it's worth bringing along a paper map when you travel.

WORTH THE SPLURGE

The Inn at Ocean's Edge (Lincolnville)

Cape Arundel Inn and Resort (Kennebunkport)

Lodge at Moosehead Lake (Greenville)

Quisisana Resort (Center Lovell)

Black Point Inn (Scarborough)

Island Inn (Monhegan)

WHERE TO STAY

Larger towns and cities have more accommodations options but are not as quaint as smaller coastal and lakeside locations. In the summer, the closer you get to the coast, the more expensive it is.

Town	Pro/Con
Portland	Walkable 'big city' buzz of art galleries, dining and Old Port alleyways. Crowded in summer.
Camden	Classic coastal town with quick access to islands. Go in off-season.
Bethel	Mountain central with ski-town vibe and river access; bring skis or canoe. Muddy in spring.
Southwest Harbor	Known as the quiet side of Acadia; less crowded than Bar Harbor. Traffic on main roads.
Augusta	Best budget options and close to the western lakes. More local, less hip.
Belfast	Harbor town, coastal exploration and less expensive lodging. Summertime through-traffic.

MONEY

Some diners or fish/lobster shacks only take cash. Making reservations ahead of time for summer locations is important.

46 Kick Back in the MOUNTAINS

SKIING | NIGHTLIFE | CANOEING

Bethel is an all-season town that becomes the mecca for hiking, cycling and floating in the summer. The winter here is pristine – rolling valleys, steep alpine runs and backcountry powder offer more than the usual ski-and-go-home experience. Come to play in the snow or sun, then relax at the pubs or inns in downtown Bethel.

How to

Getting here/around Limited public transport; driving is best. Parking can be a chore in prime season, so get up early and grab a coffee at DiCocoa's and get moving.

When to go Escape the crowds of midsummer and peak leaf-peeping fall by heading for the nearby Baldface Circle Trail for spring skiing, or take a hike at Blueberry Mountain and a dip at Rattlesnake Pool. Don't worry: there are no rattlesnakes.

Top tip Be the last one on the resort/mountains for a sunset 'snow-glow' view.

Take your pick of fresh-track backcountry, glide-zone Maine wood peacefulness, and big powder days.

Baldface Chutes A bald beauty in the quiet Evans Notch, this mountain pass between Maine and New Hampshire offers off-piste steeps and wide-open S-turn glory along empty ridge runs. North, South and Baldface Knob peaks are for the full-throttle crowd, but there are plenty of wide angles for moderate explorers. Caution: this is an avalanche zone during high-snow season, so be prepared. Hiking the **Baldface Circle Trail** in the summer offers a dip in beautiful Emerald Pool.

Bethel village trails With views of the Mahoosuc Range and rolling terrain, this is classic Nordic skiing at its best. If you want less windy winding through forest glades, connect to the **Pine Hill Trail** system for some zips and races. There are larger expeditions throughout this region on the **Inland Woods + Trails**

PEGGY NEWLAND/LONELY PLANET ©

Float the Androscoggin River Trail

Summers are made for canoeing down this wide expanse of rippling water rapids after spring melt in early June. Bring a friend and park one car in Gilead and another downriver in Bethel, and you've got a day's worth of rope-swinging leaps from granite ledges, island picnics and multiple 'jump from the boat over sandbars' swimming. Bring a fly-fishing rod and hook a rainbow or brook trout for supper, or find your perfect burger at the **Woody Food Truck** and wash it down with a Whitecap blueberry lager at **Steam Mill Brewing**.

system, easily added to a day of cross-country snow adventures.

Sunday River Surrounded by eight mountain peaks, this resort is just outside Bethel. White Heat is the steepest but Oz ski area is a wonderland during snow dumps. Après-ski heats up mid-afternoon at the pubs, so go early for a seat – or stay on the mountain for empty last runs.

Sugarloaf Near Kingfield, Sugarloaf resort is Sunday River's competitor for 'Big Maine Mountain' skiing. Try them both to pick your favorite.

Above Canoeing, Bethel.

Coastal CYCLING

CYCLING | COMMUNITY | BIRD-WATCHING

The East Coast Greenway (ECG) takes bike riders through 15 states and 450 cities, across 3000 miles from Maine to Florida. Coastal Maine has the country lanes, red barns, lake views and farm stands. Pine-laden, traffic-free rail trails combine with the most pristine bird-watching rides across a seaside marsh. Pick a route and take off for all things Maine.

PEGGY NEWLAND/LONELY PLANET ©

How to

Getting here/around Park at 'Park and Ride' lots throughout the state and take a day or longer weekend for inn-to-inn cycling.

When to go Summer and mid-fall can be crowded but it's stunning along the coast. Greenway routes are geared for country lanes and access to rail-trail riding.

Take your bike on a ferry Bring a bicycle on your visits to larger islands for backroad exploration to coves and rocky cliffs.

BEN MCCANNA/PORTLAND PORTLAND PRESS HERALD VIA GETTY IMAGES ©

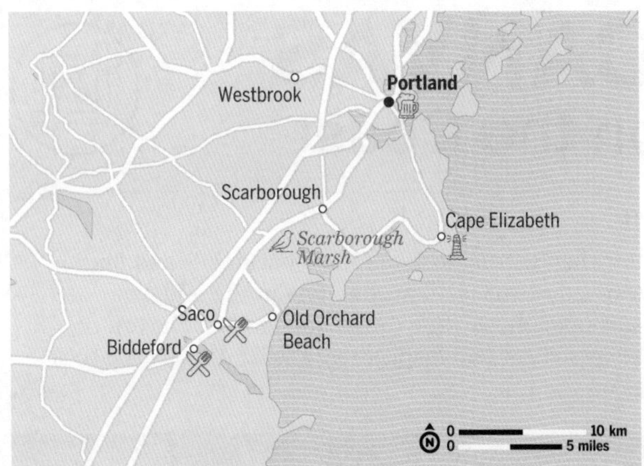

Top left Cycling, East Coast Greenway. **Bottom left** Blue heron, Scarborough Marsh.

All ECG signs are easily found as you ride the backroads of Kittery, Eliot and the Berwicks, over to Biddeford and Saco. Wind along the **Piscataqua River** and **Salmon Falls**, passing fruit and vegetable stands and fields full of sunflowers, and don't be surprised if a friendly farmer 'trackers over' to ask where you're off to.

The roads are quiet as the miles add up, and if peaches and fresh strawberries don't cut it appetite-wise, stop in downtown **Biddeford** or **Saco** where you'll find a multitude of coffee stores and places for lunch. Picnic tables are abundant in the fields before the beautiful rail trail in Saco, and you'll be encased in a tunnel of pine and oak forest as you glide over crushed gravel. There are no cars, just graded pathways through woodlands and marshes.

Don't miss **Scarborough Marsh**, complete with curved emerald-green and gold inlets – perfect cycling nirvana. Zip and zag through country lanes to the final rail trail over to **Portland** via the Million Dollar Bridge with its protected bicycle lanes. Portland is foodie-zone extraordinaire and, most importantly, full of breweries and bike-friendly inns.

If you want more for your cycling adventure, add in early morning rides around Portland's **Back Bay** and **Munjoy Hill**, or head back across the Million Dollar Bridge to the beaches of **Cape Elizabeth** with its famous lighthouses: iconic Portland Head Light and Two Lights.

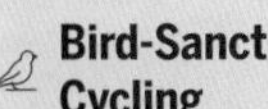

Bird-Sanctuary Cycling

A migration habitat extraordinaire, Scarborough Marsh is part of the **Maine Birding Trail** system. At this estuarine gem, watch for the zen-like ibis or the wing flash of the great blue herons and egrets. In the summer, **Maine Audubon** (maineaudubon.org) sets up a nature center for maps, tips and tours. Park your bike for a bit and rent a canoe for an estuary adventure on the twisting tributaries. If you're lucky, you'll spot willets and Hudsonian godwits.

Tip from the Scarborough Marsh Audubon Center: go at high tide to see flitting sparrows, stilt sandpipers and the occasional harbor seal.

48 CANVAS on the Coast

WALKING | ART | COASTLINE

There's nothing better than getting lost on Maine backroads and finding unique sculptures in misty meadows or plein-air painters in the midst of landscape creations. Pick a couple of coastline towns and look for the art, or explore the rocky ledges where artists find inspiration. Sunlight along the coast is special, coming at angles off the tide.

DEREK DAVIS/PORTLAND PORTLAND PRESS HERALD VIA GETTY IMAGES ©

How to

Getting here/around Stay off crowded Rte 1. Dead-end streets can lead you to beaches or picnic spots, but be aware of private dirt roads and communities. Most beaches, coves and paths have public access points.

When to go Spring is the best time to explore, but it can be muddy. Look for free museum days and summer open-studio events online.

Fairy houses Nature-inspired creations made of feather, moss, sea-shells, bark and pine are found along designated 'fairy house' trails.

S SHEPPARD/SHUTTERSTOCK ©

Ogunquit Situated on granite cliffs and with an art-colony history, the **Ogunquit Museum of American Art** has seaside sculptures, misty gardens and Edward Hopper in the house. Meander across the drawbridge to art-studio-encrusted **Perkins Cove**. Hike the 2-mile Atlantic stunner, **Marginal Way**, and find your perfect swimming cove.

Kennebunkport Explore village art walks and open studios along the wharfs at **Dock Square**. Rent a bicycle for a glide along **Ocean Avenue's** rugged coastline and spy sumptuous 'summer cottage' mansions and perfect picnic rocks. Bring a sketch pad or watercolors.

Boothbay The **Coastal Maine Botanical Gardens** has 300 acres of fairy houses, cliffside gardens and revolving sculpture events. There are meditation spaces, bee havens and a forest pond with stepping stones. Head to the local studios for root sculpture or to **Ovens Mouth Preserve** for your own inspiration.

Rockland This chic-central town is known as The Art Capital of Maine. Enjoy the **Wyeth Center** at the **Farnsworth Art Museum** or head to nearby **Cushing** to see where he was inspired. Discover your own inner artist at **ArtLab Open Studio** classes. The downtown offers occasional 'closed-street' walks.

Prouts Neck Imagine a genteel 'summer cottage' history, Atlantic on three sides and a painter with the soul of a seafarer. A hike along these rocks leads past images off Winslow Homer's canvases. The **Cliff Walk** is best traveled at sunset as you pass Homer's house, now a museum. Seagulls careen and waves crash, so bring a paintbrush.

Top left Ogunquit Museum of American Art. **Bottom left** Olson House.

Artist House Tours

Make sure to visit these unique museums:

Winslow Homer Studio Reserve tickets at the Portland Museum of Art and tour the Homer House on Prouts Neck.

Rockwell Kent – James Fitzgerald House and Studio Located on Monhegan Island; special dates with reservations required from the Monhegan Museum of Art and History.

Olson House This reservation tour will take you to the location of Andrew Wyeth's *Christina's World*. Part of the Farnsworth Museum Collection, the house is located in Cushing.

■ **Recommended by Kristen Levesque,** *a communications specialist for the arts based in Maine (kristenlevesquepr.com)*

UNIQUE GIFTS
from Maine

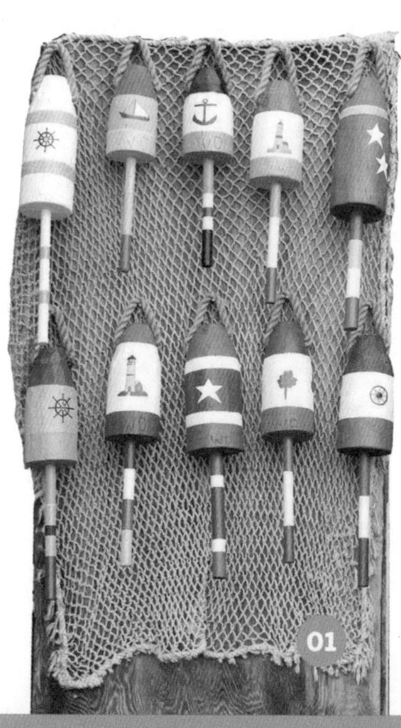

01 Painted lobster buoy

This souvenir can be found at thrift shops and lobster pounds. Look for the most colorful and decorate your garden back home.

02 Maine tourmaline

Snag yourself some earrings, or necklaces in greens and teals.

03 Sea-glass necklace

Find your own on the beaches or head to an artist studio for unique creations.

04 Maine seaweed

Soaps, shampoos, body balms, salts and dried salad toppings.

05 Painted recycled sailcloth
Purses, pillows, shirts, bags – all with nautical renderings.

06 Maine maple syrup
Head to sugarhouses for pancakes and this golden treat.

07 Shipped lobster
Any lobster pound on the coast will ship a live one to you.

08 Ayuh T-shirt
Capture this colorful Mainer saying as you walk the coastal towns.

01 CULLIGANPHOTO/ALAMY STOCK PHOTO ©, **02** GREG C GRACE/ALAMY STOCK PHOTO ©, **03** RACHELSSEAGLASS/STOCKIMO/ALAMY STOCK PHOTO ©, **04** JENNIFER BOOHER/ALAMY STOCK PHOTO ©, **05** JOHN EWING/PORTLAND PRESS HERALD VIA GETTY IMAGES ©, **06** STEACK/SHUTTERSTOCK ©, **07** ANTONIO GRAVANTE/SHUTTERSTOCK ©, **08** AIRDONE/SHUTTERSTOCK © & PABLO MASTEPANO/SHUTTERSTOCK ©

49 Windjammer WONDERS

SAILING | NAUTICAL HISTORY | SEAFOOD

There's nothing more majestic than watching the wind fill the white sails of a four-masted schooner charting its course along the rugged coast of Maine. If you're aboard one, all the better. With multiple options to get your 'sea legs' on – from day trips to longer, overnight jaunts – you'll cruise past cozy coves and coastal villages and be part of a maritime community.

PLANETPIX/ALAMY STOCK PHOTO ©

How to

When to go Summer has ideal weather but it gets crowded. For deals, go in late spring or early fall. Summer tours and exhibits abound all along the coast; book ahead. For events, check the Maine Windjammer Association (*sailmaine coast.com*).

Top tip Sleep on the deck at night if you don't enjoy tight berths. Slumber under the stars, rocked by the tide.

Nautical museums Get into the schooner mood at the Maine State Museum (Augusta), the Sail Power and Steam Museum (Rockland) or the Maine Maritime Museum (Bath).

JEFFREY ISAAC GREENBERG 2+/ALAMY STOCK PHOTO ©

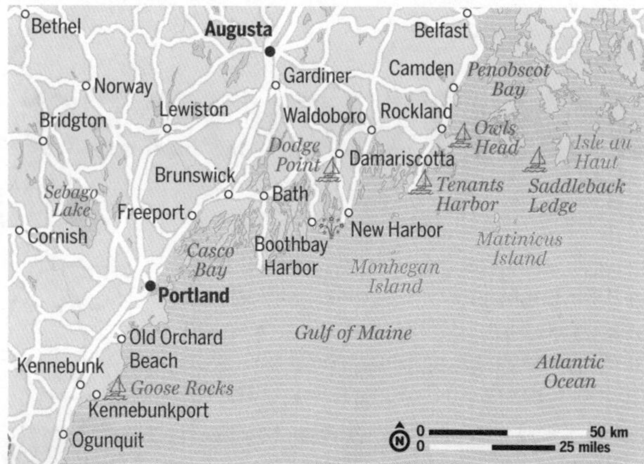

Sunsets and sea shanties Pick a smaller harbor for a schooner tour and explore hidden coves and private rocky islands along this cranny-filled coastline during the day. Perch on the bowsprit as you cruise past **Tenants Harbor**, **Saddleback Ledge**, **Goose Rocks** and **Dodge Point**, and don't miss **Owls Head**. If you are 'way Down East' near Lubec, you'll spy Canada. Afternoons can be spent lolling on the deck with après-nautical cocktails or taking a putter over to the mainland on a dinghy for a walking tour of tiny towns. Dinners are true open-air experiences with tables set for sunset views. Prepared below deck in galleys, most are hearty and locally inspired – think grilled swordfish or steamed clams, kale with cranberries, purple Aroostook potatoes, or nutty Brie flecked with herbs. Sea shanties about hauling the line and rounding the bend and Whiskey Johnnies are common refrains, and all are sung loudly, with stamping feet and clapping hands, most evenings after dinner. In the mornings, wake early so you can help raise the headsails and haul anchor for another day on the Atlantic.

What's a windjammer? Schooners, or windjammers, typically have two or more masts, with a foremast smaller than the main, but some larger vessels have up to seven whipping in the wind. The name is related to a Scottish word, meaning 'skipping across the water.'

Top left Windjammer Days parade, Boothbay Harbor. **Bottom left** Maine State Museum.

Windjammer Days

The **Windjammer Days** in Boothbay Harbor is a summer festival of all things schooner-related: pirates, parades, fireworks, codfish races, antique boats and a harbor aglow with fleets of schooners. It takes place in June every year.

50 Lobsters & LIGHTHOUSES

PHOTOGRAPHY | COAST | SEAFOOD

The Maine coast is craggy, with sheer cliffs and jagged-edged islands, and this means you'll find lighthouses wherever you explore. If it's a stormy day, you'll be treated to smashing tide and blackened clouds, and with foghorn blaring and clanging buoy, you'll be inside a symphonic landscape. Add lobster rolls and you've got a plan.

MONICA FIGUEROA/SHUTTERSTOCK ©

Trip Notes

Getting around Some lighthouses are off the mainland and require mail-boat rides or kayak rentals. Most are drive-worthy. A few are a long haul Down East but worth the sunrise settings.

When to go Spring for coastal wildflowers around the keeper's houses; summer for clear skies; late autumn for storm squalls and large waves.

Top tip Go at low tide or sunset for better photography angles and exposed shadows off rocks.

Sleeping with Seafaring Spirits

There's something romantic about sleeping in a lighthouse. If star-crossed-lover ghosts reside inside as well, you'll have a story to tell. Stay for a night if you dare and walk the spiral staircases, watching for the phantom lantern flashing over the dark sea. For options, check uslhs.org.

01 Pack your lunch and ferry over to rugged **Seguin Island** with sandy coves for foggy explorations. Cobblestone beach and trestle-built tramway lead up to the highest light in Maine.

02 Overlooking Muscongus Bay and Johns Bay, exposed rock ledges jutting upward at low tide frame the keeper's house at **Pemaquid**. Maybe you'll see the 'lady in the red shawl' on the shore while you enjoy a lobster roll from Seagull Seafood.

03 Grab a haddock melt at **Owls Head** general store and try to find the 'head of an owl' on the cliffside rocks of this whitewashed lighthouse. Stroll the pine forests overlooking Penobscot Bay.

04 You'll want a lobster and egg roll for **Bass Harbor Head**, the Hulls Cove beauty on the quiet side of Acadia National Park. Parking is limited, so go early for sunrise views over Blue Hill Bay.

05 **West Quoddy Head** (pictured opposite) is 'way up theyah' with first-in-the-nation sunrise views and empty, rocky beaches. Look over to Canada or take a boat across the border to Grand Manan Island.

TOP: PUT ARMSTRONG/SHUTTERSTOCK ©
BOTTOM: JAMES GRIFFITHS PHOTO/SHUTTERSTOCK ©

51 Find Your Island GETAWAY

SEASIDE | SOLITUDE | COVES

Unique islands dot the coast, each boasting maritime histories, generational lobstering, summering cottage and art communities and hideaway camps. According to Maine Coastal Island Registry, there are close to 4000 islands, give or take – at low tide, piles of nubble rocks. With the scent of seaweed and fir, find your rustic escape or cultured getaway.

Camp Quiet

Become your own Robinson Crusoe by going off-grid at tent sites on **Jewell**, **Tinker** or **Little Chebeague** islands. It's on a first-come, first-served basis, but the rewards are no cell reception, misty silence, empty coves, seal sightings and a full sky of stars. You'll share your time with migrating birds and squirrels. For options, check mcht.org.

Trip Notes

Getting around Stay at a hotel in Portland for day-tripping to some Casco Bay islands, or find your own island getaway. Take a mail boat to offshore islands for a true Maine experience.

When to go Ferries are easily accessible from the mainland but in the summer you'll need reservations. Fall is a great time to visit – fewer crowds, more color.

Learn more Check out the Island Institute *(islandinstitute.org)* for all things history and islands.

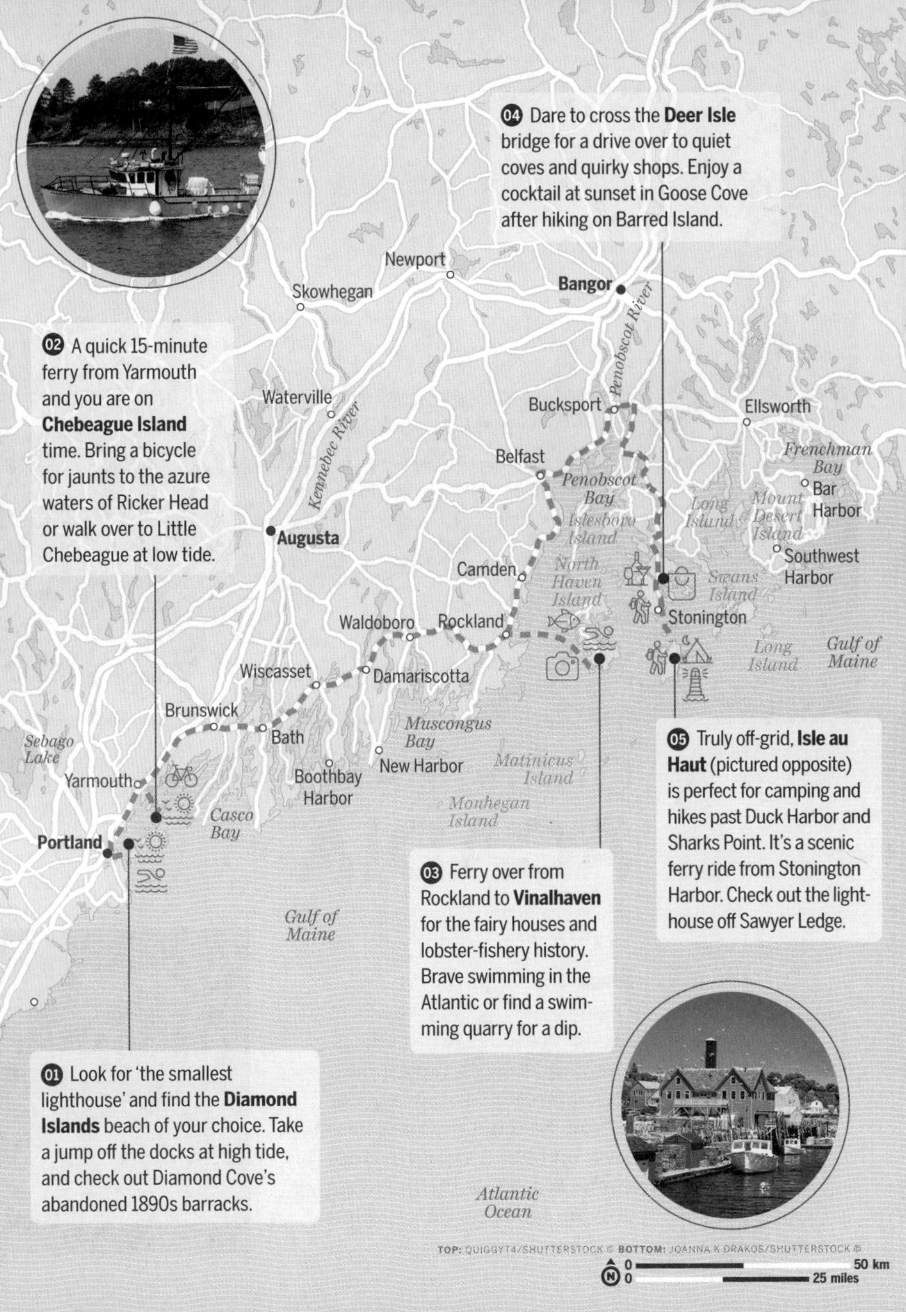

04 Dare to cross the Deer Isle bridge for a drive over to quiet coves and quirky shops. Enjoy a cocktail at sunset in Goose Cove after hiking on Barred Island.
02 A quick 15-minute ferry from Yarmouth and you are on Chebeague Island time. Bring a bicycle for jaunts to the azure waters of Ricker Head or walk over to Little Chebeague at low tide.
Newport
Skowhegan
Bangor
Penobscot River
Waterville
Kennebec River
Bucksport
Ellsworth
Frenchman Bay
Belfast
Penobscot Bay
Bar Harbor
Mount Desert Island
Long Island
Islesboro Island
Augusta
Camden
North Haven Island
Southwest Harbor
Swans Island
Stonington
Waldoboro
Rockland
Long Island
Gulf of Maine
Wiscasset
Damariscotta
Brunswick
Bath
Muscongus Bay
Sebago Lake
Yarmouth
Boothbay Harbor
New Harbor
Matinicus Island
Monhegan Island
Casco Bay
Portland
05 Truly off-grid, Isle au Haut (pictured opposite) is perfect for camping and hikes past Duck Harbor and Sharks Point. It's a scenic ferry ride from Stonington Harbor. Check out the lighthouse off Sawyer Ledge.
03 Ferry over from Rockland to Vinalhaven for the fairy houses and lobster-fishery history. Brave swimming in the Atlantic or find a swimming quarry for a dip.
Gulf of Maine
01 Look for 'the smallest lighthouse' and find the Diamond Islands beach of your choice. Take a jump off the docks at high tide, and check out Diamond Cove's abandoned 1890s barracks.
Atlantic Ocean
N
0 50 km
0 25 miles

52 Off the Beaten Paths of ACADIA

MOUNTAINS | CYCLING | HIKING

One of the best places to decompress on the East Coast, Acadia National Park with its mountains, lakes, ponds and gorgeous vistas is the gemstone of New England. Located 'Down East' on Mount Desert Island, this landscape is filled with adventure, both on land and on sea. Find your hidden cove.

JASON BUSA/SHUTTERSTOCK ©

How to

Getting around You'll need a car or bicycle for trips to hikes, lake dips and island tours. Use the free Island Explorer shuttle for easy access to trails.

When to go Bar Harbor is crowded in the summer; stay in quieter harbors or come off-season for more peacefulness.

Get festive Bar Harbor Music Festival is held in late June and July. Fourth of July has parades, fireworks and lobster races.

Where to start The Hulls Cove Visitor Center is the place to plan your adventure.

PEGGY NEWLAND/LONELY PLANET ©

Southwest Peacefulness

Summers are best spent on the quieter sides: Southwest Harbor, Trenton or Bass Harbor. Sunflowers abound and bluffs are filled with spruce-edged paths over granite ledges as you make picture-postcard memories hiking, cycling and exploring working harbors and tranquil marinas. Elevated Dorr and Cadillac Mountains can be spied atop **Acadia Mountain**. Quarried stone-stepped hikes take you up Mansell and Beech Mountains, all overlooking **Echo Lake** for après-hike dips. For unique hiking, head to the **Beehive Loop** or the **Precipice Trail** (watch for trail closures during peregrine-falcon nesting) for cliff climbs skirting up iron ladders through narrow breaks of granite. Moss gardens are abundant throughout the national park.

JOHN WESOLOWSKI/SHUTTERSTOCK ©

Tiny Beaches

Hulls Cove Swim with your dog or hunt sea glass. Get views over Frenchman Bay.

Little Hunter Camping at Blackwoods? Head to this hidden cobblestone beach.

Seawall Staying at Seawall Campground? Perfect sunrise swims here.

Seal Harbor Sandy swimming and a picnic lunch on this cove-side beach.

Top left Beehive Trail. **Bottom left** Moss garden, Acadia National Park. **Top right** Cycling, Acadia National Park.

Head to **Bass Harbor** for lighthouses and uncrowded hikes on the Wonderland and Ship Harbor Trails. Downtown **Southwest Harbor** is quaint, walkable, artful Maine. Get blueberry pie at **Quietside Cafe** and Maine brews like Thunder Hole, Wise Guys or Scuppers. Check out the **Charlotte Rhoades Park and Butterfly Garden**. End the day with a swim in Echo Lake.

Down East Islands

Bring a bike on the ferry over from Southwest or Northeast Harbor to the **Cranberry Isles** – Great and Little Cranberry – to enjoy cove-side picnics on Gilley Beach.

Ferry and bike it from Bass Harbor to **Swan's Island** and check out the beautiful Burnt Coat Harbor Lighthouse. Grab a sandwich at the Island Market and take a hike down to Fine Sands Beach.

Ride the Rock Bridges

Graded crushed stone paths meandering up scenic mountain vistas and around pristine lakesides offer 45 miles of excellent cycling.

🚲 Sunrise Cycling

Start at dawn for this beauty ride. Spy the gorgeous **Sand Beach** and iconic **Thunder Hole** and look for **Otter Cliffs**, tight ledges of granite, lupine growing wild. In the morning light, the 27-mile **Park Loop Road** is a tranquil slip through canopied pines and crashing surf. **Cadillac Mountain**, a 1530ft charmer, is a challenge – but at sunrise, you'll be treated to 360-degree views from every hairpin curve. Watch for hawks riding thermals before your last slog up to the flat-topped peak. Take a well-deserved breath before you zip the wild ride down to town for breakfast.

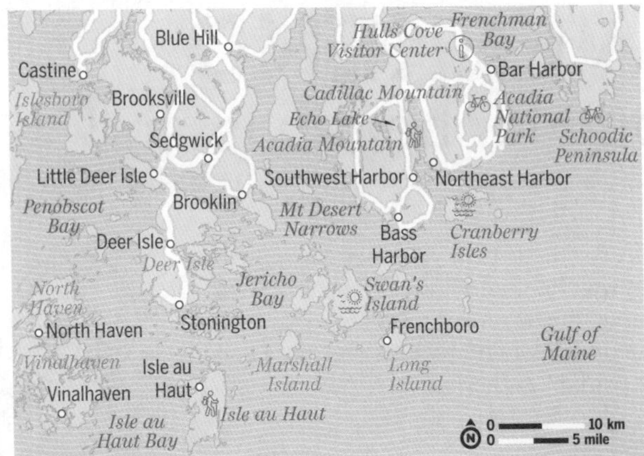

Twenty-seven years in the making, this historic trail system links various coves and villages. Originally built for horse carriages by the Rockefeller family, these routes offer quiet even in the middle of summer. A series of 17 rock bridges loop and hairpin-curve along ledges, with waterfalls abundant in the spring. It's an easy ride along **Eagle Lake** or **Aunt Betty Pond**, and some challenging loops will take you around **Sargent** and **Parkman** mountains. You'll have views over the Blue Hills, dotted Frenchman Bay islands and **Somes Sound**, the only fjord on the East Coast. Cedar signposts at most intersections help with choices, and most cyclists end up at **Jordan Pond House** for a popover and a water-bottle fill-up.

Utilize the free Island Explorer shuttle for to/from cycling ease. Most buses accept bicycles. Small parking lots fill up quickly.

Nooks & Crannies of Acadia

Pack your hiking boots and a lunch and spend the day hoofing around the **Isle au Haut** coastline, with dips along the way at Goss Beach or Long Pond. Rustic camping is available.

Take the ferry from Bar Harbor to the **Schoodic Peninsula** and bike the trails around this nook of uncrowded headlands, cliffs and beaches. Don't miss the sunset at Raven's Nest!

Left Cycling, Cadillac Mtn. **Below** Popovers and tea, Jordan Pond House.

FAR LEFT: INARTS/SHUTTERSTOCK © LEFT: JENLO8/SHUTTERSTOCK ©

53 WEEKEND on Monhegan Island

ART | HIKING | HISTORY

Once the last ferry leaves the island, you'll see artists with easels, photographers capturing light and hikers returning from cliffside jaunts. There's pop-up music on various porches and jamborees in the church on open-mic nights. Inns are spare and have communal spaces for twilight gatherings.

E.J.JOHNSON PHOTOGRAPHY/SHUTTERSTOCK ©

How to

Getting here/around Take a ferry over to Monhegan from Port Clyde, Boothbay Harbor or New Harbor (reservations are required). It's a rollicking ride on often foggy seas.

When to go There are daily ferries between Memorial Day weekend and mid- to late October. On other dates, ferry and on-island services are limited.

Tip If you're staying overnight, bring a flashlight as the rocky, dirt roads are unlit except for stars or moonlight.

MICHAEL VENTURA/ALAMY STOCK PHOTO ©

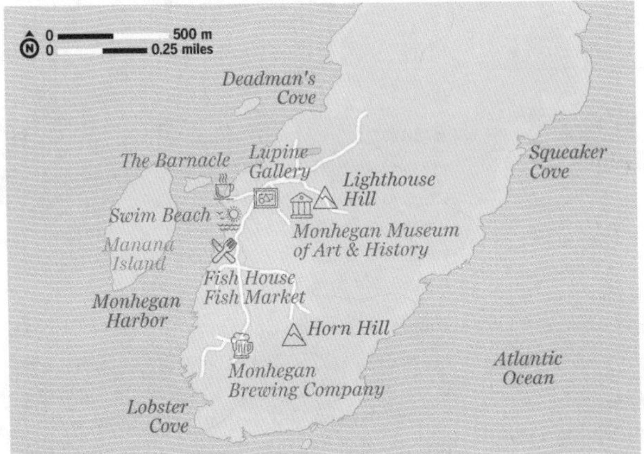

The artists' island Monhegan was established as a primary residency for artists in the mid-19th century. Join the history of the Hudson River School, American Impressionists and Modernists through the lens of idyllic coves, jagged headlands and foggy forests. Many galleries and studios have open houses. Perhaps you'll be inspired by shingled fish houses, or granite ledges filled with light and thrashing tide. Bring a paintbrush.

Morning stroll Wake up before the first ferry arrives and grab a coffee at **The Barnacle**. Head up Wharf Hill Rd and note artists setting up easels near **Lupine Gallery**. Look for **Lighthouse Hill** and hike up to the 'second-highest light' on the East Coast and the whitewashed jewel of the Monhegan Museum. Take a dirt path down **Horn Hill**, and peek into the community church. Loop down to the fish houses and take a dip at **Swim Beach**.

Hike to beer Tighten your boots and hike around the island past **Deadman's Cove**, looking for Pebble Beach and Cathedral Woods Trails. There are 17 miles of moss forests, fairy houses and rocky outcroppings, with offshoots past **Squeaker Cove** and **Gull Cove**. Once you discover the shipwreck of *D. T. Sheridan* near **Lobster Cove**, look for lobster-themed **Monhegan Brewing Company**. There's a Trap Stacker Ale waiting for you.

Sunset dinners Off-the-boat lobster, fish stew or fried-haddock sandwiches can be found at **Fish House Fish Market**. Make it dinner on the rocks for sunset – sand mixed with sea glass shines at dusk, and the island turns purple as the moon rises over the harbor.

Top left Main St, Monhegan Island. **Bottom left** The Barnacle.

Magnificent Museum

The **Monhegan Museum of Art and History** sits like a crown jewel atop Lighthouse Hill. Open from June 24 to September 30, this is the East Coast's most unique museum, with a setting to take your breath away. Created by volunteers and artists, with a focus on showcasing Monhegan's cultural, natural and community-based spirit, this is the true heartbeat of Maine. The keeper's cottage is chock-full of seafaring history: nautical maps, maritime paintings, collections of fishing lures, anchors, shipbuilding tools, and even Thomas Edison's gramophone. Rotating exhibits – incluing Andrew Wyeth, Rockwell Kent, Alice Swett, George Bellows and James Fitzgerald – will keep you mesmerized.

Listings

BEST OF THE REST

Outdoor Drinks & Nibbles

Quarry Tap Room $

Rustic spot in Hallowell with river views and music. If you want your exercise before your beer and burger, cycle the Kennebec River Rail Trail and earn your IPA or pale ale afterward.

Funky Bow Beer Company $

Enjoy microbrews in the North Woods and hear the fiddling in rural Lyman. Dance around the farmlands as you sip single batch brews to bands under the tent. Down-home fun and excellent afternoons.

Blaze $$

Patio-hopping in Bar Harbor? You'll end up here, for a ready-to-relax vibe after a day on carriage trails. Hipsters in bike shorts and hiking boots come for wood-fired pizzas and 34 draft beers on tap.

Newcastle Publick House $$

Terrace on the square in Newcastle. Organic, local and featuring famed Damariscotta oysters on the half-shell, this is a place for friendly bartenders pouring Maine Whoopie Pie stouts by the glassful.

Thirsty Pig $$

Cityscape patio for watching the cool kids drinking craft brews with their pooches. Share your flight of house-made sausages with Fido, but keep the pickles and porters for yourself.

Nocturnem Draft Haus $

Laid-back pub in bustling Bangor. Come for the retro vinyl nights and stay for the Belgian Dubbels and Munich Dunkels. German-fest-type fun with a rotating style of beer play and festive gatherings.

Bramhall $$

Hideaway garden in a historic Portland neighborhood. You'll feel in the know at this speakeasy-styled, stained-glass-lit nook of a hip zone. Get your cocktail on with a touch of urban class.

Allagash Brewing Company $$

Lumberjack-industrial vibe with Belgium brews. Located in Portland just off-center of the city, this is sustainable 'beer with a purpose' with an outward style toward community-building. Hang here for awhile.

Caffeine Fix

Northport Landing Gallery & Espresso Bar $

Art and a cup of joe in Belfast. Locals and artists join together for morning gatherings and community discussions. Bronzes, paintings and espresso – what could be more perfect?

Mornings in Paris $$

France revisited on the Maine coast in Kennebunkport. Walk along Ocean Ave for your wake-up, then come to this sunny spot for a buttery croissant and elegantly styled coffees.

Newcastle Publick House

Lil's Cafe $

Homemade doughnuts and an art-inspired latte in Kittery. Kittery Foreside is the zone for everything sidewalk and local, and Lil's is the place for starting the day. Bring some bread home.

Bard Coffee $$

Walk-up cup of Joe; located in Portland. Sunlight and single-origin brews mixed with an eclectic morning crowd make for an energy pickup in the afternoon.

Zoot Coffee $$

Vegan muffins and lots of morning light in Camden. Everything is homemade, and the vibe is sleek, European and often crowded during the summer. Go early and stay.

Choco-Latte $$

Specialty cups and plenty of sidewalk views in Bar Harbor. Chocolate is a theme, so if you like it rich and creamy, come for the coffee brews with a decadent edge for wake-up calls.

Little Notch Bakery $

Afternoon pickup and excellent sandwiches in Southwest Harbor. Nothing is more quaint and bread more fresh than this place. Have some blueberry pie for breakfast.

Lobster Every Which Way

Geddy's $$

Lobster pizza – the classic place to be in Bar Harbor, filled with college kids working the counter, folks from every corner of the world, and lobsters by the pound.

2 Cats $

Lobster omelet – hip breakfast place in an elegant house close to downtown Bar Harbor. Sit on the lawns if you're waiting for your table and watch the world go by.

STAN TESS/ALAMY STOCK PHOTO ©

Geddy's

Holy Donut $

Lobster doughnut – sounds gross, but people buy them by the dozen. There are 16 flavors to choose from if you decide against crustacean. Located in Portland.

Cook's Lobster & Ale House $$

Lobster martini – lobster spiced the Maine-bar-scene way on a beautiful lip of land on Bailey Island. Stay for dinner if you're close to sunset.

Ben & Bill's Chocolate Emporium $$

Lobster ice cream or chocolate – of course, after a full day, why not have sugar with your lobster? Ask for a double dip. Located in Bar Harbor.

Stewman's Lobster Pound $$

Lobster Bloody Mary – now you're talking! Start with this pick-me-up, and continue on to a seaweed-brined two-pounder accompanied with corn on the cob. Located in Bar Harbor.

Oxbow Brewing Company $

Lobster beer – lobster meat and a kettle full of boiled wort during the brewing makes for a limited-edition *saison* for the summer. Located in Portland.

Scan to find more things to do in Maine online

Practicalities

Right Hiking, Echo Lake (p193)

EASY STEPS FROM THE AIRPORT TO THE CITY CENTER

Boston Logan International Airport is the main entry point for New England. It's located east of the city center and across the harbor in East Boston. It's not huge but there are four terminals (A, B, C and E), connected by free Massport shuttle buses. Most international flights arrive at Terminal E.

AT THE AIRPORT

SIM CARDS
SIM cards are available for purchase at InMotion stores in Terminals B, C and E. However, the stores are located behind the TSA checkpoint, so if you arrive on an international flight you may not be able to access them.

CURRENCY EXCHANGE
International currency exchange is available in the arrivals hall of Terminal E, but rates are less advantageous than at banks in town.

2P2PLAY/SHUTTERSTOCK ©

WI-FI
Free wi-fi is available throughout Logan, including the rideshare pickup points. Select the network BOSWifi and accept the terms of service to connect.

ATMS
Cash points are available in every terminal before and after the TSA checkpoints.

CHARGING STATIONS
You can find charging stations in waiting areas throughout the airport. They are free of charge and accommodate US (type A or B) plugs or USB cords.

CUSTOMS REGULATIONS

Personal exemptions Each traveler is permitted to bring up to $800 worth of merchandise into the US without incurring any duty.

Alcohol and tobacco Each visitor is allowed to bring 1L of liquor and 200 cigarettes into the US without paying any duty, as long as they are at least 21 and 18 years of age, respectively.

GETTING TO THE CITY CENTER

BUS

Silver line buses pick up at each terminal and run through the Seaport District to South Station, where you can transfer to the red line subway. It's free from the airport but otherwise $2.40. Convenient for Seaport, Downtown, Beacon Hill and Cambridge.

BLUE LINE SUBWAY

Take the free airport shuttle No 22, 33 or 55 to the Airport T-station. Connects with the orange line (at State) or the green line (at Government Center). One-way $2.40. Convenient for West End, Back Bay and Fenway.

BOSTON WATER TAXI

(bostonwatertaxi.com) Buy tickets online. Take the free airport shuttle No 66 to Logan Dock and call for service. Runs to various points on Charlestown, Downtown Boston and Seaport waterfronts.

TAXIS

Taxis pick up right outside the terminals. Fees and tolls totaling $4.50 to $5 are added to the metered fare.

RIDESHARE

Lyft and Uber pick up in designated areas in Central Parking. Follow the signs.

MBTA FARES

A one-way fare is $2.40 for the subway or silver line bus, $1.70 for the regular local bus.

MBTA PASSES

These passes cover unlimited travel on the subway, local bus and silver line bus. Get a one-day pass for $12.75 or a seven-day pass for $22.50. Buy your pass at any MBTA kiosk at Logan Airport or any T-station.

OTHER POINTS OF ENTRY

Many international travelers fly into New York City and drive north to New England. Trains from New York arrive at South Station, located in central Boston, with a designated red line subway station. Aside from Boston and New York, several other airports in the region receive national and international flights.

Bangor International Airport in Maine is served by regional carriers.

Bradley International Airport is New England's second-largest airport, located 12 miles north of Hartford, CT, in Windsor Locks. The Bradley Flyer bus runs to the city center and takes about 40 minutes.

Burlington International Airport is Vermont's major airport.

TF Green Airport is 20 minutes south of Providence. The MBTA commuter rail runs to Providence or Boston.

Manchester-Boston Regional Airport is a quiet alternative to Logan, located just 55 miles north of Boston in New Hampshire.

Portland International Jetport serves coastal Maine. Bus No 5 runs to downtown Portland.

TRANSPORTATION TIPS TO HELP YOU GET AROUND

Driving is the way to go in much of New England, both practically and visually. While public transportation is developed in bigger cities like Boston and its suburbs, it's sparser and more sporadic elsewhere. In rural areas, public transportation is nonexistent. In the fall, nothing beats a drive through the mountains. In summer, coastal drives are especially beautiful.

PUBLIC TRANSPORT

Mass transit in New England varies wildly depending on where you are. Buses and trains are plentiful in densely populated places like Connecticut and Boston and its suburbs, but services are limited or even nonexistent in rural areas.

FERRIES

Ferries take travelers between mainland and island destinations like Martha's Vineyard and Block Island. Buses or trolleys often operate locally in heavily touristed spots like Salem, Massachusetts and Ogunquit, Maine.

TRAINS

Connecticut, Massachusetts and parts of Rhode Island are generally well served by inexpensive, reliable trains. In Northern New England, though, they're harder to come by and more expensive. For instance, Amtrak offers train service to just a few towns and cities between Maine, New Hampshire and Boston via its Downeaster line and between Vermont, Connecticut and Massachusetts on its Vermonter line.

WINTER DRIVING

New England winters are cold and snowy; driving can be dangerous during and after snowfall. Heed advice from local authorities to stay off the road. Rural or mountainous roads may close during winter. In spring, watch out for potholes and 'frost heaves' (sections of pavement that have buckled and risen from freezing and thawing water).

BICYCLES

Bike lanes are sporadic – some towns and cities have them but many don't. That's why rail trails are a good option for those who want to bike without traffic. Several, like the Cape Cod Rail Trail and the Minuteman Bikeway, connect multiple towns.

DRIVING ESSENTIALS

Drive on the right; the steering wheel is on the left.

Toll roads in Maine, New Hampshire, Vermont and Massachusetts are connected by the E-ZPass system *(e-zpassiag.com)*. Vermont and Connecticut don't collect tolls.

The blood alcohol limit is 0.08% for drivers 21 and older.

Highway speed limit is 65mph, unless otherwise posted.

Driving age ranges from 16 to 16.5 across states.

KNOW YOUR CARBON FOOTPRINT

A domestic flight from Boston to Portland, Maine, would emit about 23.5kg of carbon dioxide per passenger. A bus between those two cities would emit about 20kg per passenger. A train would emit about 1kg. There are a number of carbon calculators online. We use Resurgence at resurgence.org/resources/carbon-calculator.

ROTARIES

In other parts of the world, travelers might be familiar with roundabouts or traffic circles, but New Englanders (and their road signs) refer to these circular intersections as a 'rotary.'

TRAFFIC

Bostonians flee to points north (New Hampshire and Maine) and south (Cape Cod and the islands) on summer weekends, so be ready for wicked traffic heading out of the city on Fridays and heading back on Sundays.

PLANES

Boston's Logan is the region's busiest and biggest airport, but smaller international and regional airports operate throughout New England. Cape Air is an independent, regional carrier that services a handful of cities and towns in Massachusetts, New Hampshire, Vermont and Maine and beyond.

ROAD DISTANCE CHART (MILES)

	Southwest Harbor, ME	Boston, MA	Salem, MA	Providence, RI	Newport, RI	New Haven, CT	Hartford, CT	Burlington, VT	Montpelier, VT	Portsmouth, NH	Jackson, NH
Boston, MA	285										
Salem, MA	268	25									
Providence, RI	336	50	76								
Newport, RI	350	72	93	34							
New Haven, CT	409	138	156	105	105						
Hartford, CT	373	101	120	86	86	39					
Burlington, VT	338	217	220	265	298	273	236				
Montpelier, VT	300	180	183	230	273	237	200	39			
Portsmouth, NH	226	58	44	106	145	186	150	207	172		
Jackson, NH	223	150	133	202	234	275	238	142	102	92	
Portland, ME	107	108	95	157	196	236	201	209	222	51	70

SAFE TRAVEL

New England is one of the safest regions of the United States, with Maine, New Hampshire and Vermont regularly ranked the 'safest' states in terms of violent crime. However, wildlife, blizzards and rough seas can derail your travels.

FIREARMS

Rules about firearms vary widely between states, with New Hampshire laws being much more permissive than neighboring Massachusetts, for example. Each New England state has its own rules for the sale, possession and use of firearms, and what's allowed in one state may be illegal just across the border.

TICKS

While there are several tick varieties, in New England only the tiny black-legged (deer) ticks carry Lyme disease. Deer ticks are common in New England, especially in grassy or woodland areas. Hikers should use insect repellent, wear light-colored clothing, tuck long pants into socks, and check their body regularly.

OCEAN SAFETY

A healthy respect for the ocean and its strength is a must for any day at the beach. Beware of posted warnings about rip currents and rough swimming conditions, and use extreme caution when swimming anywhere lifeguards aren't on duty. Flat spots between breaking waves indicate a rip current.

MARIJUANA

Recreational marijuana use is legal in four New England states: Connecticut, Maine, Massachusetts and Vermont. Having small amounts will get you fines in New Hampshire and Rhode Island.

CAPPI THOMPSON/GETTY IMAGES ©

KEITH J FINKS/SHUTTERSTOCK ©

COVID-19

New England has one of the highest COVID-19 vaccination rates in the US. Mask and vaccine rules can vary by state and municipality and change according to local COVID rates. Check local sources.

BLIZZARDS

New England often gets whacked with heavy snowfall and power outages. What differentiates a blizzard from your run-of-the-mill snowstorm are high and sustained wind gusts and limited visibility from snow, known as 'whiteout' conditions.

BEARS

Campers, especially in Maine, New Hampshire and Vermont, should be cautious of black bears. If you can, lock food and garbage in your car's trunk or store it in a bear cannister. Never store food inside your tent.

QUICK TIPS TO HELP YOU MANAGE YOUR MONEY

CREDIT CARDS

Bank cards are accepted widely, even at pop-up events and farmers markets, and are often the preferred payment method. However, it's always good to have cash on hand for places that don't accept cards, such as ice-cream stands, flea markets, clam shacks and roadside farm stands. Many cash-only places have ATMs on-site, but they typically have high usage fees.

PAYING THE BILL

Servers at restaurants with table service will bring the bill to the table when your meal is finished. No need to ask.

TIPPING

Tipping 10% to 20% on a restaurant check is typical. Everyone from tour guides, bartenders, bellhops and baristas will gladly take tips, too.

CURRENCY

US dollar

HOW MUCH FOR A

Craft beer
$8

Fried-scrod plate
$15

Small cup of Dunkin' coffee
$2

STATE PARK PASSES

New England's state parks are plentiful and packed with things to do. If you plan to visit several parks in a single state, it might be cheaper to buy an annual or seasonal pass than paying to visit each individually. States have their own park services, so check their websites for information.

BANKS & ATMS Local and national banks will have branches and ATMs in even the smallest towns. Independent businesses may also have their own ATMs on-site, but they'll often have very high usage fees.

TAXES

Taxes vary by state and by the goods and services sold. New Hampshire, for instance, has no general sales tax, whereas Rhode Island's is 7%. Lodgings, liquor and meals may have different tax rates.

MARKET PRICE

The cost of seafood items on restaurant menus may say 'market price' or 'MKT price.' That means the price varies daily or seasonally, depending on current market conditions. Ask your server when ordering.

PARKING

Even in smaller cities, paying to park your car is common and rates vary depending on how long your car is parked. Metered parking may only accept coins, while others are linked to mobile apps. Smaller parking lots may have an attendant or electronic kiosks. Larger parking garages typically issue tickets that you must take with you and pay for at a kiosk before returning to your car. Posted signage for guidance will explain parking rules.

RESPONSIBLE TRAVEL

Tips to leave a lighter footprint, support local and have a positive impact on local communities.

ON THE ROAD

Calculate your travel carbon Use the carbon-footprint calculator at nature.org.

Verify green status Look for hotels with certifications like LEED, Green Key or Green Seal.

'Carry in, carry out' There are no trash barrels at many state parks, so visitors must leave with everything they brought in.

Hit the pavement Explore cities and compact downtowns on your own or with a walking tour.

Hop on See a city with bus and trolly tours.

Paddle Explore New England waters by renting kayaks, canoes or stand-up paddleboards, or by taking a guided paddle tour.

Bike share Many cities and even some hotels have bikes to rent or borrow.

Rail trails They're often decorated with local outdoor-art installations.

Rent electric or hybrid cars There are charging stations at many garages, hotels and other locations.

ENIGMA/ALAMY STOCK PHOTO ©

GIVE BACK

Run for a cause Explore a neighborhood and get some exercise by running a 5K road race that's raising money for a local program.

Sustainable brews Visit craft breweries that use locally sourced ingredients and upcycle their spent grains.

Volunteer Visit naturegroupie.org to find outdoor volunteer activities like pruning trees, maintaining trails and learning to identify invasive plants.

Join a beach cleanup Spend time picking up trash on the shoreline.

Eat seasonally Enjoy strawberries in June, nightshades in August, apples in fall, root veggies in winter and fish like haddock and Atlantic pollock year-round.

Donate Consider making a donation to the New England Forestry Foundation *(newenglandforestry.org)*, which engages in land management, education and conservation.

DOS & DON'TS

Do keep off sand dunes at the beach to prevent erosion and protect delicate plants and habitats.

Don't pick plants. Some are rare and protected, like the Robbins' cinquefoil, which only grows above the tree line in the White Mountains.

Don't go shellfishing without knowing local licensing and permitting rules and harvest limits.

LEAVE A SMALL FOOTPRINT

Stick to the trail When hiking, it's important to stick to marked trails for many reasons, including safety. It also helps you leave a small footprint. Venturing off the trail might harm plant and animal habitats, such as along protected shorelines and in the alpine region of Mt Washington. Luckily, New England has plenty of wonderful trails, including large portions of the Appalachian Trail, which passes through every New England state except Rhode Island and ends at the summit of Maine's Mt Katahdin.

ROZBEH/SHUTTERSTOCK ©

SUPPORT LOCAL

Local fishing Try locally caught 'trash fish' like hake or skate instead of popular, overfished species like cod.

Art communities Visit local galleries or take a walking tour of New England street art and murals in New London, Connecticut and East Boston.

Farmers markets Find breakfast, lunch, live music, conversations with growers and makers, and hyper-local souvenirs from local honey to handmade candles.

CLIMATE CHANGE & TRAVEL

It's impossible to ignore the impact we have when traveling, and the importance of making changes where we can. Lonely Planet urges all travelers to engage with their travel carbon footprint. There are many carbon calculators online that allow travelers to estimate the carbon emissions generated by their journey; try resurgence.org/resources/carbon-calculator.html. Many airlines and booking sites offer travelers the option of offsetting the impact of greenhouse gas emissions by contributing to climate-friendly initiatives around the world. We continue to offset the carbon footprint of all Lonely Planet staff travel, while recognizing this is a mitigation more than a solution.

RESOURCES

naturegroupie.org
newenglandforestry.org
ourwickedfish.com
massfarmersmarkets.org
greenseal.org

UNIQUE & LOCAL WAYS TO STAY

In New England, you can't throw a stone without hitting a place where something historic happened, and that's true for many of its accommodations, too. Its historic inns and grand hotels are wrapped up in stories, legends and lore. Travelers can also choose accommodations that get them closer to nature and the ocean, two other key elements of the New England identity.

JAMES KIRKIKIS/SHUTTERSTOCK ©

GRAND HOTELS Built in the 1800s and early 1900s for wealthy travelers who wanted to escape the city, old-school grand resort hotels are popular luxury destinations. These sprawling properties usually have extensive grounds, multiple dining options and dramatic locations, like the edge of an oceanside cliff or overlooking vast rolling mountains.

LIGHTHOUSES New England's lighthouses are tourist attractions all by themselves and often have incredible stories of heroism, storms and shipwrecks to go along with their iconic beauty. The lighthouse-keeper job has gone the way of the horse and buggy (Boston Light in Boston Harbor was the last officially manned lighthouse in the United States), but travelers can stay overnight either in the lighthouses themselves or the keeper's house. Many are available for weekly rentals only.

JON LOVETTE/GETTY IMAGES ©

BED & BREAKFAST

Old-fashioned B&Bs, where each guest room is uniquely decorated, the owners live on-site and guests wake to the smell of bacon, coffee and pancakes served in a common dining room, dot New England and offer a cozy and quiet alternative to the typical nondescript-room-and-continental-breakfast hotel experience.

JAMES KIRKIKIS/SHUTTERSTOCK ©

HISTORIC INNS

New England's historic inns come in many varieties, from ones that were originally built as hotels, taverns or guesthouses, to historic houses, mansions and farmsteads that have been converted into boutique hotels. But they all have one thing in common: you'll get much more than a place to sleep when you visit. Some have extensive art and antique collections that are worth a visit even if you don't stay there, historic architecture that's been preserved or restored, and on-site restaurants that are just as celebrated as the accommodations themselves. You'll hear stories about notable people and famous guests who visited throughout history, like George Washington, Thomas Edison or Grace Kelly. You might hear ghost stories and tales of hauntings in certain guest rooms, hallways or stairwells. At historic mansions that have found new life as hotels and inns, you'll get a sense of how a wealthy sea merchant or politician lived more than 100 years ago and sleep in their former bedrooms. Some historic inns and hotels have been preserved to look and feel as they did in their heyday, while others have been completely renovated to marry historic features with modern amenities and furnishings. Both options are truly one of a kind.

BOOKING

Booking online is usually the best option for all accommodations. Rates vary by season and locale, with waterfront accommodations more expensive in the summer, for instance. Although some accommodations might close for winter, others (like mountain resorts) are popular all year, thanks to the winter ski season. Book in advance for the summer beach season, fall foliage season and October in Salem.

Discover New England *(discovernewengland.org)* The official tourism site for New England with links to each of the states' tourism boards.

Visit New England *(visitnewengland.com)* Provides New England travel information broken down by state, as well as things to do and places to stay.

New England Lighthouses *(newenglandlighthouses.net)* Provides links to New England lighthouses with overnight accommodations.

Historic Hotels of America *(historichotels.org)* Has a New England section that lists hotels included in the National Trust for Historic Preservation.

Reserve America *(reserveamerica.com)* Features a campground directory that's searchable by state and reservation tools.

CAMPING

Campgrounds are everywhere in New England (even in Boston!) and campers can get lots of diverse experiences within just a few hours' drive: mountains, backwoods, beaches, islands and more.

ESSENTIAL NUTS & BOLTS

FIND A GUIDE

New England has some areas of true wilderness. Considering hiring a guide, like a Registered Maine Guide, to explore safely and ethically.

CANADA

Canada shares a border with Maine, New Hampshire and Vermont, and requires a passport to visit. Check the latest COVID-19 vaccine and testing requirements.

SMOKING

Indoor smoking in public places is prohibited. E-cigarettes are included in indoor-smoking rules.

FAST FACTS

Time Zone
GMT-5

Country Code
+1

Electricity
120/240V
60Hz

GOOD TO KNOW

Most New Englanders are Boston Red Sox fans, but allegiance switches to the New York Yankees in Western Connecticut.

Passports usually must be valid for at least six months after your planned departure from the US.

Stay on the right when driving, cycling and walking on trails and sidewalks.

The US drinking age is 21.

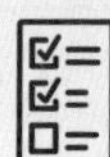

Citizens from 40 countries can travel to the US for business or tourism without a visa.

ACCESSIBLE TRAVEL

Major hotels will have elevators and wheelchair-accessible rooms, but many small B&Bs may not.

Historic buildings, like the House of the Seven Gables (Salem) or the Mark Twain House (Hartford), often aren't fully wheelchair-accessible.

Boston's public transportation is quite wheelchair-friendly, but a few subway stations lack elevators between the subway and street levels. Green line train operators will lower the ramp on request.

Many museums and theaters offer sensory-friendly programs, performances and visiting times.

Many parks and forests have accessible trails and resources. Acadia National Park offers a free, wheelchair-accessible Island Explorer shuttle bus and services for people with visual or hearing impairments. The White Mountain National Forest maintains a list of its accessible trails online.

Some beaches have services like sand and floating wheelchairs, boardwalks, access mats and beach transportation.

Take care on cobbled streets, which can be challenging for those with mobility issues.

Check resources like accessible go.com, accessiblenature.info and wheelchairtravel.org.

BRAKE FOR MOOSE

These iconic signs dot New Hampshire byways for good reason. Car-moose collisions can be deadly.

RELIGION

New England is among the United States' least religious regions, especially New Hampshire and Vermont.

CLAM CHOWDER

New England clam chowder is cream-based. An old Massachusetts law prohibits tomatoes in clam chowder.

FAMILY TRAVEL

Many restaurants have children's menus and highchairs. At the 99 Restaurant & Pub, a local chain, kids eat free the day after the Red Sox win.

Museums often have free or discounted rates for children, depending on their age.

Some theaters provide booster seats for kids who are too short to see the stage.

Children aged 11 and under (up to two per paying adult) ride free on the Massachusetts Bay Transportation Authority (MBTA).

TOILETS

Popping into a gas station or fast-food restaurant to use the toilet is acceptable in most places. In cities like Boston, though, public toilets are harder to find and may require a small fee, a key, or electronic code (available from merchants) to enter.

PATRIOTS' DAY

This is a public holiday in Maine and Massachusetts. It's the third Monday in April and commemorates the start of the American Revolution. Traditionally, the Boston Marathon and a Red Sox home game happen on Patriots' Day, earning it the local nickname, 'Marathon Monday.'

LGBTIQ+ TRAVELERS

New England is very LGBTIQ+ friendly. Many places, like Northampton in Massachusetts and Providence in Rhode Island, have thriving LGBTIQ+ communities.

Provincetown, Massachusetts (aka P-town; pictured left), located at the very tip of Cape Cod, holds annual LGBTIQ+ events, like Provincetown Carnival in August and the Fantasia Fair, celebrating the trans community, in October.

Ogunquit, Maine, is a beachside LGBTIQ+ resort town that's quieter, easier to access and cheaper than P-town.

Read *The Rainbow Times*, New England's largest LGBTIQ+ newspaper, at therainbowtimesmass.com.

Index

000 Map pages

000 Map pages

'A witch in Salem gave my daughter a crystal for under her pillow to prevent bad dreams. It worked.'

ALEXANDRA PECCI

'While cycling in the Champlain Islands, a wrong turn led to a pleasant discovery – South Hero's tiny stone castles.'

LISA HALVORSEN

'I had a peaceful day canoeing with the dog on the Androscoggin River – just before she leapt out and the canoe flipped over.'

PEGGY NEWLAND

'Standing alone on the Stony Creek dock, waiting for someone I didn't know to take me to his Thimble Island home, I felt rather cloak and dagger, but pleased to have wrangled an invitation to the private islands.'

STASHA MILLS HEALY

'My four-year-old twins were intrigued by the evocative gravestones on Copp's Hill, but the highlight of our North End field trip was the cannoli.'

MARA VORHEES

TOP: PEGGY NEWLAND/LONELY PLANET ©, BOTTOM: SERGIO AMITI/GETTY IMAGES ©

THIS BOOK

Design development
Lauren Egan, Tina García, Fergal Condon

Content development
Anne Mason

Cartography development
Wayne Murphy, Katerina Pavkova

Production development
Mario D'Arco, Dan Moore, Sandie Kestell, Virginia Moreno, Juan Winata

Series development leadership
Liz Heynes, Darren O'Connell, Piers Pickard, Chris Zeiher

Commissioning editor
Sandie Kestell

Product editor
Clare Healy

Cartographer
Anthony Phelan

Book designer
Gwen Cotter

Assisting editor
Brana Vladisavljevic

Cover researcher
Kat Marsh

Thanks Gwen Cotter, Alison Killilea, Laura Motta, Charlotte Orr, Gabbi Stefanos, John Taufa